PRAISE FOR SINGLES AND SMILES

"Artie Wilson was one of the guys who watched out for me when I played for the Birmingham Black Barons in 1948. In turn, I watched Artie. That year, he hit .402! That was a lesson in hitting that I always remembered."—**Willie Mays, legendary Hall of Famer, 2-time National League MVP, 12-time Gold Glove Award winner, and 24-time All-Star**

"Artie Wilson was my idol growing up in Puerto Rico. He inspired me to be a ballplayer. *Singles and Smiles* is a well-deserved tribute to a great man and player, and a beautiful dresser. Artie was amazing in everything he did."—**Orlando Cepeda, Hall of Fame first baseman, 1958 National League Rookie of the Year, 1967 National League MVP, and seven-time National League All-Star**

"I'm delighted the story of Artie Wilson is being told. He was amazing both on and off the field—a role model for younger Birmingham Black Baron players like me and Willie Mays. We were rookies on the highly respected 1948 team that raised the bar of excellence for our race, our city, and ourselves."—**Rev. Bill Greason, former pitcher for the Birmingham Black Barons and first black to pitch for the St. Louis Cardinals**

"Artie Wilson might not have been blessed with the baseball career he deserved—damn segregation—but all these years later, he's finally got the biography he deserves."—**Rob Neyer, author of *Rob Neyer's Big Book of Baseball Legends***

"I broke into the big leagues in 1947—the same year Jackie Robinson broke the color barrier. Jackie had a belly-full of guts and didn't give an inch to all the pitchers who threw at him. Artie Wilson showed the same courage, winning the Coast League batting title his first season in Organized Baseball. *Singles and Smiles* recognizes Artie for doing in the minors what Jackie did in the majors."—**Wally Westlake, power-hitting outfielder for the Pittsburgh Pirates**

"I always had the feeling Artie Wilson shaved several years off his age a la Satchel Paige. He was like Satch in other ways, too—a barrier breaker and great example for the black players that followed."—**Chuck Stevens, first baseman for the St. Louis Browns, the first to get a hit off of the legendary Paige in the majors**

"Breaking up a double play at second base is a lost art. That's too bad because we'll never see another Artie Wilson—the greatest I ever saw at evading guys like me trying to knock him into the next county. I enjoyed reading about Artful Artie, and so will you."—**Gale Wade, former Chicago Cub and minor league star renowned for rolling-block slides at second base**

SINGLES AND SMILES

HOW ARTIE WILSON BROKE BASEBALL'S COLOR BARRIER

Gaylon H. White

ROWMAN & LITTLEFIELD
Lanham • Boulder • New York • London

Published by Rowman & Littlefield
An imprint of The Rowman & Littlefield Publishing Group, Inc.
4501 Forbes Boulevard, Suite 200, Lanham, Maryland 20706
www.rowman.com

Unit A, Whitacre Mews, 26-34 Stannary Street, London SE11 4AB

British Library Cataloguing in Publication Information Available

Library of Congress Cataloging-in-Publication Data

Names: White, Gaylon H., 1946– author.
Title: Singles and smiles : how Artie Wilson broke baseball's color barrier / Gaylon H. White.
Description: Lanham : Rowman & Littlefield, [2018] | Includes bibliographical references and
index.
Identifiers: LCCN 2017043270 (print) | LCCN 2017059353 (ebook) | ISBN 9781538107911 (elec-
tronic) | ISBN 9781538107904 (hardcover : alk. paper)
Subjects: LCSH: Wilson, Artie. | Baseball players—United States—Biography. | African American
baseball players—Biography. | Negro leagues—History. | Discrimination in sports—United
States—History—20th century.
Classification: LCC GV865.W46 (ebook) | LCC GV865.W46 A3 2018 (print) | DDC 796.357092
[B] —dc23
LC record available at https://lccn.loc.gov/2017043270

∞™ The paper used in this publication meets the minimum requirements of
American National Standard for Information Sciences Permanence of Paper
for Printed Library Materials, ANSI/NISO Z39.48-1992.

Printed in the United States of America

My wife, Mary Lynn Joette White, is the wisest person on this planet. Long before 2016 when the Chicago Cubs won their first World Series in 108 years, she said: "If the Cubs win the World Series, they won't be the Cubbies anymore." As usual, she was right. The Cubbies were America's lovable losers. Now, they're just another baseball team.

CONTENTS

ACKNOWLEDGMENTS

A familiar thing happened on my way to finishing the baseball book I started in the 1970s. I took a detour.

It's not the first time I wandered off in a different direction.

My first two books, *The Bilko Athletic Club* and *Handsome Ransom Jackson: Accidental Big Leaguer*, a collaboration with Ransom Jackson, a two-time National League All-Star, were pleasant side trips down memory lane.

In fact, I was with Ransom and his delightful wife Terry at historic Dodgertown in Vero Beach, Florida, when I got an e-mail from Christen Karniski, acquisitions editor at Rowman & Littlefield.

She expressed interest in a biography on a sports pioneer—"not just a great athlete, but someone who impacted sport and society beyond the game itself."

That described Artie Wilson to a tee.

It so happened I was going to devote a chapter to Artie in the epic I was working on. There was enough material to make it a book, so that's what was proposed. Christen liked the idea, and I was off on another detour.

My wife Mary has waited patiently for me to retire and enjoy our beautiful surroundings in the mountains of northeast Tennessee. She's still waiting, and for that, I am forever grateful.

Mary met Artie in 1994. I wrote down what she said: "This man is a gentleman. A fine, gentle man. How grateful he was for the opportunity to play baseball."

Mary encouraged me to write this book. She also used her keen ear for Southern accents to make a quote from Mississippi-born Clay Hopper sound like the way he said his name—Clayhoppeh.

Ed Mickelson played for the Portland Beavers in 1955, when they were managed by Clayhoppeh. He wrote a book, *Out of the Park*, about his outstanding minor-league career, one that included cameo appearances in the majors with the Cardinals and Browns in St. Louis and the Chicago Cubs. He also did a nice job capturing Clayhoppeh's Southern drawl. It's a fun read—just like the foreword he did for this book.

Most of the photographs in *Singles and Smiles* are from the collections of Doug McWilliams and David Eskenazi. Both should have busts at the National Baseball Hall of Fame in Cooperstown, New York.

Of course, 11,000 color negatives of baseball player photos taken by McWilliams are housed at the Hall of Fame. The images he donated are estimated to be 12 percent of everyone who has played baseball.

Doug's collection of photographs and memorabilia covering Artie's career is equally remarkable. I spent an entire day with Doug at his home in Berkeley, California, poring over the material and listening to him share memories of his favorite baseball player. His respect for Artie and the friendship that came out of it inspired the chapter "The Ballplayer, the Boy, and the Cigar." Photos from five albums devoted to Artie are scattered throughout the book. They are priceless—just like Doug.

Eskenazi's treasure trove of Seattle baseball photos can be traced to his grandfather, Albert Alhadeff, and uncle, Leon Alhadeff, who befriended players for the Rainiers, as well as those from other Pacific Coast League teams. He kindly shared Seattle-related photos of Artie.

The other photos in the book are from the Center for Negro League Baseball Research, founded by Dr. Layton Revel. He's also the driving force and guiding spirit behind the Negro Southern League Museum in Birmingham, Alabama. It's well worth a visit.

Unfortunately, we were unable to use a black-and-white photo of Artie colorized by Jason Barber to look like a vintage 1952 Topps baseball card. Topps even granted permission to use the image but we couldn't make it work as a book cover design.

Rene Anderson of the San Francisco Giants arranged for me to interview Willie Mays by telephone. A big thanks to Rene and the "Say

Hey Kid" for taking time to reminisce about Artie and his first pro team, the 1948 Birmingham Black Barons.

Bertha Fajardo of the Giants set up an interview with Hall of Famer Orlando Cepeda, who was a big Artie Wilson fan growing up in Puerto Rico. A high five to Bertha and Orlando.

Rev. Bill Greason was a rookie pitcher on the '48 Black Barons. He graciously sat down with me on the next to last day of 1999 to talk about Artie and that special team, and tell his personal story.

Artie Wilson Jr. gave me a glimpse of his father that only a son can provide. He answered seemingly endless questions and contributed some wonderful photos.

Incidentally, my youngest son, Rory, a talented photographer, reviewed the photos to make sure they are as good as the day they were taken.

Charley Dressen managed Artie when he played for the Oakland Oaks in 1949 and 1950. Dressen guided the Brooklyn Dodgers in 1951 when Artie finally got a chance to play in the majors for the New York Giants and their boss, Leo Durocher. I wanted to better understand the relationship between the two managers, as they played an important role in Artie's career.

Carl Erskine, a pitching star for the 1951 Dodgers with 16 wins, took time to talk about Dressen and the still-painful loss to the Giants in the third and decisive game of the 1951 National League playoffs.

The list of players interviewed for this book is a long one, and I'm grateful for their valuable contributions. In addition to those already mentioned, they are: Dwight "Red" Adams; Eddie Basinski; Charlie Beamon; Jim Brosnan; Alvin Dark; Lorenzo "Piper" Davis; Bob Dillinger; Jim Fanning; George Freese; Allen "Two Gun" Gettel; Elijah "Pumpsie" Green; Don Gutteridge; Sam Hairston; Bobby Hofman; Monte Irvin; Chet Johnson; Jim Marshall; Clint "Butch" McCord Jr.; Roger Osenbaugh; Les Peden; Herm Reich; Dino Restelli; Chuck Stevens; Bobby Usher; Gale Wade; and Bud Watkins. Also sharing their memories were Bill Veeck, owner of the Cleveland Indians in 1949; Cece Carlucci, a Pacific Coast League umpire; Bill Conlin, sports editor of the *Sacramento Union*; and Chuck Christiansen, Artie's breakfast buddy at the Bomber Inn restaurant in Gladstone, Oregon.

Working quietly inside the libraries of this country are some amazing people like Tim Spindle and Samantha Vickery, dedicated to helping find the newspaper articles needed to fill in the research blanks. Tim works for the Oklahoma City Metropolitan Library and Samantha for the Kennewick branch of the Mid-Columbia Libraries in the Tri-City area of Washington. Samantha went out of her way to find stories covering Artie's brief stint with the Tri-City Braves at the end of the 1962 season.

Before starting this book, I planned on traveling to the Amazon region of Brazil to fish the Rio Roosevelt, best known as the "River of Doubt," because Teddy Roosevelt almost didn't survive his expedition there in 1913–1914. I had some doubts myself whether I'd make it back home. Fortunately, my three fishing buddies—Rogerio Dias, Pedro Fortes, and Damon Warmack—looked after me so I wouldn't fall out of the boat and into the piranha- and alligator-infested waters.

Writing has its own perils, and Leann DeBord has protected me from them by diligently editing the stories and taking care of the niggling details that have caused me to lose most of my hair. I only wish she was around to help when I still had hair.

I was blessed with a father, Rev. Hooper W. White, and an uncle, Herbert Hoover White, who was like a second father. They were born and raised in the segregated South but treated everyone with the highest regard and respect.

I was 10 years old in 1956, when my father took the family to a Rockwood, Tennessee, church he pastored in the early 1940s. It was a weekday. No one was there except a man high up on a ladder painting the exterior of the church.

Dad parked the car and got out to speak to the man.

Upon seeing my father, he immediately climbed down. They hugged.

There's no photo of my dad and the black man he embraced. I don't need it.

PREFACE

It was April 1943. Sixteen months earlier, the Japanese had attacked Pearl Harbor, plunging the United States into two wars. Almost 3 million childless, married men had just been reclassified 1-A by their draft boards, making them immediately eligible for military service and possible combat on the front lines.

In Oakland, California, the local professional baseball team, the Oaks, couldn't beat college kids. They had lost seven of eight exhibition games, including an embarrassing 9–0 drubbing by the University of California. Games were being cancelled because they didn't have enough able-bodied pitchers.

A crystal ball wasn't needed to see what was ahead for baseball.

Fifteen-year-old Joe Nuxhall would become the youngest player in major-league history. He pitched two-thirds of an inning for the Cincinnati Redlegs in 1944, allowing five runs on five walks and two hits.

A one-armed outfielder, Pete Gray, played 77 games in 1945, for the St. Louis Browns.

Older players left shuffleboard courts to fill depleted rosters.

Desperate times require desperate measures, reasoned Art Cohn, a sports columnist for the *Oakland Tribune*.

Cohn was known for calling a spade a steam shovel. "Many a man tried to punch Art in the nose for what he had written," one colleague quipped.[1]

He was saying good-bye to the sports world for the real one so he could report on General Douglas MacArthur's first assault against Japanese-occupied islands in the South Pacific and his own U.S. Navy ship that was torpedoed by a Nazi submarine. Why not stick a bomb in the middle of one of his columns just before leaving?

"NEGROES COULD SAVE OAKS," the small headline read.

"The Oaks are in a bad way, and no one knows it better than Vic Devincenzi, the owner," Cohn began. "The good man is desperate. And helpless. He needs players, but he has no one to turn to. Everyone else needs players too."[2]

Nine months earlier, baseball's iron-fisted commissioner, Judge Kenesaw Mountain Landis, insisted Negroes were not barred from the game. "A manager can have one or 25 Negroes if he cares to," said Landis.[3]

"Bravo, Ken, bravo," Cohn mockingly cheered. "If Negroes are not barred from baseball, why are they so bashful about playing?"

Negro players were discriminated against in baseball, Cohn needled. "It is a pity such prejudice and intolerance should exist."[4]

Cohn urged Devincenzi to "make himself the biggest man in baseball" and call Judge Landis's bluff by signing three or four Negro players that could save the Oaks and break the game's color barrier. He listed a dozen Negro boxers, including Sugar Ray Robinson and Henry Armstrong, who saved their sport.

"Without Negroes, boxing would have collapsed last year," Cohn said. "With them it is enjoying the greatest boom in two decades." He added, "What they have done for boxing they could do for baseball—if baseball would let them. But baseball won't."

He fired this parting shot: "It is a sad commentary on American 'tolerance' that even if the bars are lowered, it will be only because of the shortage of white players."[5]

Cohn knew no team would defy baseball's unwritten ban of blacks. But he stirred up enough controversy that the Oaks' Devincenzi agreed to look at first baseman-outfielder Lou Dials and pitcher Chet Brewer, prior to the team's season opener at Wrigley Field in Los Angeles.

In mid-March, Dials and Brewer were among four black players to appear at the Los Angeles Angels' spring training camp in Anaheim, California, after the club's president, Clarence "Pants" Rowland, promised them a tryout. They were accompanied by Herman Hill, a correspondent for the *Pittsburgh Courier*, a black newspaper.

The Angels were a Chicago Cubs farm team owned by Philip K. Wrigley, head honcho of the chewing gum company by the same name.

Just before Christmas 1942, Wrigley told a group of black leaders that the big leagues would soon be integrated but more time was needed to educate the public.

"What must be done is to get people talking," Wrigley said. "If there was sufficient public demand at this time, I would put a Negro on my team now."[6]

The black players never got a tryout.

Rowland told them he had no objections to their playing on the team, but he was only the president, and it was up to Angels manager Bill Sweeney to decide who he wanted on his club.

Sweeney made a speech deploring discrimination but said he couldn't risk the potential friction with white players on the team. Besides, he couldn't establish policy. That was up to Rowland and Wrigley.

In a *San Francisco Chronicle* story published in 1993, Dials said Wrigley told him, "I know how good you are, but I don't have a place for you."[7]

Despite orders from his boss, Devincenzi, Oaks manager Johnny Vergez refused to give Dials and Brewer a tryout. "I can't do it. I'll lose my job first. I'll be damned if I do it," he said.[8]

One Oaks player confided to a *Courier* reporter that the 36-year-old Brewer was one of the best pitchers he'd faced and far better than any hurler on the team, saying, "Why, you can catch their fastest pitches in your bare hand."[9]

Vergez didn't want to be the first white manager to use black players. "He said they'd crucify him," Dials said later, "and I believe they would."[10]

Six years passed. Vic Devincenzi sold the Oaks at the end of the 1943 season; Johnny Vergez was fired by the new owner, Clarence "Brick" Laws; Judge Landis died; World War II ended; Jackie Robinson broke baseball's color barrier; and Art Cohn became a prolific screenwriter in Hollywood.

Finally, on May 18, 1949, the Oaks had their first black player— shortstop Artie Wilson. They acquired him from the San Diego Padres, the first Pacific Coast League (PCL) team to integrate when they signed catcher John Ritchey in 1948. The Seattle Rainiers were the last, Artie crossing the white line in 1952.

The story of Jackie Robinson is well documented. Every year on the 15th of April, baseball celebrates Jackie Robinson Day. Jackie's uniform number "42" is on display in every big-league stadium. The movie *42* ensures that the latest generation of baseball fans knows the hardships Jackie endured.

But little is known about Artie and the other blacks who integrated the minors. They are mostly footnotes in baseball history, their achievements in need of resurrection and telling so they won't be forgotten.

Almost lost in the fog of time is the remarkable story of Bill Greason, one of Artie's teammates on the 1948 Birmingham Black Barons team—usually remembered for a 17-year-old kid named Willie Mays, who went on to become the greatest center fielder ever.

At age 18, Greason joined the U.S. Marines. He fought in the bloody Battle of Iwo Jima.

"I was taught that God is the creator and sustainer of everything," Greason said. "He controls our whole being. He is responsible for our being. He'll take care of you, look out for you. Of course, you have to experience it for yourself. And I did."

Greason landed at Iwo Jima on the fourth day of the American invasion in 1945. He recalled:

> I didn't even feel that I was going to get off. So many marines were killed. We had 20,000 casualties, over 7,000 killed. Two of my best friends were killed. Several other members of our squad were wounded. I prayed. My Mom told me to always pray. So, I carried a Bible with me. One night when things got pretty rough, I prayed that if the Lord spared me, whatever He wanted me to do, I'd do it.

Greason found out God works in mysterious ways.

"I never dreamed that I would've been a baseball player," he said in a CNN interview in 2014. "Nobody taught me how to play. It was a gift."

He could hit, but he was especially gifted at throwing the ball. "I had a good downer. I threw overhand. It would fall off the table."[11]

The slender right-hander had a smoking fastball too, and he could throw either pitch different ways—overhand, three-quarters, and side-armed.

The Black Barons got their first glimpse of Greason in a spring exhibition game in Asheville, North Carolina. He was pitching for the hometown Blues. "It so happened that the Barons needed some pitching strength. They saw me. I had pretty good talent," he reflected.

That talent helped the Barons win the Negro American League pennant in 1948. Greason beat the Kansas City Monarchs in the final game. Against the powerful Homestead Grays in the Negro World Series, he accounted for the Black Barons' lone victory.

Greason served another stint in the marines during the Korean War but didn't go overseas. "I had a good camp commander." He said, 'That's a no-win war. You stay here. I'm going to have a baseball team.'"[12]

He was the only black on the Camp Lejeune club.

A marine recruiting sergeant based in Oklahoma City brought Greason to the attention of E. J. "Jimmie" Humphries, owner of the Oklahoma City Indians, a Class AA Texas League club.

"I've been following a pitcher in the marines in camp papers we exchange," the sarge informed Humphries, continuing:

> He's lost only one game in more than two years that I know of. He beat Don Newcombe, 1 to 0, in a camp game in Virginia the other afternoon.
>
> The last paper I got from his camp said he was due to be discharged pretty soon. Maybe he'd be worth looking at. His name's Greason—Bill Greason.[13]

The Indians signed Greason on July 28, 1952, making him the team's first black player and the second in the Texas League.

Blazing the trail earlier in the year was Dave Hoskins, a former Homestead Grays pitcher signed by the Dallas Eagles. He won 11 of his first 15 decisions and was being hailed as the "savior of the Texas League" for packing ballparks with black fans. Bus excursions were arranged from cities 100 miles from Dallas so as many people as possible could see the "sensational Negro pitcher" in action. Hoskins finished with 24 victories, including two in the playoffs, and is credited with personally adding 92,850 to league attendance.[14]

Shortly before his first start for the Indians, Humphries called Greason into his office.

"I am, in a sense, employing you," Greason recalled the owner saying. "But I want you to play with us because we are beginning to bring blacks into the league. You can't be as good as these white boys. You've got to be better. I brought you here not because you are as good as them but because I believe you are a better pitcher than these fellows are."

"That really lifted me up," Greason said.

A season-high crowd of 5,731 showed up to see Greason's first game, an impressive win over the Shreveport Sports. "Every fastball he threw me was alive and doing something," said Shreveport's Grant Dunlop, the league's top hitter.

"Few ballplayers will ever be on a larger, warmer spot than was Greason when he was called on for his debut," John Cronley wrote in the *Oklahoman*.[15]

Three days later, in Dallas, more than 11,000 people, half of them black, saw Greason toss a four-hitter to best Hoskins, 3–2, in the "first all-Negro duel in Texas League history."[16]

He went on to post a 9–1 record and miniscule 2.14 earned run average.

"How Greason came out of the Marine Corps unnoticed by the majors, I'll never know," Cronley marveled.[17]

By the end of the summer, at least six major-league teams were in hot pursuit of Greason. "He's a fine prospect with good pitching knowledge for a man with so little experience," the New York Yankees' cagey super-scout Tom Greenwade said, downplaying his three years pitching for the Black Barons.[18]

The Yankees and the Boston Red Sox got into a bidding war, reportedly offering as much as $60,000 for Greason's services. That was a large sum of money for two teams that had previously shown little interest in signing black players.

Jimmie Humphries turned down both clubs, explaining, "Bill's one of the most amazing athletes I've ever seen in baseball. Cool at all times, he's going to be a great major leaguer one of these days, but he needs further time in the minors to learn the little tricks."[19]

Humphries was trying to jack up the price. If he didn't get what he wanted, he could cash in on his biggest drawing card for one more year and then sell him for $100,000.

Humphries's decision was called a "grave injustice" by Wendell Smith, a highly respected columnist for the *Pittsburgh Courier*. "The player is nothing more than chattel, a piece of property that lives or dies in accordance with the whims of the owner of the club for which he is playing." Smith concluded, "Abe Lincoln set people like Greason, and others caught similarly, free a long, long time ago."[20]

In 1953, the extra money Humphries made off Greason at the box office was offset by the pitcher's sore arm and a 16–13 won–loss mark, which cut his market value in half.

In October 1953, the St. Louis Cardinals acquired Greason and teammate Joe Frazier, the Texas League batting champion, for an estimated $25,000 in cash and four players.

The Cardinals didn't have any black players, and they weren't ready for them either.

They sent Greason to their minor-league spring training camp in Albany, Georgia. Upon arriving there, he received a manual covering team rules for meals, transportation, and housing. It read, in part, "A colored player will come directly from Albany State College in a special bus. All white players will be roomed in private homes, while colored players will be housed in Gibson Hall, Albany State College for Colored."[21]

Greason opened the 1954 season at Columbus, Ohio, the Cardinals farm club in the American Association, a Class AAA league.

He had a three-game winning streak going when, in late May, the Cardinals tabbed him to be the first black pitcher in the franchise's history. "I didn't want to go. Eddie Stanky was the manager. He was from Mobile. We were in the middle of the season. The Cardinals were losing."

Nicknamed "the Brat," the hot-headed Stanky grew up in Philadelphia, Pennsylvania, but he was more closely associated with his adopted state of Alabama. "You could take the 'B' off the Brat. He bullied people," Greason said.

The Cardinals had lost five of six games and were in sixth place when Greason joined them. "Eddie Stanky didn't greet me or say nothing."

The players didn't have much to say to him either. "I was kind of lost up there. It just didn't feel good to me."

One reason was because the Cardinals paid him only $900 a month, 25 percent less than his Columbus salary. "I thought, 'This is the majors, I'm supposed to get more here than I did in the minors.'"[22]

Greason made his debut against a power-packed Chicago Cubs lineup at Wrigley Field.

"This is a rough way to break in, pitching at Wrigley Field with the wind blowing out and against a club of fly-ball hitters," New York Giants scout Tom Sheehan said before the game. [23]

Greason started and lasted three innings, allowing five runs on three Cub homers—two by Hank Sauer and one by Ernie Banks.

In his next start, against the Philadelphia Phillies, Stanky yanked him after he faced just three batters, giving up a home run and two walks.

Greason explained:

> In Philadelphia, Stanky asked me to throw batting practice. I had not pitched in two or three weeks. Naturally, you're going to be a little wild. He came out and said, "Get the damn ball over the plate!" I said, "What the hell do you think I'm trying to do?" He turned and walked away. Those were the only words he ever said to me.

Greason pitched one inning of scoreless relief against the Giants in his third and final game in the majors.

"I tried to get there for years, and then when I got there, I didn't want to stay," he lamented. [24]

Back in Columbus, he finished the season with a 10–13 record. In 1955, he won 17 games for Houston in the Texas League and 10 more in 1956, before heading to Rochester in the International League, where he was primarily a relief pitcher until he retired after the 1959 season. Overall, he had a 78–62 record in the minors.

Greason spent three weeks in the big leagues—a cup of coffee in baseball terminology. He likened his cup to the one Artie Wilson had with the Giants in 1951. There were no refills.

"He just didn't get a chance," Greason said of his Black Barons teammate. He continued:

> They wanted you to be a success in one game. You had to be almost perfect in that one game if you were going to impress them. With me and Artie, it didn't happen. We had the tools, but they just expected so much out of us.
>
> They expected us, coming out of the Negro Leagues into the white leagues, to be better than those other fellows. And they were looking at an instantaneous thing. They were not willing to give you the time. They wanted it just like that.

He snapped his fingers, adding, "People ask me, 'Do you regret anything?' I say, 'No, I have no regrets at all.'"

In Greason's mind, what happened to him in the majors was part of the deal he made with God on Iwo Jima. "It was in God's plan. He knew all about it," he said.

That plan had him playing baseball in Tuscaloosa, Alabama, on a Sunday morning in 1963, when the Sixteenth Street Baptist Church he attended in Birmingham was bombed by the Ku Klux Klan, killing four girls, ages 11 to 14.

That plan led to him becoming a Baptist minister and leading Birmingham's Bethel Baptist Church since 1969.

That plan had him returning to St. Louis in 2014, so he could be honored with a Living Legend Award on the 60th anniversary of him becoming the Cardinals' first black pitcher.

That plan kept him around long enough to receive a Congressional Gold Medal for his service in the Montford Point Marines, the all-black squadron that spilled its blood on the shores of Iwo Jima.

That plan had him passing on to young people the lessons he learned in baseball and the ministry.

Greason said:

> Life is not so much what you can get; it's what you can give. It's not so much the material or the monetary, but giving somebody a good example to follow. Somebody is watching you; somebody wants to be like you. And if you're going to be a good example for them, you've got to help somebody else along the way.

Art Cohn was right in 1943, when he wrote that Negroes saved boxing and could do the same for baseball, if given a chance.

Boxing supplied Cohn with the story lines for such films as *Glory Alley*, *The Set-Up*, and *Tennessee Champ*. It also provided the metaphorical 10-count on his life, as well as material for a book he was writing about Mike Todd, an award-winning film producer and husband of actress Elizabeth Taylor.

"I've got it all finished except for one thing," Cohn told friends. "I haven't got an ending."[25]

That was decided for him on March 22, 1958.

Cohn and Todd were flying to New York City on the filmmaker's private plane, *Lucky Liz*, when it crashed in the mountains near Grants, New Mexico, killing them both. Cohn was 48 and Todd 50.

Todd's biography was going to be called *The First Nine Lives of Mike Todd*. The word "first" was dropped.

Cohn's death coincided with the arrival of the San Francisco Giants and the Los Angeles Dodgers on the West Coast. The biggest star on both teams was Willie Mays, the "Say Hey Kid," who had broken into pro baseball 10 years earlier with a Black Barons team led by Artie Wilson, the game's last .400 hitter.

Willie Mays, Jackie Robinson, Henry Aaron, Ernie Banks, Roberto Clemente, and other blacks saved baseball, just as Cohn predicted. We can only imagine what might've happened if more of them had a better chance sooner.

FOREWORD

Ed Mickelson

Little did I know on a fateful day in December 1954, that my life's trajectory was set in motion to become a teammate of Artie Wilson, one of the greatest shortstops in baseball history. It was the seventh year of my pro baseball career and a lucky one at that. At the minor-league draft, held in Houston, I was the first pick out of some 8,500 eligible minor leaguers, and I was deeply honored by the selection. I went to the Portland Beavers of the Pacific Coast League (PCL), the team with the worst won–lost record in the country's highest minor league, which gave them the right to pick first.

As the only "open classification" league, the PCL was ranked higher than Class AAA. In those days, the St. Louis Cardinals were the only major-league team west of the Mississippi River. With eight teams on the West Coast, the PCL was often considered a third major league, only in some ways it was even better than that for players and fans. As a matter of fact, if a Major League Baseball team bought the contract of a PCL player, he had the right of refusal. Some players made more money in the Coast League than major leaguers and wouldn't accept the "demotion."

The PCL had other advantages. Teams traveled by plane, not train, and road trips lasted a week in one city, not two days here and three days there, as in the big leagues. In a week-long series, Monday was always an offday. We played the rest of the week's games at night. Saturday was a day game, with a doubleheader on Sunday. The weather was always comfortable and rainouts few and far between. When we landed in Los Angeles, we stayed at the Hollywood Plaza Hotel, playing the Los Angeles Angels for a week and the Hollywood Stars the next week, meaning we spent two weeks in the same hotel.

It felt like the big leagues to me, and for the West Coast fans, it was. Los Angeles' Wrigley Field—a smaller replica of the Cubs' "Friendly Confines"—seated about 25,000 fans; San Francisco's Seals Stadium held about 15,000 and Portland's Multnomah Stadium 26,000.

It was in this context that I had the privilege of sharing an infield with Artie. I knew he had been a great player in the Negro Leagues, but I had no idea how formidable his skills were in every aspect of the game.

He was widely known as the best shortstop in the Negro Leagues. Artie had sprinter's speed, and although a left-handed hitter, he took everything to the left of the diamond. Left fielders played him almost on the line. He could leg out base hits on nearly any ball to shortstop or third, and he was known as the "Octopus" for his defensive skills. Artie always hit well above .300 and one year won the batting title. Until he was scratched from the lineup at the last minute, he was going to start at shortstop, with Jackie Robinson serving as his backup in the Negro League's East–West All-Star Game in 1945. And if that's not impressive enough, remember Wilson was the last .400 hitter in the Negro Leagues.

Like Robinson in the major leagues, Artie was a trailblazer coming into the PCL in 1949. He was a tablesetter for other African Americans in the PCL and won the batting championship that year. Frankie Austin was another groundbreaker in the league. He had made a name for himself as a smooth-fielding shortstop in the Negro Leagues. While not the hitter Artie was or blessed with speed, he was a great fielder. Like Artie, Frankie also broke into the PCL in 1949, and suffered through the same indignities as Artie—not being served in restaurants or housed in hotels. It was nothing like Robinson's abuse, but it was abuse nonetheless.

By 1955, Artie and Frankie were fan favorites in Portland, and Austin was feted at a "Frankie Austin Day" with gifts galore and many honors. Both stellar players had overcome any enmity toward them as African American ballplayers by being pillars of strength and gentlemen in every situation.

I liked the way the two men treated everyone with a smile and respect. They were not only good teammates, but also wonderful human beings. As a first baseman, I also liked them for their fielding.

In 1955, Frankie was 38. He had lost power in his arm, but every throw was chest high. Catching his throws to first was like picking cherries from a tree. Artie had a little more zip from second base, maybe because he was "only" 34. But every throw was upstairs. Don Eggert, our third sacker, had a cannon for an arm, and fortunately his throws were chest high, too. Those guys helped me set a new fielding percentage record for the PCL of .996, which I still hold for first basemen in 150-plus games. Currently the PCL plays only 145 games, so our record may be eternal.

I had the privilege of playing with another Negro League All-Star, Luis Marquez, who also became a PCL All-Star. In 1956, Luis, who by then was 32, hit .344, with 110 RBIs and 25 home runs.

How I would have loved to have seen those three men play in their prime and in the major leagues where they belonged. I was lucky to have played with Negro League royalty—All-Stars in the Negro Leagues in their prime playing years and then All-Stars in the highest minor league and at ages well past their prime.

What a travesty it was that they did not get a chance to play in the major leagues. Artie, Frankie, and Luis were great role models and even greater human beings. In my dreams, I still hear Artie yelling, as he often did in spring training in Glendale, California, in 1955, "Never fear, Artie's here."

I was fortunate to have played in the majors with Stan Musial, Satchel Paige, and Ernie Banks. From what I saw playing with a 34-year-old Artie Wilson, he might have come close to them playing in the big leagues. But we'll never know, and, unfortunately, neither did Artie. Rest in peace, Artie. You are loved and admired.

ABOUT ED MICKELSON

Ed Mickelson was a standout first baseman for 11 years in the minors, three of them (1955–1957) with the Portland Beavers in the PCL, where he was an All-Star, batting over .300 each season. He appeared in 18 games in the majors for three different teams, the St. Louis Cardinals (1950), St. Louis Browns (1953), and Chicago Cubs (1957). Mickelson accounted for the last RBI by a Brownie, hitting a single off Billy Pierce of the Chicago White Sox in the team's last game in St. Louis September 27, 1953. The Browns moved to Baltimore the next year and renamed the Orioles. Mickelson wrote about his career in the book *Out of the Park* (2007).

LIST OF ILLUSTRATIONS

INTRODUCTION

"There ought not never have been no time called too early!"[1]

When American playwright August Wilson penned those words for *Fences*, the play that was made into a movie in 2016, he could well have been thinking about another Wilson—Arthur Lee "Artie" Wilson.

Artie was the best shortstop in the Negro Leagues in the mid-1940s—and perhaps in all of baseball. The color of his skin, and then his age, kept him out of the big leagues until he made a cameo appearance in 1951, with the New York Giants. He was 30 years old.

That didn't stop *Sport* magazine, in its February 1951 issue, from naming Artie to a dream team of black baseball players. "The All-Star Team that couldn't happen," the magazine proclaimed.[2]

"Five short years ago," the story began, "if anyone had stood up in public and predicted that in the very near future there would be enough Negro players of proven brilliance in Organized Baseball to man an all-star team capable of holding its own against the best performers in the business, he would have been laughed to scorn."

The team featured four future Hall of Famers: second baseman Jackie Robinson and catcher Roy Campanella of the Brooklyn Dodgers and outfielders Larry Doby of the Cleveland Indians and Monte Irvin of the Giants. Rounding out the squad were Dodgers pitcher Don Newcombe; Indians first baseman Luke Easter; Giants third baseman Henry "Hank" Thompson; outfielder Sam Jethroe of the Boston Braves; and Artie at shortstop, the "only non-major-leaguer," as he had yet to play a game for the Giants.

"When you look this team over," *Sport* concluded, "you are bound to ask yourself: If they have done so well in so little time, what sort of all-star team will the Negro stars be able to field a few years from now?"

Only 12 blacks had played in the majors when the all-star nine were selected. Artie was the 13th, making his big-league debut on April 18, 1951, in the seventh inning of a game against the Braves. Teammate Rafael "Ray" Noble and the Braves' Luis Marquez appeared in the ninth to hike the number to 15. By year's end, that number had increased to 20, with one of them being Willie Mays, a 20-year-old whiz kid and Artie's former Birmingham Black Barons teammate.

"Artie was a superstar before the term was invented," Monte Irvin told author Roger Kahn for his book *A Season in the Sun*. "He had tremendous range, wonderful speed, a super arm. Besides that, he was a first-rate punch hitter, always on base, always making trouble for the pitcher. But by the time they let him join us on the Giants, he wasn't the player we'd known."[3]

Artie was still the best handyman in the league, and Giants manager Leo Durocher wanted to keep him around.

"He could play all the infield positions, and he could pinch-hit or whatever you needed him to do," Willie Mays said. "Artie was better than Bill Rigney."

Rigney could play second, shortstop, and third, plus he was white. The Giants already had four blacks, one more than the unwritten quota of three established by the major-league team owners.

Artie knew Mays was destined for greatness and, early in the 1951 season, urged Durocher to bring up Willie and send him back to Oakland in the Pacific Coast League (PCL), the best of the minor leagues. "I'm a singles hitter, and I've got to play every day to keep my timing," he said.

When Mays joined the struggling Giants in late May, Artie returned to the minors. Rigney stayed put.

"Colored guy has to be twice as good just to be on the team," lamented Troy Maxson, the fictional Negro League star played by actor Denzel Washington in *Fences*. "I just wasn't the right color."

Artie was the same color as Maxson, but he didn't let it bother him.

"My father was comfortable in his skin and with his ability," said Artie Wilson Jr., a basketball star at the University of Hawaii in the early 1970s. "He honestly didn't think there was a pitcher he couldn't get a hit off. Even when he was 65 and 75, he thought he could still get in the batter's box and slap out three out of 10 shots somewhere."

The racial bigotry of the times was beyond Artie's control. All he could do about it was slash singles and flash smiles, breaking color barriers and endearing himself to players and fans alike.

"His personality and temperament was perfect," said young Artie. "He'd just look off and keep playing. He felt racism was really the problem of others. It wasn't his problem. That's not who he was. He could turn the other cheek."

"He was one of the great players in the Coast League and a great in-between guy because he got along with the white guys as well as he did with the black guys," said Eddie Basinski, who played with and against Artie during his nine years in the PCL. "Artie was a credit to baseball."

Even umpires adored Artie.

"Boy, was he joyous," said Cece Carlucci, a PCL umpire for 12 years. He added:

> He was jumping up and down and laughing. One of the best-liked fellows in the entire league. They loved him. Just a fabulous guy. We loved to see him come to bat because we knew we weren't going to have any trouble on a ball and strike call. I don't remember calling a strike on him. Anything close, he was swinging.

Most of Artie's hits were singles.

"He was tough to play against because he sprayed the ball," said Basinski. "It was hard to position yourself and for a pitcher to pitch to him because he was pretty good at hitting almost any kind of a pitch—high or low, inside or outside."

Singles and smiles were Artie's trademarks.

"My dad had a classic smile," said Artie Jr. "He had a smile that made you smile and made you want to know him because it was such a sincere smile."

Artie was always smiling because, for him, baseball was still a child's game. And he was getting paid to play it.

"He loved baseball more than any guy I ever run into," said Basinski, a teammate at Portland in 1955. "On an offday, he'd call me and some of the other guys and say, 'Hey, let's go out to the ballpark anyway and play pepper.' The guy just loved the game so much."

That love was particularly obvious the last few times I saw him, in September 1994 and early 1995.

Artie grew up in Birmingham, Alabama, the most racially divided city in the United States at the time. In 1955, he moved his family to Portland, Oregon, and upon leaving baseball in 1958, he began selling used cars as a full-time salesperson for Gary-Worth, a dealership in nearby Gladstone.

The longest strike in the history of Major League Baseball (MLB) started on August 12, 1994, and lasted 232 days, until April 2, 1995.

It was the last day of September when I walked into the Gary-Worth showroom with my wife Mary.

"Can you believe it's September and they're not playing baseball?" Artie asked incredulously.

"You look like you could play too," I said.

"I can still play. Played ball this summer," he responded.

He was almost 74 and weighed the same 162 pounds he did as a player.

"I don't worry about my weight," he said. "I eat anything I want. And I sleep like a baby."

He looked spiffy in a double-breasted pinstripe suit.

"Still have my clothes from 1944. Fit good. Good quality," he continued. "Little pleats in front. Wear them to play golf. My daughter sent me a new pair of pants and shirts. Still haven't unwrapped them."

He smiled. "My wife and daughter want me to get rid of my old clothes."

Artie turned serious, "Baseball is the greatest game. I think about the baseball strike every day. Almost every minute of the day."

"Would you rather play then or now?" he was asked.

"Then!" he said emphatically. "I wouldn't trade the good times we had then."

He later elaborated, "If I had it to do over again, I'd do the same thing—over and over again. All the riding on the buses we did. All the hassle we had. I still enjoyed it. Made a good living at it. I would do it again."

In fact, Artie's biggest regret had to do with another player—Josh Gibson, the legendary Negro League slugger. "Boy, I wish he could've got into the major leagues," he said. "Powerful hitter. Best hitter I ever saw walk up to the plate."

The MLB strike was still unsettled the following February, when I accompanied Artie to the Allen Temple Christian Methodist Episcopal Church in Portland.

It was the same church I had attended with Artie 20 years earlier. Roger Kahn also visited the church when he wrote about Artie.

"Is your church integrated?" Kahn asked in advance.

"Of course, it's integrated," Artie said.

Kahn was the lone white face in the crowd.

"You remember when you asked if my church was integrated?" Artie said afterward.

"You told me it was," Kahn replied.

"What I meant was that God don't know no color."[4]

I sat in the middle of the church. Artie was sitting with other church elders in a pew near the pulpit.

Everybody stood up to sing the Negro National Anthem, *Lift Every Voice and Sing*:

> God of our weary years,
> God of our silent tears,
> Thou who has brought us thus far on the way;
> Thou who hast by Thy might, led us into the light,
> Keep us forever in the path, we pray.[5]

After the singing, prayers, and reading of the scripture, Artie got up to introduce me. "I think if I was in trouble, he'd come to my rescue," he said. "I feel the same way about him. He was here a few years ago. And when he arrived the other day, he mentioned coming to this church. He could've gone to other churches. But he came here, and I'm grateful."

While the ushers passed the offering plate, Artie moved next to me.

The pastor, Rev. James E. Smith Jr., stepped to the pulpit.

"The baseball players are on strike, worrying about how much money the owners make," he began. "What about how much *they* make?"

He gestured toward Artie and said, "I saw Artie Wilson this morning. I said, 'Brother Wilson, you need to go play baseball.'"

Artie smiled as several people shouted, "Amen!"

The sermon topic was, "A God Who Remembers."

"And God heard their groaning," Rev. Smith said, citing the second chapter of Exodus, verses 23 through 25. "God remembers because he hears."

After church, we had lunch at a restaurant in Gladstone.

"If I could change my age now, I'd go back and play," Artie said.

I brought up the newly released television documentary series on baseball by director Ken Burns, which was creating widespread interest among the Negro Leaguers still living.

"Double Duty was on there," he said. "He was in New York a couple of weeks ago when I was back there."

Ted "Double Duty" Radcliffe was a pitcher-catcher in the Negro Leagues who lived to be 103. He'd hurl the first game of a doubleheader and catch the second game. He and Artie were Black Barons teammates in 1944. They were reunited at a baseball-card show, one of many events throughout the country that celebrated the Negro Leagues and their mostly unknown players.

"'You're finally getting the recognition you deserve,' I told Artie, asking: 'How does it make you feel?'"

He replied:

> It's something that never happened before in the history of baseball. It's great. I couldn't thank the Lord enough for being alive to participate in this activity. It's something that no ballplayer could dream would ever happen. We're getting a little benefit, a little recognition. People are beginning to know about us. Every day I get 10 to 12 letters, people wanting my autograph. They send me pictures. I sign them and send them back. It makes tears come to my eyes.

Of course, they were tears of joy. Artie wouldn't have it any other way.

When Artie died in 2010, at the age of 90, he left a legacy of the abiding love and respect he oozed for the game and the singles and smiles that won the hearts and minds of so many white folk along the way.

1

JUST LIKE JACKIE

Artie Wilson once was considered the best shortstop in baseball.

"In 1944, Artie Wilson at shortstop and Lorenzo "Piper" Davis at second base made up an all-star combination that was hard to beat anywhere in baseball," Hall of Famer Monte Irvin said.

"He was right at the top—him and Jackie Robinson," Piper agreed. "He was at the top all the way in hitting."

After Artie put on a spectacular performance in the Negro Leagues' East–West All-Star Game in 1946, the *Chicago Tribune* reported how he almost became the one chosen by Branch Rickey of the Brooklyn Dodgers to break the color barrier in Organized Baseball, or "white folks' ball," as Piper referred to it.

"His agility, hitting, and powerful throwing arm had caused colored baseball magnates to pitch strong recommendations in his behalf," the *Tribune* said.[1]

Rickey passed Artie by and picked Jackie Robinson.

White folks' ball passed Artie by until 1949—three years after the Dodgers signed Jackie. Except for the New York Giants, every big-league team passed him by because he was black or too old.

In 1951, at the age of 30, Artie quickly passed through the majors with the Giants. He started just one game, batting a mere 24 times. He slapped four singles, walked twice, swiped two bases, scored two runs, and batted in another run to hit .182—barely more than the 162 pounds he weighed.

The singing of the spiritual hymn *Pass Me Not* was particularly poignant on Sunday, May 25, 1975, at the Allen Temple Christian Methodist Episcopal Church in Portland, Oregon. On the same date in 1951, Artie's fling with the Giants ended when he was let go to make room for a 20-year-old phenom named Willie Mays.

Standing at the altar, facing the congregation as he sang, Artie's slender body swayed gently with the music until the singing stopped. In a soft, tender voice, Artie briefly mentioned his baseball career and then, sounding the theme of the day's sermon, "A Day to Remember," said, "Baseball gave me a lot of wonderful memories. But there's one day I'll always remember—the day I was converted."

Artie was 12 years old at the time, living alone with his mother Martha in Birmingham, Alabama.

"Everything changed that day," he said. "I made up my mind to go all the way for the Lord. Do everything I can to help somebody. And that's what the Good Lord leaves me here for now—to help someone."

After the church service, an elderly woman, wearing a white straw hat, testified to that fact.

"He was a brother to me when I met him, a brother to me when my husband died, and he's a brother to me today," Mattie Larsen said, as tears welled from her eyes. "He's a man with a beautiful heart."

Big-league baseball passed him by, but Artie knew from five All-Star seasons with the Birmingham Black Barons in the Negro American League that he belonged in the majors.

He batted .402 for the Black Barons in 1948, the last pro player in a top-level league to surpass the .400 mark, the Holy Grail of hitting.

The following year, his first in white folks' ball, he hit .348 to win the batting title in the Pacific Coast League (PCL), the highest and best of the minor leagues. He spent most of the next eight seasons in the PCL, consistently batting over .300 and fielding his positions with flair.

"There wasn't nobody who saw me and Jackie in 1945 who wouldn't tell you but one thing," he told author Roger Kahn. "I was the best shortstop. There isn't nobody with intelligence who wouldn't tell you something else. For integrating baseball, Jackie was the best man."

"A brevity of pathos," Kahn said in describing Artie's big-league career.[2]

Artie focused on the big picture, not the big leagues. He looked at the entirety of his baseball career—seven years playing for the

American Cast Iron Pipe Company (ACIPCO) in the Birmingham Industrial League and seven winters of baseball in Puerto Rico, sandwiched among five years with the Black Barons and 10 years in white folks' ball.

He had a career batting average of .312 in the minors.

In 22 seasons as a semipro and pro, the Center for Negro League Baseball Research calculates he batted .338 to win six batting championships and finish second five times. His .376 average in Negro League play ranks third all-time. He played on 10 championship teams and was named Manager of the Year for leading Mayaguez to the Puerto Rican League title in 1948–1949.[3]

"Had Artie been given the opportunity to play with the Giants or anybody in the major leagues, there's no doubt in my mind that he would've been up in the top 10 hitters of the league," said Chuck Stevens, who played against Artie and coached him in the PCL.

They called him Artful Artie in newspaper headlines because of the amazing things he did with a bat and glove.

The bat was a wand in Artful Artie's hands. He waved it and base hits, mostly singles, magically appeared on the left side of the diamond, where opposing players were bunched together in a futile attempt to prevent the left-handed-swinging Artie from dumping one between them. He was like Houdini, the famous escape artist. "We called him Houdini," Stevens said. "We couldn't get him out."

Stevens played first base for the Hollywood Stars. They tried everything to stop him.

Hollywood catcher Eddie Malone threw dirt on his shoes when he stepped into the batter's box. "I'll stop you from running," Malone told Artie.

Artful Artie kept on beating out infield hits and stealing bases.

When Artie batted, the Stars moved their shortstop closer to the third baseman guarding the left-field foul line. "They could shake hands," Artie said.

George Raft, the movie star famous for his roles in gangster films, always attended Stars games when Artie was in Tinseltown. "He was a good buddy of mine," Artie said.

"They're bunching up on you," Artie recalled Raft yelling.

"They'll fall," Artie answered. "Some of them will fall in there."

The Stars couldn't keep Artful Artie from getting his hits. "I just racked them up. They couldn't get me out."

Yogi Berra of the New York Yankees was a notorious bad-ball hitter. So was Artful Artie.

Jerry Priddy was Artie's manager at Seattle in 1954. During batting practice, he threw a ball at least six inches over Artie's head. Artie whacked it into left field.

"Even an umpire could see that was a ball," Priddy hollered. "Learn to lay off those pitches."

"Skip," Artie yelled, "that's the pitch I hit best."[4]

Artful Artie's motto was, "Thou shall not pass." He said, "I didn't want a base on balls."

"Get ready, I'm going to have him throw it right down the middle of the plate," an opposing catcher said, trying to trick him.

"I'll take it, too."

Artie watched the pitch zip past him.

"How come you didn't swing?" the catcher asked.

"I didn't want it there."

"Only time I'd swing was if I had two strikes on me," he explained. "I wanted it outside, not down the middle of the plate."

Think of how Rod Carew, seven-time American League batting champion, handled the bat, consistently making contact with the ball. Or think about Ichiro Suzuki simultaneously swinging the bat and speeding off to first base.

"I always classified him as the greatest singles hitter," Piper said. "He hit off his front foot moving. He was one of the best running to first base because of that."

That was Artful Artie.

He was a black version of Richie Ashburn, the sprinter-quick leadoff hitter for the Philadelphia Phillies in the 1950s, who averaged 30 to 35 bunt singles a year.

"He could lay that ball down that third-base line, Podner," Piper Davis marveled.

That was Artful Artie.

Imagine Ozzie Smith, the acrobatic shortstop known as the "Wizard of Oz."

Artie was called the "Octopus" in the Negro Leagues because he covered so much ground, it seemed he had eight arms. In Puerto Rico, he was nicknamed "Barre Minas" as in ground-sweeper. "He catch everything," said Orlando Cepeda, a Hall of Fame first baseman who grew up in Puerto Rico watching Artie play against his father, Pedro. "I love Artie Wilson. He was my idol. He was amazing and really inspired me to be a ballplayer."

"Artie backhanded a ball with so much ease that people would just ooh and ah over the way he played," recalled Bill Greason, a pitcher for the Birmingham Black Barons and later the St. Louis Cardinals.

That was Artful Artie.

Picture someone with a big, infectious smile, a can-do attitude, and a wonderful sense of humor that made others around him feel better by quipping, "Never fear, Artie's here."

That was Artful Artie. He was an artist other great artists admired.

Lionel Hampton, the jazz legend known as the "King of the Xylophone" and the "King of the Vibes," was a close friend and one of Artie's biggest boosters.

"Going out to Artie Wilson's, the terrific shortstop of the Seattle, Washington, ball club, to whom I am the godfather of his newborn son, Artie Wilson Jr.," Hampton wrote in his column for the *Pittsburgh Courier* in early 1953.[5]

"We met in the 1940s," Artie said. "Best man at my 40th wedding anniversary. Good ballplayer. He could hit. Good fielder."

Joe Louis, the world heavyweight boxing champion from 1937 to 1949, went to see Artie play every chance he got.

In September 1949, Louis was a boxing promoter and organizing a fight for Ezzard Charles, his successor as king of the boxing world. He took Charles's manager, Jake Mintz, to a game at Wrigley Field in Los Angeles, where Artie's Oakland Oaks were playing the hometown Angels. Joe and Artie posed together for a picture before the game.

"Wilson only got four hits out of five times at bat," Mintz said afterward. "What's the matter with that guy, Joe?"

"He's just having an off night," Joe deadpanned.[6]

That's what Joe Louis, the renowned "Brown Bomber," thought of Artful Artie.

Near the end of his playing career, Artie played second base for the Portland Beavers in the PCL. Ed Mickelson was the first baseman.

"God! How I would have liked to have seen Artie Wilson play in his youth," he wrote in his autobiography, *Out of the Park*.[7]

Best of friends, Artie Wilson and Lionel Hampton, the "King of the Vibes," could light up a hotel ballroom with their smiles and shared passion for baseball and jazz. Hampton was the godfather of Wilson's son, Artie Jr., born in Birmingham, Alabama, in 1952. *Doug McWilliams Collection*

"He was missing the top of his right thumb," Mickelson said in amazement. "All he had there was a nub."

The tip of the thumb on Artie's throwing hand had been cut off in a machine shop accident when he worked for ACIPCO.

Alvin Dark, star shortstop for the New York Giants, checked out Artie Wilson's thumb on his right throwing hand when he reported to the team's spring training camp in 1951. Artie played without the tip of the thumb, severed in an accident when he worked for the American Cast Iron Pipe Company in Birmingham, Alabama. *Courtesy Artie Wilson Jr.*

"That was certainly a strong hindrance to him," said Roger Osenbaugh, a teammate at Sacramento in 1957. "Without the thumb, you
can't put that much mustard on the ball."

Or grip the bat normally.

"If he had the thumb, case closed," Osenbaugh added. "He would've
been a great major leaguer because of his hitting ability. He was a great
Coast League hitter."

Artie saw plenty of the dark side of life, but, consistent with his
smile, he always accentuated the bright side. "I have no qualms over the
way I was treated," he reflected. "I was able to cope with the situation,
able to get along with every player. I never had any problems with the
opposing team. I respected people. And they respected me."

That respect is best summed up by Stevens, a white player:

> Artie carried the banner well when it was important. The only guys
> who get credit [for integrating baseball] are the guys with big-league
> careers. But the Artie Wilsons were as important as the Jackie Robin-
> sons. They handled themselves in a difficult time with great dignity.

Jackie broke Major League Baseball's (MLB) color barrier with a
relentless fighting spirit. Artie did it in the minors with singles and
smiles.

In 1975, Artie lived in a modest house on a wide, tree-lined street in an
integrated neighborhood about three miles from downtown Portland.

Everyone seemed to know Artie, waving at him as he cruised by in a
new, sparkling white Chrysler Cordoba.

He moved to Portland in 1955, when he joined the hometown Beavers, a team in the PCL. "I got turned down in Portland more than any
other Coast League town," he said. "Eight times. And I wind up living
here."

Artie laughed at the irony.

"This is your home," Artie said upon welcoming a guest. "Act as if
you were home."

Artie's mother-in-law served a good, old-fashioned lunch of fried
chicken, hot buttered rolls, mixed vegetables, tossed green salad,
peach-apricot cobbler, and a tall glass of milk. It was as scrumptious as
the spring weekend was beautiful, the flowers and shrubs in the Wil-

son's well-manicured yard picture perfect. The living room was immaculate and tastefully decorated.

Artie was batching it. His wife Dorothy was in San Francisco, attending a church convention.

They shared their home with Dorothy's parents, David and Annie Daniels. "They're good people. Great people. I love them both like they were my own parents."

They could be heard that evening whooping and hollering in the family room downstairs as they watched pro wrestling on television. "They like that wrestling. Man, do they like it."

Artie looked just as dapper as he did in his playing days, when he was called "Dude" for his spiffy pinstriped suits and Kangol® berets with tassels. He sported a closely cropped mustache and a gray-speckled "soul patch"—a small amount of facial hair just below the lower lip and above the chin. He wore tan Dingo boots and an olive green double-knit suit with a matching turtleneck sweater, accented by a green-and-white necklace made from rocks and shells.

"I bought this in Hawaii," he said, fingering the necklace. "Brought a bunch of 'em back as gifts for friends. I don't know what these things are. I just like 'em."

The 1975 season was underway, and MLB finally had a black manager—Frank Robinson of the Cleveland Indians. Black players dominated the game, with Rod Carew and Bill Madlock capturing league batting titles, George Scott leading the American League in RBIs and tying Reggie Jackson for most home runs, and Mickey Rivers and Davey Lopes topping their respective circuits in stolen bases.

"There are a number of players that I would've picked for a manager over Frank Robinson," Artie admitted. "I'm just hoping he settles down to be a good manager since he's the first black."

Artie questioned whether Frank had the patience and temperament needed to succeed, saying, "It takes a player sometimes two, three years to develop. I hope he plays it cool and don't get everybody riled. He could make a good manager. He knows baseball. But you've got to understand people. There are no two alike."

Frank wound up managing 16 years in the majors, winning American League Manager of the Year honors in 1989, by guiding the Baltimore Orioles to an 87–75 record and a second-place finish in the

American League East after losing 101 games the year before. Overall, his teams won 1,065 games and lost 1,176.

Artie favored someone else:

> Junior Gilliam was my number-one choice as the first black manager. I would've taken Gilliam over any of them. He was an underrated ballplayer. Never got the publicity that he should have got. Same way with Hank Aaron. Used to tell them all the time, "Hank Aaron was one of the best ballplayers in the National League." Every day he did the same thing. He did his job year after year. Nobody ever heard of him until he got close to Ruth's record. Then all you could hear was "Hammerin' Hank." Before that, you didn't hear much of him. And he gave you 100 percent every day. Every day.

Jim "Junior" Gilliam was cut from the same cloth as Artie—a gang of one with the glove and a maestro with the bat in his 14 years with the Dodgers in Brooklyn and Los Angeles. He was National League Rookie of the Year in 1953, enabling Jackie Robinson to move from second base to third, where he mostly played for the rest of his career. Junior played every position except pitcher and catcher. He batted behind Maury Wills in 1962, when he stole 104 bases, a single-season record at the time.

Artie continued:

> Junior Gilliam was one of the best ballplayers Brooklyn ever had on the field. But they never gave him credit. I played against him; I've played with him. I've yet to see him throw the ball to the wrong base. When he fielded it, he knew where that ball was going. And he played heads-up ball all the time. Any position he played, he played like he'd been playing it all the time. Yet, he never got the credit.
>
> He was the reason Maury Wills stole as many bases as he did. He could see if Wills had the base stolen. He'd let the ball go. If he saw where Wills didn't have a good jump, he'd foul off the ball. A good second hitter, that's what he's good for—protecting that man on in front of him. Gilliam was one of the best.

Artie loved talking baseball.

"He was always extremely humble and extremely quiet," Artie Jr. said of his father. "But you start talking baseball and there was a switch that went on. He was very proud of what he could do."

"Why did they pick Jackie?" Artie asked, answering his own question:

> Jackie had been a football player at UCLA—something a lot of us hadn't had the opportunity to do. Playing football with white ballplayers. He'd mingled with them; he knew how to get along with them. You couldn't just pick any Negro ballplayer out of the Negro League who would've gone through what Jackie did.

He rattled off the names of other Negro League players—Larry Doby, Roy Campanella, Monte Irvin, Hank Thompson, Joe Black, Don Newcombe, Hank Aaron, and Willie Mays. He added Bob Gibson and Lou Brock, two black superstars who came along a few years later. "I'm naming players with a lot of baseball knowledge," he said.

Artie paused to make sure his next point came through a lot louder than his usual soft voice:

> Jackie is the *only* man who would've gone through with what he did. He had everything. He had the tools, the know-how. I'm not saying these other guys couldn't do it now. I just don't think they would've gone through with it like Jackie. This is why I like Branch Rickey. He picked the right man.

Artie faced the same racial bigotry in the PCL, relating, "Jackie had gone through more than I had. I could whip it."

John Ritchey was the PCL's first black, joining the San Diego Padres in 1948, the year following Jackie's breakthrough with the Dodgers.

Artie signed with the Cleveland Indians in 1949, after leading Mayaguez to the Puerto Rican League championship as a player-manager. The New York Yankees challenged the contract, claiming Artie belonged to them because of a deal they made with the owner of the Black Barons. A public feud erupted between Indians owner Bill Veeck and Yankees general manager George Weiss.

Frank "Fay" Young of the *Chicago Defender*, the dean of black sportswriters, broke the controversy down to its basics in a column titled "Who'd a 'Thought It'":

> Weiss called Veeck's practices "unethical." Veeck threatens to sue Weiss. Weiss claims he will toss the Wilson deal into Chandler's lap. Veeck says he will sue Weiss—perhaps for slander.

All of it makes good reading matter. We laugh. Here are two millionaire white men (or at least they represent millions and two top-notch ball clubs) fighting over a Negro ballplayer.

Ever think you'd live to see that? We didn't, but there it is as plain as your nose on your face. [8]

Artie went to spring training with the Indians and played 31 games for their PCL affiliate, the Padres, before baseball commissioner Albert "Happy" Chandler ruled in favor of the Yankees.

Artie explained:

I didn't want to report to no Yankees. Not to Newark for what they wanted to pay me. Going through some of the same things I knew Jackie had gone through I couldn't see leaving the Negro League going with Newark. I wasn't improving any. And then taking less money. So, I said I'd go home. I can still play in the Negro League.

Charley Dressen was manager of the Oakland Oaks, another PCL team, and he needed a shortstop. "Charley got on the phone and some-how or another bought my contract from the Yankees. That's how I got to Oakland."

Artie became the first black to wear an Oaks uniform. "I had prob-lems when I first went to Oakland."

One player quit the team and baseball in protest. "They had a couple of others, but then they said, 'Well, he's going to be here. You can play or you can go.' So they left."

The Oaks' second baseman, a skinny, hot-tempered kid named Billy Martin, offered to room with Artie on the road. "Billy Martin didn't have a prejudiced bone in his body. He was a super guy."

Artie also was befriended by Jackie Jensen, a young outfielder who would go on to star with the Boston Red Sox. "Another super guy," he said. "We named our daughter Zoe Ann after his wife."

The oldest of Artie and Dorothy Wilson's two children, Zoe Ann was born on June 12, 1950. Zoe Ann Olsen-Jensen won a silver medal in springboard diving at the Olympic Games in 1948 and a bronze in 1952.

Earlier in the 1949 season with San Diego, Artie played alongside Luscious "Luke" Easter.

"Super guy," Artie said of his former teammate. "Not many could hit the ball further than Luke Easter."

To Artie, most baseball players were super guys. Fans and sports-writers felt the same about him.

In Seattle, another PCL city, the media referred to him affectionate-ly as "Li'l Arthur."

He was the first black to play for the Seattle Rainiers. He joined the Rainiers in 1952 and played three full seasons, batting .316, .332, and .336, and piling up 200-plus hits in each of them. After batting .307 for Portland in 1955, he returned to Seattle and hit .293 in 1956.

"He is as regular as the phone bill," *Seattle Times* sports columnist Lenny Anderson opined.[9]

Artie was liked and respected by everyone, especially Gale Wade, a kamikaze-style baserunner who was personally responsible for the PCL banning rolling, cross-body, block-type slides. Wade played for the Los Angeles Angels from 1955 to 1957.

"The biggest kick I got out of baseball was breaking up a double play at second base," Wade said. "I'd rather do that than hit a home run."

"I saw him go in there and just roll over some of those guys," said Cece Carlucci, a longtime PCL umpire.

"Any way to break up a double play, he would do it," Artie said. "He never got me."

"Artie was just about as slick as you could get," Wade said. "He was the only guy that I couldn't take out at second base. I tried everything in the world. If he thought he was going to get got, so to speak, he dodged out of the way and just grinned at you. He had a great attitude."

More than once, runners tried to spike him sliding into second.

"You do that again, I'll make you eat the ball," he warned.

"They tried to low-bridge me, too," Wade said. "That was part of the game."

So were pitches that flattened batters or hit them in the head. "I never got mad when pitchers threw at me," Artie said. "I could make them jump rope out there. I'd hit the ball back through the box."

"Every time you brushed Artie back, he hit a line drive down the left-field line," said Sacramento pitcher "Chesty" Chet Johnson.

"Dusting him off was a virtual impossibility," the *Times*' Anderson observed. "He not only slashed the knockdown pitch into left field for a single, but [also] didn't even know he was being thrown at."[10]

"He was the most even-dispositioned fellow I ever saw in my whole life," Stevens said. "He was a great asset to a ballclub because he was that type of guy."

In many ways, Artie was just like Jackie.

"I went through some of the same things," he conceded, "but my experience was nothing compared to what he put up with. Knowing what he went through made it a little easier for me when I did get in the Coast League."

He pondered the similarities a little more:

> I might've been able to do the same thing he did, but I don't know whether I could've gone through with it or not. So, I think he's the only man. You build a solid foundation, and it's hard to wash it away. Jackie had the foundation. He knew it was going to be rough. If he'd failed, we might be struggling yet to get into Organized Baseball.

Artie was inducted into the Oregon Sports Hall of Fame in 1989, the Puerto Rican Baseball Hall of Fame in 1994, and the PCL Hall of Fame in 2003. Some 60 years after he broke into pro baseball with a .346 batting average, the *ESPN Baseball Encyclopedia* named him both Rookie of the Year and Most Valuable Player in the Negro American League for 1944.

The Negro Leagues Baseball Museum in Kansas City, Missouri, opened in 1997, with life-sized bronze sculptures of 12 Negro League stars on display: Leroy "Satchel" Paige, Josh Gibson, James "Cool Papa" Bell, Walter "Buck" Leonard, Leon Day, Andrew "Rube" Foster, William Julius "Judy" Johnson, Ray Dandridge, Oscar Charleston, John Henry "Pop" Lloyd, Martin Dihigo, and John "Buck" O'Neil. Ten of them are also enshrined at the National Baseball Hall of Fame in Cooperstown, New York.

Missing from both places is Artie Wilson, the last .400 hitter in the Negro Leagues and the highest echelon of white folks' ball. Once again, he was passed by.

"It's very exciting, but it's painful too," said Jackie's widow, Rachel Robinson, upon unveiling the statues of the Negro League greats. "You can't just celebrate. Somehow, it's painful because we paid a big price with segregation. These boys were great ballplayers. But it's painful to look at these statues because I think, 'What if?'"[11]

2

LET'S PLAY BALL!

The Birmingham Civil Rights Institute is located across the street from the Sixteenth Street Baptist Church, where one Sunday morning in 1963, a bomb blast killed four young girls.

From the late 1940s to the mid-1960s, almost 50 unsolved, racially motivated bombings prompted Alabama's largest city to be called "Bombingham." The racial tension of the period was best summed up in April 1960, by Harrison Salisbury, writing in the *New York Times*:

> Every channel of communication, every medium of mutual interest, every reasoned approach, every inch of middle ground has been fragmented by the emotional dynamite of racism, reinforced by the whip, the razor, the gun, the bomb, the torch, the club, the knife, the mob, the police, and many branches of the state's apparatus.[1]

A visit to the Birmingham Civil Rights Institute is a journey through Birmingham's segregated past.

The trip begins with a short movie of Birmingham's early history and its emergence as the American South's industrial powerhouse. The movie screen lifts to reveal two drinking fountains. The newer, cleaner one is designated for white people; the other one is for "colored" people. Nearby is a vivid reminder of the racism that once divided baseball in Birmingham—a display recognizing the Birmingham Black Barons of the Negro American League. From 1940 to 1962, Birmingham had two professional teams—the all-white Barons of the Southern Association and the Black Barons.

This was the Birmingham Artie Wilson experienced growing up and playing baseball, first in the city's industrial "colored" leagues for the American Cast Iron Pipe Company (ACIPCO) and then for the Black Barons.

"My first baseball suit, I bought it myself: $2.98. That was a lot of money back in those days. But I was the only one that had a baseball uniform," Artie said.

Artie had a glove that cost him $1.98. "Kept that glove a long time."

He made the money for the glove and uniform shining shoes at a barbershop for a man named Swan. He started at age six and continued into high school.

"People used to see me, and I'd have a ball glove or mitt on my belt buckle, hooked on the side," Artie said. "Anybody who stopped me and said, 'Let's play ball!' I was ready to play ball. Rain, snow, sunshine, it didn't make any difference. I was ready to play ball."

Artie made his own baseballs. He took a golf ball, wrapped twine around it, and taped it up tightly. If he couldn't finagle a bat from someone, he cut a branch off a tree and made one.

Games were played by a big pond near the three-room house he lived in with his mother. "We'd be playing and somebody would hit the ball in the pond. We'd wade out and find it. I cried many times when the ball went into the pond and we couldn't play."

A man at Artie's church was the father he didn't have at home, providing guidance and discipline. "I had no alternative but to learn the game and go straight. I'd run around shagging flies with the men. I'd grab a mitt and warm up the pitchers. They'd throw so hard it would knock me down. I'd fall back on my seat, get back up, and catch it again. Hold onto it, though. I grew up that way."

At Hooper City High School, Artie was well prepared to play in a league against grown men representing Birmingham's largest companies. "We beat those men. Lost only one game the whole year," he said proudly.

He also played every other Saturday on a men's team from the National Cast Iron Pipe Company. "I wasn't old enough to work there, but finally they decided to give me a job so I could take care of my mother."

Artie worked three days one week and two days the next. Eventually, he quit high school to work full time.

Arthur Lee Wilson was an only child, born on October 28, 1920, to Martha Wilson, in Springville, Alabama, about 30 miles northeast of Birmingham. Martha wasn't married, and Artie's father, Lonnie Hicks, flew the coop. He went by his mother's family name of Wilson.

Artie was 20-something the first and only time he met his father.

"Listen to this: He only lived 101 miles from Birmingham. That was down in Montgomery, Alabama."

Artie had just returned home from a month-long road trip with the Black Barons and was looking forward to a home-cooked meal by his cousin, Lillie Mae, who lived with him. While Lillie Mae prepared dinner in the kitchen, Artie chatted in an adjoining room with his Uncle Willie and another man. Artie soon noticed Lillie Mae standing in the doorway.

"If you're through cooking, we're ready to eat!" Artie said.

Lillie Mae burst into laughter.

"What are you laughing about?" he asked.

"Fool, that's your father there!"

"You're kidding!"

Uncle Willie confirmed the stranger was, indeed, his father.

"Why didn't you tell me? You've been here all this time," Artie asked his uncle.

"Well, we just wanted to see what you'd do," Uncle Willie said.

Artie never saw his father again.

Meanwhile, Martha Wilson was a mother, father, sister, best friend, and everything wrapped into one for her son.

"She used to sit down and talk to me just like a man," Artie said fondly. "I could go to her and talk about anything. She was more or less like a sister to me. She'd get out in the streets and play ball with me. Hit from the left side just like I could. And she could run . . . keep right up with me."

Martha juggled housekeeping jobs, one of them working three days a week for a judge and his family. "She'd never been sick until she died in 1938. She was in her 40s. She worked and worked. She and I cut wood like two men. Worked every day. That's why I gave up school. I wanted to stop her from working."

Artie talked about his mother wistfully, saying, "Boy, I wish my mother was living. I'd give anything. I'd give the whole world. Kids don't realize what a mother means to them. I think of that now. That's why I appreciate things."

The big things that happened to Artie later in life didn't bother him much because he grew up appreciating the little things. Artie said:

> I can remember when I didn't have money. Pair of shoes . . . not a decent pair of shoes. If I had a pair, a hole was in the bottom. I'd go to the grocery store and I'd have to pay to get cardboard boxes. I'd go home at night, sit down, take my shoes off, and put my feet on the cardboard and draw. I'd take a razor blade and cut it out. Put it in my shoes and it was the sole of my shoes.

In 1937, Artie went to work for ACIPCO, one of the largest employers in Birmingham and a baseball powerhouse.

"Baseball is the major attraction and recreation for the employees of the plant," management stated in the company newsletter in 1929.[2]

ACIPCO fielded black and white teams in the city's industrial leagues. Players received uniforms, socks, sweatshirts, and sometimes gloves and baseball shoes.

Artie recalled:

> I was making more money at ACIPCO than some of the guys playing in the Negro Leagues. I know of many players who left to play in the Negro Leagues but had to fight to get their way back home. They didn't make the money. They got promises, that's all. I didn't see any sense in me leaving the good job I had until the Negro Leagues were paying good money.

ACIPCO attracted the best players around.

One of them was Piper Davis, a versatile infielder who would go on to play 17 years in the Negro Leagues and white folks' ball. "See," Piper said, "your better ballplayers were right here working, that had experienced life on the road a little bit."[3]

Piper and Artie would go on to star for the Black Barons, along with three other ACIPCO players—outfielder Ed Steele, catcher Herman Bell, and pitcher Bill Powell. "That's five Black Barons on the same company team," Piper pointed out.[4]

"The ballplayers piddled around in the machine shop," Artie explained. "You still had to work, but if we had a game during the week, we'd work something out. We'd go to the Y—colored YMCA—and get dressed, take a bus to the stadium, and play."

Games were played at Sloss Field in the Negro Community Center.

When ACIPCO played its archrival, Stockham Valves and Fittings, 10,000 to 12,000 people showed up to watch. "We were like the Dodgers and Giants in New York. We outdrew the white Barons easily," Artie said.

Artie lived a block from the ballpark. "Ten o'clock Saturday morning I'd be sitting out on the porch. People would be on their way to the stadium so they could get a good standing place."

Piper and Artie often arrived early to throw one another short hops that they caught between their legs.

"Okay, Piper and Artie, put it on," appreciative fans yelled. "Let's have some fun!"

And they did.

Artie was a defensive wizard at shortstop and won four Birmingham Industrial League batting titles in his seven years at ACIPCO, with a career batting average of .438, the all-time high for the league.

What makes his record at ACIPCO even more amazing is that he did it without part of his right thumb.

Artie worked in machine shop number three at ACIPCO. Most days he took equipment apart for a machinist named Gilliam to do the necessary repairs.

"I could do most anything," Artie said. "But at that time they didn't allow no black man to run any machines."

Sometimes on weekends, Gilliam looked the other way.

Artie was running a machine when he heard something fall and instinctively grabbed for it with his right hand. The machine pulled his hand down and cut off the top of his thumb.

He was not supposed to work with gloves on, but he was wearing a brand-new pair. It wasn't until the bloody glove was removed that he realized part of his thumb was gone.

"When they were taking me to the dispensary, they said, 'Don't look, it will make you sick.'"

Artie looked anyway.

The first question he asked the doctor was, "You think I can play ball?"

The doctor shook his head in disbelief, saying, "You've done lost your thumb and here you are talking about playing ball."

"It's gone. Can't do anything about it."

The doctor replied, "You'll be able to play ball."

Artie Wilson compiled a .438 batting average in the seven years he played for the ACIPCO Pipemen, to rank as the greatest hitter in Birmingham Industrial League history. Like Piper Davis before him, he joined the Birmingham Black Barons in 1944, and during the next five years, they teamed to become the best double-play combination in the Negro Leagues. *Center for Negro League Baseball Research*

A stub of a thumb wasn't going to keep Artie from playing ball. "It healed up in about three weeks. I carried a golf ball in my pocket. I kept squeezing it. Next year I didn't even miss it."

The accident occurred in October 1939 as World War II was beginning. It kept him off the battlefield, but not the ballfield.

Artie adjusted by throwing three-quarters instead of overhand.

"He had to learn to throw with the middle finger holding most of the ball," explained Piper. "He laid the ball on those other two fingers."

The injury caused his batting average to drop 13 points, to .398, the second time in seven years he failed to top .400. In 1943, his last at ACIPCO, he batted .559.

Artie followed his sidekick Piper to the Black Barons in 1944. "If I can make it playing baseball, why not?" he said. "It's something I love to do. They were paying good money. I had nothing to lose; I had everything to gain. So, I left—took a leave of absence."

When Artie tried to turn in his employee identification badge at ACIPCO, no one would take it. "You'll come back after a while," he was told.

In 1944, the second baseman for the Black Barons was Tommy Sampson, a slick fielder despite missing the index finger on his right throwing hand, severed in a coal-mining accident.

Artie and Tommy put on a show, teaming up on stylish double plays that had fans hollering, "Nub to nub!"

It was a popular yell that meant hell for opposing teams.

Artie quickly became an All-Star in the Negro Leagues, a starter in the 1944 East–West All-Star Game at Chicago's Comiskey Park, called the "dream game" because it annually showcased the greatest black players.

He returned to ACIPCO in 1946, with his employee badge and the key to his locker in the pipe shop. This time someone took them, telling Artie, "If you ever decide to come back to work, come on back anytime."

He never went back.

3

"LEAVE THE BUS HERE!"

A Negro League ballplayer spent more time on a bus than in his own house or apartment. The bus was how he got from town to town and game to game. The bus was where he ate when a restaurant owner wouldn't serve him a meal inside. The bus was where he slept when there was nowhere else to sleep.

The bus was home to Artie Wilson and his Birmingham Black Baron teammates.

When Artie returned to his house in Birmingham, his cousin, Lillie Mae, told the bus driver, "Leave that bus here! Cause Artie can't sleep!"

Artie slept on a bed about once a week. "Didn't get much sleep. Only in the bus. But those were good days. We had a good bus driver, and we had a lot of fun."

A bus driver was paid as much as the average player, and it helped if he was as good a mechanic as he was a driver. The Black Barons' Charlie Rudd was both. "God bless him," Piper Davis said, "he saved our lives many a day."[1]

The Black Barons bus was a 22-seat model with no air conditioning. It was easy to spot, since "BIRMINGHAM BLACK BARONS BASE-BALL CLUB" was printed in capital letters above the six windows on each side of the bus.

After one all-night ride, Piper recalled a teammate rushing to get that morning's newspaper. "I wonder what Joe DiMaggio's doing this morning?" the player said sarcastically. "Laying up in that big, fine bed, done been out last night."

The Birmingham Black Barons spent more time on the bus than on the baseball field. It served as a restaurant, hotel, and locker room, as the players often couldn't eat, sleep, or change clothes anywhere else because of segregation laws. The bus driver, Charlie Rudd, was as valuable as any player on the team, and he was rewarded with a comparable salary. *Memphis and Shelby County Room, Memphis Public Library and Information Center*

"Always reading about them damn white boys," another player chided. "Why don't you do something yourself?"

"Man, they love me in the South," Piper joked. "They got signs that say white go here and black go here. They look out for me."[2]

Humor bonded the players and helped them look beyond the snubs and inconveniences to the pleasures of getting paid to travel throughout the country and play the game they loved.

"We made fun out of our lives as players," said Bill Greason, a pitcher for the Black Barons in 1948. He continued:

> If we went to a hotel and couldn't get a room, we didn't have a fit about it. We'd just laugh about it, get back on the bus, stop, and somebody would buy cold cuts, cake, and bread to make homemade

sandwiches. We just laughed about it. It was a lot of fun. That's how we looked at it—something to enjoy.

The Black Barons were the Harlem Globetrotters of baseball, going wherever they were booked by Abe Saperstein, the roly-poly Jewish founder and mastermind of the world-famous basketball team.

Tom Hayes Jr., the black president and owner of the Black Barons, acquired the team with money he made from his undertaking business in Memphis, Tennessee. He made sure the Black Barons didn't go under financially by partnering with Saperstein, a sports promoter dubbed "the Great White Father of Negro Baseball."

Saperstein had the connections and a simple strategy: "Book it and they will come."

He booked the Black Barons at Yankee Stadium. Between 25,000 and 30,000 people showed up.

Saperstein scheduled Black Barons games at major-league ballparks in Washington, DC, Philadelphia, Cincinnati, and Chicago, as well as smaller cities ranging from Wilmington, Delaware, on the East Coast to San Bernardino, California, on the West Coast.

The Black Barons were part of the Negro American League, along with the Memphis Red Sox, Kansas City Monarchs, Cincinnati Clowns, Cleveland Buckeyes, and Chicago American Giants. They played about 70 league games a year, plus dozens of nonleague contests against Negro National League teams and such local semipro clubs as the Bushwicks of Brooklyn and Autos of Benton Harbor, Michigan.

"We played every day, doubleheader on Sunday," Artie said.

"See," Piper added, "you had places that didn't have baseball, and they were glad to see you."[3]

The Black Barons played most of their home games at Birmingham's Rickwood Field, the ballpark they shared with the white Barons of the Southern Association. As supportive as the black community in Birmingham was, it didn't have the disposable income needed for the Black Barons to prosper throughout an entire season. They hosted some games in New Orleans, Shreveport, Nashville, and other Southern cities.

The Black Barons once played five games in two days.

"We played in Birmingham on a Sunday—doubleheader," Artie said. "Got in the bus after the game and went to Memphis."

They arrived in Memphis at about noon on Monday, Labor Day, and played another doubleheader. There was one more game to play—a night contest in Jackson, Mississippi, 210 miles from Memphis. "Got in the bus with our uniforms on and went to Jackson," Artie recounted.

The last game in Memphis went into extra innings. "We called and told them we were on our way."

The Black Barons got to Jackson at 9:00 that evening, the ballpark crammed to capacity. "Took us about 30 minutes to get through all the people."

And then, the Black Barons played their third game of the day. "We were off the next day, but we played five ballgames in two days."

Saperstein arranged trips to Hawaii and, in 1944, a series of 12 games in San Francisco and Oakland, against all-star teams made up mostly of Pacific Coast League players and ex-major leaguers. They won 11 of them.

"Every bit as good as they claim to be," a *San Francisco Chronicle* sportswriter said of the Black Barons after Artie and James "Cool Papa" Bell had three hits each in a 7–4 victory over a squad headed by Augie Galan, a three-time National League All-Star with the Chicago Cubs and Brooklyn Dodgers.[4]

The game at San Francisco's Seals Stadium attracted a crowd of 7,000, prompting a local sports columnist to ask why in the middle of football season "more people paid to see just another baseball game" than the "top local gridiron contest of the year" at nearby Kezar Stadium. "You furnish the answer—I can't," he wrote.[5]

One reader observed that the Black Barons are "capable of playing any white team in major- or minor-league ball on a basis of equality," and "thousands of Negro fans" went to the game for "visual proof."[6]

Saperstein was a sugar daddy to the players.

Artie explained:

> When we came back from Hawaii into Frisco, he had a party for all the players, their girlfriends, their wives, whoever they wanted to bring. He footed the bill. This happened many times. When he'd get ready to leave, he'd come around and give every ballplayer a $20 bill. You could write or call him and say, "I need $100, Abe." He'd send it. Why wouldn't you play for a guy like that?

In the winter, Piper and Ted "Double Duty" Radcliffe, a pitcher-catcher for the Black Barons in 1944, played for the Globetrotters. At one point, Winfield Welch managed both teams.

Saperstein was the consummate promoter, ballyhooing the 1944 Barons as "one of the great Negro teams of all time."[7]

Only the Homestead Grays, with the mighty Josh Gibson, were better. They beat the Barons in seven games in the 1943 Negro World Series.

Prior to the start of the 1944 season, the black-owned *Pittsburgh Courier* billed the Barons as the "whipping boss" of Negro baseball. The story mentioned 12 players but not a single word about Artie.[8]

Some of the old-timers on the star-studded team didn't look kindly upon a newbie like Artie. "They weren't going to show you anything. They were afraid you were going to take their jobs," he said.

When Welch announced Artie was his shortstop, one teammate groused, "You'll never make the All-Star Team."

"Why?"

"You're a rookie."

"So what?" Artie retorted. "If a player can make it, I'll make it."

Halfway through the season, Artie's box-office appeal was being likened to Satchel Paige, the legendary black pitcher. "Hottest Negro player, now that Satch is in eclipse," the *Cincinnati Enquirer* reported. "He's leading the Negro American League in hitting."[9]

Even Satch was impressed.

The first time they faced one another, Artie belted a double. Satch sauntered to second base for a private chat.

"Yeah, young buck," Artie recalled Satch saying. "They told me you could hit, but I didn't know you could hit like that. You won't get that pitch anymore. You can sit down there on second base because that's as far as you're going."

Artie didn't get past second, but he made it to the Negro Leagues East–West All-Star Game in Chicago. He was the starting shortstop for the West and wowed a "sweltering throng of 50,000 hilarious baseball fanatics" with two hits and fancy fielding. This inspired the *Courier*'s Wendell Smith to write, "Everyone agreed that classy, little Art Wilson of Birmingham has 'it' plus. . . . He played shortstop like a 15-year veteran."[10]

In the Negro Leagues, he was referred to as Art or Arthur and, in Smith's opinion, the silver lining in the Black Barons losing the 1944 Negro World Series to the Grays in five games. "Art Wilson," wrote Smith, "may someday be rated alongside Willie Wells, the peer of all shortstops."[11]

This was lavish praise from a highly respected black sportswriter, as Wells was the best shortstop in black baseball for two decades.

Artie's performance was even more impressive because he was one of five players injured in a car crash the week before the World Series.

"Our second baseman got broke all to pieces," Piper explained, "and the third baseman . . . he got a hole knocked in his head; and the catcher, one of our catchers . . . he got his arm hurt, and our utility infielder . . . he got his leg hurt."[12]

Artie played with a sprained wrist and Johnny Britton, the third baseman, with a patch over one eye. The others never made it onto the field.

Artie finished the season with a .346 batting average, seven percentage points behind the Negro American League batting champ, Sam Jethroe—the first black to play for the Boston Braves and National League Rookie of the Year in 1950.

The *Courier* named Artie to its Negro League "dream team," along with Satchel and four other future Hall of Famers—catcher Roy Campanella, first baseman Walter "Buck" Leonard, second baseman Ray Dandridge, and outfielder James "Cool Papa" Bell.

Another brilliant shortstop appeared on the black baseball scene in 1945, a second lieutenant in the U.S. Army signed by the Kansas City Monarchs—Jackie Robinson. He was already a familiar name in the sports world, starring in football, baseball, basketball, and track at UCLA before entering the military.

Soon after reporting to the Monarchs, the *Courier's* Smith arranged a tryout with the Boston Red Sox for Jackie, Jethroe, and Marvin Williams, a smooth-fielding second baseman.

Facing political pressure from a Boston city councilman to ban Sunday baseball, the Red Sox and Boston Braves promised in writing to give black players a chance. When Smith arrived in Boston with the trio, the general managers for both teams went into hiding. "We have been here almost a week now, but our appeals for fair consideration have been in vain," Smith said.[13]

The players eventually got their tryout at Boston's Fenway Park. Red Sox coach Hugh Duffy conducted the 90-minute drills, while manager Joe Cronin watched from the stands. Afterward, Duffy told the players they would hear from the team "probably within the near future."[14]

Meanwhile, at the Brooklyn Dodgers' training facility in Bear Mountain, New York, Dodgers president Branch Rickey was quietly sizing up two black players—pitcher Terry McDuffie and first baseman Dave "Showboat" Thomas. They were taken to the camp by Joe Bostic, sports editor of the *People's Voice*, a black newspaper in New York City, and a *Courier* sportswriter.

At first, Rickey refused to see them, explaining he would look at a "devil with a forked tail and horns" if he could play baseball, but he didn't like being pressured by the scribes.[15]

The tryouts were dismissed as a "travesty" by Cum Posey, owner of the Homestead Grays. "It was the most humiliating experience Negro baseball has yet suffered from white Organized Baseball," he said, adding, "Any white rookie one-half as good as any of these players would have been kept for at least a week and sent to some minor-league club."[16]

One positive that came out of the tryouts is that they rallied such white newspapers as the *New York Post* to join the *Courier* in its crusade to tear down the wall between blacks and Organized Baseball. The *Post* editorialized:

> Baseball is not a monopoly of lily-whites or gray-greens. It belongs to all the people. It is the typical American game. And so it is part of the American melting pot. Into this sport have come men like Joe Di-Maggio, an Italian; Hank Greenberg, a Jew; Alejandro Carrasquel, a Cuban; Lou Gehrig, a German; Sigmund Jacucki, a Pole; and others. There should be a place waiting in it for the 10 percent of Americans who are Negro.[17]

Carrasquel was Venezuelan, but no one quibbled with the key point of the editorial or Jackie's statement to the media the day before the Red Sox tryout: "We can consider ourselves pioneers. Even if they don't accept us, we are at least doing our part and, if possible, making the way easier for those who follow. Someday, some Negro player or players will get a break. We want to make that day a reality."[18]

The clock was ticking louder than ever, and by the end of the 1945 season, it couldn't be ignored.

Jackie, Artie, and a third shortstop, Avelino Canizares, had the Negro Leagues abuzz with their electric play. "Probably at no time in the history of organized Negro baseball has there been three shortstops who were so near equal," Smith said.[19]

Jackie was living up to the star status he achieved at UCLA. Artie was again near the top of the league in hitting and dazzling afield. The unheralded Canizares, nicknamed the "Cuban Wonder," was a speedy rookie and the sparkplug of an infield that helped the Cleveland Buckeyes win the 1945 Negro World Series.

Smith compared their numbers midway through the season. Artie had the highest batting average, Jackie had the most stolen bases, and Canizares was tops in RBIs. He concluded they "should be given a chance to play in the major leagues."[20]

All three shortstops were selected to play for the West in the East–West All-Star Game, but, curiously, only Jackie saw action. Artie was benched by Winfield, the Black Barons manager who guided the West squad, even though he was announced as the starting second baseman.

The so-called dream game was a nightmare in 1945, because Negro League greats Josh Gibson and Satchel Paige didn't play. Satchel refused to pitch because the game's promoters didn't show him the money he wanted to see, and Gibson was held out for "flagrant and consistent training violations."

As for Artie's absence, "Dissatisfaction is running rampant through the Birmingham Black Barons," Smith said. "Captain Art Wilson is in the doghouse and as a result was not permitted to play."[21]

Piper was expected to start at second for the West, with Artie at shortstop, but in late July, just before the All-Star Game, he was suspended for hitting and breaking the nose of an umpire. The Black Barons struggled to finish second in the American League standings, a distant 14 games behind Cleveland. Artie ended up batting .372, runner-up to Jethroe (.393) for the second straight year.

The careers of the three shortstops went in entirely different directions.

Canizares wound up playing mostly in Mexico for lower-level minor-league teams.

Jackie signed with the Dodgers to trigger the integration of Organized Baseball. As Rickey said, "It's the inevitable, not a move; it's a movement."[22]

Artie carried on in Birmingham, waiting for the movement to sweep him onto a big-league club. "I believed I could hit .300 in any league. Against anybody. Might not hit many home runs. But I bet you I could hit .300."

But would anyone notice? That was the question for Artie and other Negro League stars left behind.

Black fans were losing interest in the Negro Leagues. "We couldn't draw flies," bemoaned Buck Leonard, a hard-hitting first baseman nicknamed "the Black Lou Gehrig."

Black newspapers became fixated on the exploits of Jackie and the other four blacks playing for Dodgers farm teams.

While Jackie made news and history at Montreal in the International League, Roy Campanella and pitchers Don Newcombe, Bill Wright, and Roy Partlow grabbed headlines at Nashua, New Hampshire, and Three Rivers, Quebec, Canada, in the lower minors. The *Courier* published the statistics for these players at the top of a sports page every week during the 1946 season. Stories on their games got top billing over Negro League contests.

Box scores for Negro League games virtually disappeared, making it impossible for historians to compile reliable numbers for Artie and some other stars in 1946. "Records not available," the Center for Negro League Baseball Research noted in its comprehensive listing of Artie's career statistics.[23]

What's well documented is Artie's brilliance in the 1946 East–West All-Star Game and his presence that fall on an All-Star Team headed by Satchel.

The lead paragraph of the *Chicago Tribune* story on the East–West All-Star Game mentioned that Artie "almost made a trip to Organized Baseball" the previous spring, "but Branch Rickey instead chose Jackie Robinson for his Montreal club." It goes on to describe his "spectacular performance," which included a rare steal of home.[24]

The *Courier* gave this vivid account of the play, the highlight of the West's 4–1 victory:

> With Piper Davis at the plate, the West pulled a perfect double steal.
> Jethroe broke from first and stopped midway. Josh Gibson, one of
> the greatest throwing catchers in baseball history, whipped the pellet
> down to second.
>
>   Wilson came high-tailin' it home, sliding under Garcia's erratic
> return throw. Jethroe, naturally, continued on to second base. It was
> a neat bit of base running, and the near-capacity throng gave the
> Western "thieves" a roaring salute.

Smith raved, "Art Wilson proved conclusively that he's the best shortstop in the American loop."[25]

In October, a *Sporting News* story posed the question, "Can a good
major-league club beat a good Negro team?"[26]

The answer supposedly was to come from a series of games between
the Bob Feller Major League All-Stars and the Satchel Paige Negro All-
Stars.

A press release promoting the games hailed Satchel's team as a
"Who's Who in Negro League Baseball." This was an apt description,
because Artie and the other players selected by Satchel were unknown
to most white baseball fans. They knew more about "Who," the imagi-
nary first baseman in the Abbott and Costello comedy routine "Who's
on First?"

Satchel needed no introduction. He was an incomparable showman
who liked to boast that he was the "greatest man in the world with a
baseball in [his] hand."[27]

He said he was 40, but there was evidence he was at least 48. Satchel
had fun with his age. "They want me to be old so I give 'em what they
want. Seems they get a bigger kick out of an old man throwing strikeouts." [28]

In 1946, Feller was 27 and at the peak of a Hall of Fame career,
leading American League pitchers in victories (26), strikeouts (348),
shutouts (10), complete games (36), and innings pitched (371).

Feller loaded his team with Mickey Vernon, American League bat-
ting champion; outfielder Charlie "King Kong" Keller, a five-time
American League All-Star; and pitchers Spud Chandler and Johnny
Sain, both 20-game winners. Another pitcher, Bob Lemon, would win
207 games on his way to the Hall of Fame. Stan Musial, the National
League bat king, joined the club late in the tour.

The teams started on the East Coast and ended up on the West Coast, flying separately in chartered DC-3 planes and staying in different hotels. It was "segregated luxury," as one black All-Star referred to the arrangements.

The games gave fans their first glimpse of baseball's best black and white players on the same field.

Two games at Yankee Stadium combined to attract nearly 50,000 spectators. The crowd of 27,462 at the second contest was the largest to watch a black team in New York City. Satchel and Feller usually started and pitched three innings, but on this occasion, they went five innings, Satchel outshining Feller in a 4–0 win.

In Chicago, 20,811 fans watched Feller's team prevail, 6–5.

The Fellerites won 4–3, in Los Angeles, as 22,577 people jammed into Wrigley Field, 2,000 more than the number of seats in the ballpark.

Most of the games were close.

In October 1948, Artie Wilson (in white coat, first row on far right) and the Satchel Paige All-Stars had their own airplane to travel throughout the country and play a series of games against a team of white major leaguers led by pitcher Bob Feller. One player called it "segregated luxury." Satchel is wearing a hat and standing in the doorway. *Center for Negro League Baseball Research*

They were exciting, the Negro All-Stars winning, 3–2, in Kansas City, on a three-run, walk-off homer in the bottom of the ninth.

They were entertaining. In a game at Council Bluffs, Iowa, Satchel caught Frankie Hayes of the Chicago White Sox napping at first base and picked him off, but not with the usual snap throw and tag by the first baseman. "Instead he ran over in person and was standing squarely on the sack with the ball when Hayes finally woke up," the local newspaper reported. "The Sox catcher was an easy out."[29]

Feller organized the exhibition games to make money. He reaped an $80,000 bonanza—$30,000 more than his annual Indians salary.

Members of Feller's team received $100 per game, or approximately $3,500, for the 35 games they played—about half of what the average major leaguer made in 1946.

Henry "Hank" Thompson, a slugging third baseman for the Negro All-Stars, called the tour a gravy train, claiming he was paid as much as $7,500 for 17 days' work.

Satchel didn't get the money he wanted and quit near the end of the tour, suing Feller for $3,800. Satchel and company were replaced by a black All-Star Team headed by Jackie.

The *Sporting News* reported Feller's All-Stars won 13 of the 18 games played against Satchel's All-Stars. Researchers later discovered two additional games the teams played, with Satchel backed by a patchwork cast and losing both. Either way, the major leaguers lost only five games.

Did this mean they were vastly superior?

Not at all.

What the games really proved is the Negro League players belonged on the same field with white baseball's finest, and, most importantly, there was a lot of money to be made because white and black fans alike wanted to see them play.

"The whole trip was because of racial rivalry," Feller said. "We knew that was what would happen, and we knew that it would draw very well."[30]

For Artie, the games proved what he knew all along: "If you could play Negro League baseball, you could play Major League Baseball."

He believed he could hit any pitcher, white or black, the fastest or the most baffling. "My masterpiece was to swing that bat up there. A guy believed he could strike me out. I don't believe it. I believe I can hit him."

Against the hard-throwing Feller, Artie singled in Chicago, hit a ground-rule double in Council Bluffs, and doubled and scored a run in Richmond, Indiana. "We had guys [in the Negro Leagues] that when they threw at you, you had to hit the dirt in a hurry. Didn't have any time to wonder whether you should get out of the way. You *knew* to get out of the way."

At Richmond, he also singled twice off Dutch Leonard, a knuckleball specialist who won 191 games in the majors. "Dutch Leonard could throw a good knuckleball. But he couldn't throw no knuckleball compared to Porter Moss. Submarine pitcher; everything underhand. He could make that ball do tricks. It was like a butterfly coming up there. He was tough to hit—tough."

The Paige–Feller All-Star Games paved the way for Jackie to break into the majors the following year.

At Montreal in 1946, Jackie batted a league-leading .349 and stole 40 bases to spark the Royals to the International League and Junior World Series crowns. In 1947, he paced the Dodgers to the National League pennant, hitting .297 and swiping a league-high 29 bases to earn Rookie of the Year honors.

Jackie also tapped into the racial rivalry Feller referred to and filled thousands of empty seats in National League ballparks. In Chicago, a record crowd of 46,572 packed Wrigley Field to see Jackie in a major-league uniform for the first time. The Dodgers set league attendance marks at home and on the road, drawing 3.7 million fans.

By the end of the summer, four more blacks were in the majors—Larry Doby of the Cleveland Indians, Hank Thompson and Willard Brown of the St. Louis Browns, and Dan Bankhead of the Dodgers.

"And the day is close at hand when every last one of the major-league clubs has a Negro in its lineup," Saperstein told a San Francisco sports columnist.

As part owner of the Black Barons, Saperstein had a vested interest in this happening. But, he also knew Negro Leaguers had the same box-office potential of his Harlem Globetrotter teams that were highly popular with white and black audiences worldwide.

The record crowds attending Dodgers games "opened the eyes of the major-league owners," Saperstein said. "Primarily they are businessmen. They saw they had tapped a new and undreamed-of source of revenue. They are getting their normal trade, augmented by thousands in colored trade."

Saperstein predicted that the "next five years will see the greatest Negro players that ever lived," and he touted Artie at shortstop and Piper at second as the "best double-play combination Negro baseball has ever seen" and the "biggest Negro League plum of them all."[31]

When the Browns purchased Thompson and Brown from the Kansas City Monarchs, they also made a deal to buy Piper from the Black Barons. There was one catch: They had to play him at first base during a 30-day option period so one of their scouts could evaluate his performance at that position.

"Never saw a more versatile player," Mel Ott, former New York Giants slugger, would say after managing Piper five years later.[32]

Upon hearing Ott say he was going to play Piper at all nine positions during a single nine-inning game, someone said, "Let's make it a 10-inning game and have Piper sell beer in the 10th."[33]

Only 478 fans showed up at one game, so the last-place Browns didn't need a beer vendor. They wanted to send Piper to their Elmira, New York, farm club in the lower minors, but he balked. It was St. Louis or bust.

Thompson and Brown were released five weeks after they were signed. After no one would take responsibility for the decision, the *St. Louis Star and Times* observed, "No double-play combination ever passed the ball around as fast as Brownie officials."[34]

Piper was more surprised when the Browns announced plans for three black players than when they let them go. "Do you know what the quota was? The quota at first was three. It wasn't a written thing, but just among the owners, they said, 'We'll have about three of 'em.'"[35]

Saperstein continued to promote Artie and Piper, suggesting, "If the Pirates don't take them the Cubs might, in another year."[36]

Three years earlier, in 1944, the Cubs had showed interest in the dazzling duo. "We heard about it," Artie said, adding that Hayes knew about it. "But nobody dreamed of Negroes getting into the majors at that time."

Artie and Piper played together so long they knew what the other was going to do before he did it.

"We made plays and people would say, 'Gee, how in the world did you get over there?'" Artie said. "Well, we knew what was going on."

They had nicknames for one another. Piper was "High"—short for "Highpocket," because he was 6-foot-3. Artie was "Squeak," although he never knew why Piper called him that.

"What's the matter, Squeak?"

"Everything okay, High."

After an All-Star Game in Chicago, Artie and Piper traveled to Chattanooga, Tennessee, for a Black Barons game that was delayed until they arrived. "The people came to see us play," Piper explained. "We dressed, threw a couple of balls, and said, 'We're ready to go.'"

In the second inning, a ball was hit to Artie behind second base. "If the ball was hit that way, one of us was to say right away if he could get it," Piper said. "There were never two of us in short right field or short left field."

"I got it, High."

Artie scooped up the ball and flipped it to the bag, where Piper was waiting to rifle it to first for a nifty double play.

"That was worth waiting for, folks," the public-address announcer bellowed.

"Two of the greatest," raved Bill Greason, who went on to pitch in the majors for the St. Louis Cardinals, before becoming a Baptist minister. "They looked like magicians on double plays. The ball would come off the heel of Piper's glove, and he was throwing. Artie could catch everything. Some just have a flair in fielding and throwing, and people love to see it. Artie had that. Same thing with Mays."

Greason was one of four rookies to join the Black Barons in 1948. Another was a 17-year-old outfielder—Willie Mays. Piper was player-manager.

"They were veterans," Greason said. "And they were not quick to help you. You either had it or you didn't stay because they were afraid of being replaced. There wasn't much teaching that they were willing to give."

Willie was the exception.

"We called him a phenom," Greason said. "He had all the tools, except hitting. He didn't know anything about sliders, sinkers, or stuff—breaking pitches. He could hit a fastball. He had the good glove, the good legs, and the good arm, all of this on his side."

Piper patiently worked with Mays on his hitting. But he didn't need any help in the outfield.

Norman "Bobby" Robinson in left field and Ed "Stainless" Steele in right were average fielders, so they welcomed Willie in center field.

"They were so happy, they didn't know what to do," Greason said. "Anything hit between them and Mays, they would just stand and watch to see if Mays would catch up with it. Most often he would."

The Black Barons won the Negro American League pennant. In the Negro World Series, they lost for the third time in five years to their old nemesis, the Homestead Grays.

"We never could beat 'em in the World Series," Artie said, continuing:

> Of course, nobody could beat the Homestead Grays. They had a powerful team. You could've taken the Homestead Grays along with some Birmingham Black Baron players and put them in the major leagues, and you'd seen a heck of a team. They would've won. Any records that go in baseball, you'd had it.

Artie won his second-straight league batting title with a .402 average. In 1947, he hit .377, three points higher than Piper, the runner-up.

"The Birmingham Black Barons of 1948 were not only mighty, they also had some outstanding gentlemen," Greason said. "It was not the greatest in ability, but the camaraderie and togetherness, the unity, the working and helping each other, it was the greatest ball club I ever played on. We had a lot of respect for each other."

Piper set the tone on the bus and the field.

After a night game in Tuscaloosa, Alabama, an umpire hitched a ride on the team bus back to Birmingham.

"I was saying some word that I shouldn't have," Greason said. "I was just doing it out of the devil."

"You don't need to do that," Piper scolded. "You need to have respect for this man."

On another occasion, Greason was pitching in a close game and became visibly upset after third baseman Johnny Britton muffed an easy grounder.

"Piper stormed in from second base and jumped all over me," Greason recalled.

"Do you throw strikes every time?" Piper asked.

"There we all are grinning like kids on Christmas morning," Willie Mays (arrow) once said of this famous photo, which someone else described as exuding "exhilaration and exhaustion." The Birmingham Black Barons had just beaten the Kansas City Monarchs to win the 1948 Negro American League championship. Artie Wilson is on Willie's right and Alonzo Perry on his left. Directly below Artie in a gray shirt is Bill Greason, the winning pitcher in the decisive eighth game. *Center for Negro League Baseball Research*

"I try," Greason answered.

"What do you think he was doing?" Piper fired back.

"I used to be kind of hotheaded," Greason said, adding:

> That turned me completely around. I was able to recognize that we all try. We all fail sometimes. Piper had everything. Good ballplayer. Good manager. He could have managed in the major leagues. He had all the savvy. He was smart. He knew the game. He was pretty strict. He set up rules with fines for how much it would be for staying out too late or being caught at a nightclub. If we broke them, he said, "You took your own money; I didn't."

The 1948 Black Barons were a mirror image of Piper—serious but fun.

There was the Sunday doubleheader at sold-out Rickwood Field in Birmingham. They were shorthanded and picked up a young player with far more speed than baseball sense.

He was on first base when Steele hit a ball that got past the center fielder.

"The kid roared around second base and went to third base, turned around, and came back and met Steele at second base," Artie said. "Steele was going on the inside; the kid was going on the outside. As he slid back into first base, he got up and asked Pepper, 'How am I doing?'"

Pepper was Lloyd Bassett, the first base coach when he wasn't catching.

"What in the world are you doing back over here?" he fumed.

"Pepper was boiling," Artie said, laughing. "The fans just went wild."

Pepper was a fan favorite, sometimes catching while sitting in a rocking chair. "He could catch and he could put on a good show," Greason said.

The rocking chair came in particularly handy when Bill Powell was pitching. "One of the slowest-working pitchers," Greason said. "Some of his games took three hours."

That was an hour longer than most Negro League games.

Powell was a stickler for conditioning, the opposite of fun-loving Jimmy "Schoolboy" Newberry, a hard-drinking, rubber-armed pitcher with a crazy streak that sometimes got him and others into trouble. "I was with him one night at a club, and he got into it with somebody," Greason said. "I went to help him and ended up with a pistol in my side."

Listen to Greason describe his teammates and a picture emerges of rugged individualists who became selfless together. "If Ed Steele was told to bunt, he'd bunt. He could hit the long ball, but that was the kind of person he was. That's what makes a winner."

Alonzo Perry was a party animal off the field, but on it he was all business, with a reputation as a big-game pitcher and clutch-hitting first baseman.

"We were not concerned too much about going to the majors and playing with the white boys because we had one of the best leagues with some of the best ballplayers," said Greason. "We were just concerned about making a living. We enjoyed playing. We played emotionally."

Pitcher Bill Greason was one of four rookies on the 1948 Birmingham Black Barons, along with Willie Mays. He went on to pitch briefly for the St. Louis Cardinals. After baseball, he became a Baptist minister. *Memphis and Shelby County Room, Memphis Public Library and Information Center*

That emotion is what *Courier* sportswriter Rollo Wilson was referring to after Artie sparkled afield, socked four singles, and scored as many runs in an All-Star Game. He "made all of the other players look verra, verra ordinary," Wilson said, "and surely rated a second and third look by big-league clubs."[37]

Artie played with the passion of the most zealous fan.

"The Negro ballplayer gave big-league baseball the unexpected—daring," Piper said in a 1977 magazine interview. "Because we loved the game, and we played more for the fans than for ourselves."[38]

The Dodgers had Jackie, and in April 1948, they added Campanella. The Indians had Doby. The most entertaining and flamboyant black player of all was still available—Satchel.

The ageless wonder was biding his time, waiting to hear from Indians owner Bill Veeck.

The day after Veeck signed Doby in 1947, Satchel sent him a telegram reading, "IS IT TIME FOR ME TO COME?"

Satchel had heard through Saperstein, a mutual friend, that the Tribe boss was interested in signing him. Veeck wired back. "ALL THINGS IN DUE TIME."[39]

That time came in July 1948, when Satchel joined his All-Star touring partners, Feller and Lemon, on the Indians pitching staff.

Satchel's box-office appeal proved to be just as "interracial and universal" as he was. Fans turned out in droves to see him pitch, with 201,829 attending his first three starts. Satchel won all of them, two on shutouts, and six of seven decisions.[40]

The Indians won the American League pennant and the World Series. They had two of the four black players still active in the majors, and Veeck had Saperstein looking for more.

Artie knew Saperstein was one of his biggest fans. As he left for Puerto Rico to play winter ball in 1948, Artie was hoping his nights of sleeping on a bus were almost over. Like Satchel, his time was coming soon.

4

THE BATTLE FOR ART WILSON

On one side, there was Bill Veeck of the Cleveland Indians, a maverick in the good ol' boys club of major-league team owners that controlled everything in baseball except him. On the other side was George Weiss, general manager of the New York Yankees empire, which ruled baseball both on and off the field. In the middle was Artie Wilson, the "pawn in the scuffle" between the newly crowned world champion Indians and the Yankees, the team they dethroned.

Wendell Smith of the *Pittsburgh Courier* coined the showdown the "Battle for Art Wilson." Said Smith, "Major-league teams are now fighting each other over ballplayers they once fought to keep out of the big leagues."[1]

Making matters worse was the bad blood between Weiss and Veeck.

To Weiss, the Tribe boss was a loud-mouth con man making a mockery of the game with his crazy gags and reckless wheeling and dealing.

In his autobiography, *Veeck—As in Wreck*, Veeck described Weiss as his "unfavorite person." He also called him a "serious, humorless man, as befitted a man with the fate of the Yankee empire on his shoulders."

Veeck's disdain for Weiss was surpassed only by his contempt for the Yankees. "Hating the Yankees isn't part of my act," he said, "it is one of those exquisite times when life and art are in perfect conjunction."

He conceded Weiss was a "good operator" that "always came up with a fine crop of young players," noting: "The possibility exists that I was never able to get along with him because I was jealous of his success."[2]

Going into the 1949 season, the shoe was on the other foot.

Veeck outfoxed Weiss and other American League executives by signing Satchel Paige. At first, they scoffed that it was another one of his publicity stunts, a view shared by J. G. Taylor Spink, publisher of the *Sporting News*. He wrote in an editorial, "To sign a hurler at Paige's age is to demean the standards of baseball in the big circuits. Further complicating the situation is the suspicion that if Satchel were white, he would not have drawn a second thought from Veeck."[3]

Satchel made Veeck look like a genius, posting a 6–1 won–loss record and a 2.48 earned run average. After he tossed a three-hit shutout to beat the Chicago White Sox, Veeck tweaked Spink in a telegram, saying, "Paige pitching—no runs, three hits. Definitely in line for THE SPORTING NEWS' Rookie of the Year Award. Regards, Bill Veeck."[4]

Weiss was anxious to reestablish Yankee supremacy with a big, headline-making trade that would put Veeck in his place.

At baseball's annual winter meetings, he had a deal lined up with the Washington Senators for Mickey Vernon, the American League's 1946 batting champ, and Early Wynn, a pitcher starting to show the potential that put him in the Hall of Fame with 300 victories. In the wee hours one morning, while Weiss was sleeping, Veeck nabbed the pair and the national limelight.

"I went to bed last night with a pennant-winner and woke up this morning in second," moaned Casey Stengel, the Yankees' new manager.[5]

Veeck had the league's only two black players, and based on their success, he was ready to add more.

Weiss knew Veeck had no quota that would keep him from filling his roster with blacks.

In 1944, Veeck tried to buy the cash-starved Philadelphia Phillies and stock the team with Negro Leaguers assembled by Abe Saperstein and Doc Young, sports editor of the *Chicago Defender*. "I had not the slightest doubt that in 1944, a war year, the Phils would have leaped from seventh place to the pennant," he wrote in his book.[6]

He was equally confident that with black and white soldiers fighting side by side in World War II he couldn't be stopped. Of course, he was wrong. The National League took over the bankrupt Phillies and sold them to someone else for about half of what Veeck was willing to pay.

Early in the 1948 season, Veeck hired Saperstein to find the best black players available. Saperstein assured Veeck that Satchel was still the greatest pitcher alive and worth the $50,000 it was going to take to land him. He also encouraged Veeck to sign Artie as insurance for Indians shortstop-manager Lou Boudreau, who was nursing fragile ankles and legs.

The Yankees scouted Artie and his sidekick at second base for the Black Barons, Piper Davis. A report was filed anonymously after the St. Louis Browns considered signing Piper. Historian Robert Burk has identified the author as Weiss. He mistakenly said the Browns scouted Piper in 1946, not 1947.[7]

The typed document reads in part:

> Davis is 32, they tell me, and Wilson is about the same age. Wilson has a finger off his throwing hand. They are both good ballplayers. The St. Louis Browns scouted Davis in 1946, took [an] option on him, then wanted to send him to Elmira. He wanted to go to the Browns so they released their option on him. If he wasn't good enough for the Browns two years ago I don't believe he could make it with the Yankees now.
>
> There isn't an outstanding Negro player that anybody could recommend to step into the big league[s] and hold down a regular job. The better players in Negro baseball are past the age for the big leagues. . . .
>
> I am aware of how these committees apply the pressure on the big leagues to hire one or perhaps two players. If you hire one or two, then, they will want you to hire another one. There will be no compromise with them, and they are mostly bluff.[8]

The report referred to the "failure of the Negro National League," so it was filed after three teams disbanded and the league dissolved in December 1948. This was at about the time the Yankees dispatched scout Tom Greenwade to Puerto Rico to look at Artie, player-manager for Mayaguez in the Puerto Rican League.

The February 2, 1949, edition of the *Sporting News* featured a picture of a beaming Artie being interviewed by one of its correspondents. The heading above the photo reads, "SHORTSTOP SCOUTED BY YANKEES."[9]

An accompanying story reported that Greenwade offered contracts to Artie and three other players: first baseman Luscious "Luke" Easter, outfielder Luis Marquez, and pitcher Ford Smith.

Why would the Yankees want Artie?

They already had Phil Rizzuto, an outstanding shortstop, and someone in their organization was on record as saying none of the Negro Leaguers were good enough.

The answer was simple: They wanted to prevent the Indians from signing the four players.

Veeck didn't do anything when Saperstein first recommended Artie. Boudreau was burning up the American League with a .355 batting average and on his way to winning the Most Valuable Player (MVP) Award. Upon learning that the Yankees had signed Marquez and were close to wrapping up a deal with Artie, Veeck made an emergency call to Saperstein's office in Chicago.

"Mr. Saperstein is somewhere in Alaska," he was informed.

"When will he return?" Veeck inquired.

"In a week or 10 days."[10]

The Yanks were about to snatch Artie, and Veeck's "number-one espionage agent was running between snow drops in the frozen wastelands of barren Alaska with his basketball circus," Smith wrote.[11]

Artie declined the Yankees' offer of $500 a month, as it was less than the $750 he was making in Birmingham. "They wanted me to go to Newark, which was alright, but then they didn't want to pay me anything."

Greenwade said Artie wasn't concerned with salary and would "play for nothing, just to get the chance."[12]

The Yankees weren't in a rush, as they had a telegram from Black Barons owner Tom Hayes that read, "Agree to assign Art Wilson contract to Newark (Yankee farm club) for $5,000 on signing and reporting, $5,000 additional if retained June 1, 1949."[13]

It so happened that when Saperstein returned to Chicago from Alaska a week later, Hayes was in town for a meeting of Negro American League owners.

"Offer him $15,000 for Wilson," Veeck instructed Saperstein. "Tell him we'll pay the money on the spot."[14]

A personal check for $15,000 from Saperstein was better than a promise of one-third that from the Yankees. They had yet to produce a penny.

Veeck called Artie in Mayaguez to tell him he had bought his contract and was flying to Puerto Rico to complete the deal.

Confusion about the meeting place led to a chase scene straight out of an old-time movie. Veeck jumped on a plane in Mayaguez and ordered the pilot to fly directly over the highway to San Juan, 100 miles away.

Smith provided the following account: "Startled farmers looked up as the plane raced at a low altitude over the highway with Veeck leaning far out the window, inspecting every automobile going in the direction of San Juan."[15]

There was no sign of Artie, so Veeck asked area radio stations for help.

"It is vitally important that Art Wilson, Mayaguez ballplayer, get in touch with Mr. Bill Veeck immediately," one announcer said on the air. "He is looking for you in his airplane."[16]

Artie heard one of the appeals and went to a San Juan hotel, where Veeck was waiting with a generous contract that was to his liking.

"Bill Veeck took care of his players—a players' owner," Artie said.

The dramatic signing turned a behind-the-scenes tug-of-war into a highly public war of words usually found on the cover of national tabloids. The battle was filled with irony.

One of the nicest guys to play the game triggered the biggest, nastiest front-office feud in the history of the game.

Artie went from being ignored on the sports pages of white newspapers to being in the headlines almost daily, and it had nothing to do with what he did on the field.

The biggest irony was white folks' ball fighting over a black player it had fought to keep out because of the color of his skin.

"The Wilson sale has caused more headlines than the signing of Jackie Robinson," Hayes said. "The Yankees just did not want Wilson because they offered him much less than I told them I was paying him. So how did they expect him to sign, when we both wired that the deal was off, as no money had been posted or paid?"[17]

Weiss was furious, accusing Veeck of "unethical tactics."

"When Weiss calls my action 'unethical,' he'd better be able to prove it," Veeck retaliated. "That sounds like a court word to me."[18]

Veeck defended his actions by going on the offense.

He chided Weiss, saying, "I did not dilly or dally. I flew to Puerto Rico, then hired a plane and chased around the island half a day trying to locate Wilson. I found him, signed him to a Cleveland contract, and completed my deal."

He needled: "Weiss probably feels like the player who was caught off second base on the hidden-ball trick and now is trying to save face with higher-ups in the Yankee organization. The Yanks ignored Negro players for a long time and now suddenly have decided to sign a few."

He lectured: "I wish to point out to the New York club that if you want to get anywhere, you have to be fast. You have to hustle."[19]

The Yankees were not going to beat a street fighter in a street fight. But they could win the fight at City Hall because they were, after all, City Hall.

Weiss took his case to baseball commissioner Albert "Happy" Chandler, contending, "There is no place in baseball—major league, minor league, or Negro league—for tactics of the sort encountered in this case."[20]

At the same time, he said the Yankees "no longer would take Wilson, even if he were awarded to us."

With Yankee interest in Artie "now being nil, the entire Wilson case should be reduced to a similar status," Spink concluded in a *Sporting News* editorial.[21]

That didn't happen.

In fact, Veeck had another case for Chandler to review.

"We want Marquez," he said. "I'll turn the facts of the case over to Chandler."[22]

Marquez was a speedy Puerto Rican outfielder for the Homestead Grays until they folded after the 1948 season. He was claimed by the Baltimore Elite Giants before being sold to the Yankees, despite an option Veeck had to buy him from the Grays.

If Veeck wanted to cause a logjam and confuse everyone, he succeeded.

Chandler was mulling over the two cases in early March, when Artie reported to the Indians spring training camp in Tucson, Arizona. Artie was still wondering what the controversy was all about.

"New York made me an offer," he told a wire-service reporter. "I didn't accept it. Cleveland came along with another offer. I like it. I accepted and signed. That's all there is to it. As far as I'm concerned, I'm with Cleveland."[23]

Artie had picked up a new nickname in Mayaguez—the "Lou Boudreau of Puerto Rico."

Boudreau was Cleveland's manager and starting shortstop, a seven-time American League All-Star coming off the best season of his career. Joe Gordon and Ken Keltner, both perennial All-Stars, started at second and third base, respectively. The average age of the infielders was 33.

"Sure, it's an old infield," Boudreau admitted, "but it was an old one last year too when we won the pennant. I'd rather call it a veteran infield."[24]

Artie was 28, but few people believed him. "Artie Wilson is a seasoned old-timer who has been around just about as much as Paige," one sportswriter said.[25]

Going into spring training, the Indians had 14 black players, six of them with the big leaguers at Tucson.

"How many Negro players can be assigned to one ball club without upsetting balance and harmony?" asked Jim Schlemmer, a sports columnist for the *Akron Beacon Journal*.

The question was posed because of the "occasional fear and worry expressed over the possibility that the Negro will eventually dominate Major League Baseball, as he already dominates in boxing."

Blacks ruled boxing in 1949. Sugar Ray Robinson was the world welterweight champion, and Ezzard Charles and Jersey Joe Walcott were vying to replace the retiring Joe Louis as king of the heavyweights.

The columnist said the question wasn't so much about skin color as it was "self-defense and self-preservation"—the same feeling the team's white veterans had toward younger whites trying to replace them.

"What does concern some of these men," he continued, "is the proven fact that the Negro baseball player runs faster, throws harder, and hits farther or more often than most of the white players whose positions are endangered."[26]

At second base, Gordon didn't show any signs of feeling threatened by Artie. "Joe taught me how to get out of the way from guys trying to

Artie Wilson got married in February 1949, and went to spring training with the Cleveland Indians in March, while the Tribe and the New York Yankees battled over his contract. In a highly controversial ruling, baseball commissioner Albert "Happy" Chandler awarded Artie to the Yankees on the basis of a verbal agreement. *Center for Negro League Baseball Research*

break up a double play," Artie said. "I'd make the double play, but I was making it the hard way."

The trick, Gordon instructed Artie, was to get to the bag, stop, and stay on the other side. Cheat a little, but know how and when to cheat. "Joe showed me one step made the difference," Artie said.

The only problem Artie had at spring training was with Larry Doby, the first black to play in the American League and a budding star.

They lived in the home of a black family, Chester and Lucille Willis, along with Satchel, first baseman Luke Easter, pitcher Jose Santiago, and third baseman Orestes "Minnie" Minoso—the "Tan Tribesmen." That's the nickname given to them by Sam Lacy, sports editor of the *Baltimore Afro-American*.

"Humble but clean," Lacy described the modest five-room house four miles from the training camp and three miles from the swank Tucson resort hotel where the white players stayed.

"Who is responsible for this segregation?" Lacy wondered.

"Everybody and anybody," he concluded, explaining, "It's one of those buck-passing things" that no one was responsible for, even though the local media condemned the practice and the Tucson Chamber of Commerce boasted of "progress in developing an integrated school system."[27]

Lacy offered readers a detailed account of the players' activities, ranging from an "occasional visit to the 'colored balcony' of the local movie house" to Doby "engrossed in a magazine or newspaper, and Wilson and Minoso engaged in a card game with the Willises or newspapermen."[28]

Nothing was said about the time Artie tried stopping Doby from badgering Santiago, a Puerto Rican.

"Wilson, stay out of this or I'll take care of you!" Doby declared.

Artie was holding a bat.

"You and who else?" he asked.

Doby backed down, but the next morning he took off in the car used by the players during spring training. "I went to management and got a car for the rest of us," Artie said, "and Doby rode by himself from then on."

Providing the fireworks on the field was Minoso, a 24-year-old Cuban. "He can run faster, he can throw a ball with more speed, and he can rap one for greater distances than anyone in camp," gushed Schlemmer.[29]

"I wish I had that Minoso," raved Leo Durocher, manager of the New York Giants. "He can hit, run, field, and throw. What else is there to this game?"[30]

The Indians didn't know what to do with Minoso. At third base, they had Keltner and Al Rosen, a rookie and future American League MVP. Minoso was outplaying both. He was too good to be sent back to the minors unless the time was used to convert him into an outfielder. That's exactly what happened.

Artie posed a similar problem. He hit .417 in exhibition games, tying Minoso for the second-best batting average on the team. His glove work was as fancy and colorful as his off-the-field wardrobe—ensembles in "blues, browns, tans, or greens," nicely complemented by a "French beret of blending color."[31]

At one point, Veeck said he thought so highly of Artie that he would not trade him for the Yankees' Rizzuto.

"He was one of the most popular players on the team with his quick wit and colorful attire," Schlemmer said. "Everybody is bidding for one of his berets."[32]

Backing up Boudreau at shortstop was Ray Boone, a rookie who went on to play 13 seasons in the majors. Gordon was entrenched at second base. There was no place for Artie to go except to the Indians' San Diego farm club in the Pacific Coast League (PCL).

Easter was already in San Diego. Artie joined his former Mayaguez teammate at the end of March.

Earlier in the month, Veeck met personally with Chandler "to see what Weiss is popping off about" and if he "has a right to pop off."[33]

Veeck was told to stop needling Weiss and the Yankees organization.

Chandler and Weiss huddled in early May to discuss the Wilson and Marquez cases. "Nothing to report on that yet," Chandler said afterward. "I'm still listening."[34]

Chandler didn't meet with either player to listen to what they had to say.

In mid-May, the Commissioner ruled that Artie belonged to the Yankees and Marquez to the Indians. The basis for the decisions was the verbal agreements the Yankees and Indians had with the owners of the Negro League clubs.

"Dude" was one of Artie Wilson's many nicknames, as he favored sports clothes topped off with snappy berets and bebops. "His togs are neat, not gaudy," one newspaper reported. *Doug McWilliams Collection*

The key factor in Artie's case was the January 29 telegram the Yankees received from Hayes agreeing to contract terms. This was more important than the wire the Black Barons boss sent the Yankees on February 4, saying Artie would not accept the offer and the deal was off. It also didn't matter that Hayes hadn't signed anything or been paid any money by the Yankees.

The Indians were awarded Marquez because the option they had to buy him from the Grays gave them prior rights over the Yankees, who without knowing it, purchased a contract the Elite Giants didn't even own.

Marquez was playing for Newark in the International League, and Artie was in San Diego. The ruling had them swapping roster spots.

"ALL IN PROPER PLACES NOW," a headline in the *Sporting News* announced. [35]

At the beginning of the feud, Weiss said, "There is no likelihood that Wilson, even if assigned to Newark, would be a satisfied player," and he had "no interest in acquiring Wilson." [36]

Marquez was happy in Newark and didn't want to leave. "I'm sorry I wasn't given a chance to state my case to the Commissioner." [37]

He threatened to return home to Puerto Rico but changed his mind, reporting to the Portland Beavers in the PCL.

The Yankees didn't want Artie, so they sold him to the Oakland Oaks, also in the PCL. Minoso replaced Artie in San Diego, learned how to play the outfield, and returned to the majors to play 17 seasons and parts of four decades, and earn the nickname "Mr. White Sox."

For all their bombast during the "Battle for Art Wilson," Veeck and Weiss were mum in the end, perhaps saving energy for their next war.

The Yankees empire struck back to win nine of the next 10 American League championships. They did it without any black players until 1955, when catcher Elston Howard donned the team's pinstripes.

The Indians tumbled to third in 1949, Boudreau's last full season as a player. The batting averages of the infielders plummeted as well—Boudreau's from .355 to .284, Keltner's from .297 to .232, and Gordon's from .280 to .251. Keltner retired after the 1950 season and Gordon became a player-manager for Sacramento in the PCL.

"I'll never understand Commissioner Chandler's decision to award the Yankees Wilson's contract," Veeck wrote in a letter 27 years later. "Commissioner Chandler's decision definitely hurt Artie's career."

The decision cost Artie the chance he wanted to play in the majors. He'd have to wait two more years to get it.

5

TOILING ON TRIBE PLANTATION

The *Sporting News* headlines were a sign of the times in 1949, and, believe it or not, also an indicator of the progress blacks were making in white folks' ball.

One headline in baseball's so-called bible announced, "14 NEGRO PLAYERS GIVE TRIBE CORNER ON COLORED TALENT."

On the same page, a second, smaller heading above a photo read, "TOILING ON TRIBE PLANTATION."[1]

Pictured were Artie Wilson, Luke Easter, and John Ritchey, three black players for the San Diego Padres, the Cleveland Indians farm club in the Pacific Coast League (PCL). Ritchey broke the PCL's color barrier the year before. The Padres began the 1949 season as the league's only integrated team.

San Diego was a world apart from the Mississippi plantation Artie had played on with Satchel Paige and other Negro League stars.

"An owner of a plantation hired players to work for him," Artie explained, adding:

> The next plantation over, the man had maybe one or two players working for him. They all got together and formed a team.
>
> You didn't go in there and beat those boys. They had men riding around the field on horses with shotguns. They gave you the money. But you had to let them win.

In one game against a plantation team, the Negro Leaguers scored 10 runs in an inning. "Satchel was pitching. He was throwing that ball,

The San Diego Padres opened the 1949 season with three blacks in their starting lineup: left to right, first baseman Luke Easter, shortstop Artie Wilson, and catcher John Ritchey. A farm club of the Cleveland Indians, the Padres were the first Pacific Coast League team to integrate, Ritchey leading the way in 1948. *San Diego History Center*

and it looked like that." Artie made the shape of an Aspirin tablet with his fingers and laughed. "Had to take Satchel out . . . couldn't let him pitch. Then we put little Dave Barnhill in there."

Barnhill was only 5-foot-7 and 145 pounds, but he could throw almost as hard as Satchel. "He was scratching that ball up and making it do tricks. They were questioning whether he was cutting the ball. They knew something was going on."

The plantation team finally won. "We were just trying to get out of there," Artie admitted.

The PCL was as good as it got in the minors and, in some ways, better than in the majors.

"Here we are playing in the Coast League, and every team in the league is flying from city to city," said Dino Restelli, a hard-hitting outfielder who split his time in 1949 between San Francisco in the PCL and the Pittsburgh Pirates in the majors. "And the big leagues are still taking trains. You know, how much better can it get?"

Road trips were more like vacations, as teams had two weeks at home and two away, playing an entire week against one another. "You got a chance to take your clothes out of a suitcase and live a week in one town," said Restelli. "The same thing happened for the second week that you were away."

Summers in PCL cities were mild and pleasant compared to the sweat-box conditions in the ballparks of St. Louis, Chicago, Boston, Philadelphia, and New York City, home to 11 of the 16 teams in the majors in 1949.

The league was filled with players who'd been there and done that in the majors and didn't want to go back.

"You were making more money, and the working conditions were better," Restelli said. "You had a better family life."

Clay Hopper managed in the PCL, as well as in the International League and the American Association, the upper tier of the minors.

Upon entering the PCL in 1952, he described it as a "brother-in-law" league, saying, "The players are all nice and friendly with each other and inclined to go along and be satisfied with a single or double, instead of being as alertly set to dig out for an extra base as he's accustomed to in the two other circuits."[2]

He clarified this later by saying Coast League players are older and "play smarter ball" because they "don't take chances on the bases they take in the two other leagues."[3]

By the end of the season, Hopper decided PCL pitching was the best of the three. "These older pitchers don't give much good stuff to hit at, and they put the ball in your eye on control," he said.[4]

The more Hopper saw of the brother-in-law league, the less brotherly it got.

Max West, an older gentleman, didn't take it easy on any pitcher, regardless of his relationship.

West belted 19 homers for the Boston Bees in 1939, and was the hero of Major League Baseball's 1940 All-Star Game with a three-run circuit blast. After six full seasons in the majors, he joined the Padres in 1949, and pounded 48 homers. He hit 100 more the next three seasons. "Still rapping the ball good," Artie said. "Made more money at San Diego than he did in the majors."

The same was true for Artie.

"When I came to the Coast League, that was a dream," Artie said. "I could play 100 years in the Coast League."

He reeled off the reasons: "I didn't have to worry about sleeping on the bus trying to get to the next town . . . going to the grocery store buying peanuts, sardines, and all that stuff, and riding along in the bus eating . . . getting a decent meal once a week . . . jumping into the bus in my uniform after a game."

The PCL was heaven compared to the Negro Leagues.

Artie elaborated:

> They had limousines to take you to the airport. You get to the next town, they got a charter bus to take you to your hotel. You get to the hotel, the bellboy takes your bags up to your room. You lollipop around.
>
> Playing in the Coast League, it was like taking candy from a baby. They asked me, "How you going to hit that screwball, curve, and slider pitchers are throwing?" Well, they wasn't throwing nothing like the Negro League pitchers were throwing.
>
> Those pitchers could throw that ball out of sight . . . make that ball sail like a kite. One of the infielders—somebody—would have a piece of sandpaper inside of a hole cut in his glove. He'd take that ball, rub it to scratch it up a little bit. They could make that ball get up there and just glide. I'm telling you it was like taking candy from a baby.

First, Artie needed a chance to play regularly. That didn't happen in San Diego, as Padres manager Stanley "Bucky" Harris was ambivalent about his new shortstop. "He doesn't impress you with any super grace, but he gets the ball to the spot quickly," Harris said. "He isn't going to pull and he won't overpower anybody, but he does not give up at the dish, and when somebody says he's always on base, I think maybe they knew what they were talking about."[5]

Artie started the first four games before being replaced by Steve Mesner, a former big leaguer and PCL fixture. "You couldn't get him out when he got hot," Artie said.

Mesner sizzled in a doubleheader, reaching base in eight of nine at-bats on two doubles, three singles, and three walks. He remained in the lineup, going 6-for-6 in another game and hitting safely in 14 straight games. Artie was reduced mostly to pinch-hitting and running roles. On

Artie was 28 years old in 1949, when he took his first swing in Organized Baseball, leading off the San Diego Padres' season opener. Artie singled and stole a base in the game. "He's a spidery little Negro, clever afield and dangerous from the south-paw side of the plate," reported Mitch Angus of the *San Diego Union*. *San Diego History Center*

one occasion, he filled in for an injured Mesner and went 4-for-5. He was still considered infield insurance.

In 31 games with the Padres, Artie had 22 hits in 67 at-bats for a .328 average. Mesner batted .353 during the same period.

Artie was best known throughout the league as the "colored player over whose signing Veeck had his big quarrel with the New York Yankees." That's how L. H. Gregory, grizzled sports editor of the *Oregonian*, referred to Artie when the Padres visited Portland in early April. [6]

Lost in the commotion about Indians owner Bill Veeck signing Artie is that he also sealed a deal with one of Artie's Mayaguez teammates—Luscious "Luke" Easter.

Artie was named mayor of Mayaguez for two days after he batted .373 and guided the city's Puerto Rican League entry to its first title in 11 years. The other Mayaguez players became honorary members of the city's board of directors, although Luke's .402 batting average—18 homers and 83 RBIs in 80 games—qualified him to be chairman of the board for life.

During their time together in San Diego, Artie and Luke lived together and cruised around town in Luke's 1949 Buick—"one of those racy models with four portholes on each side amidships." [7]

Luke liked Artie to drive so he could sit in the back seat and look like a big shot. Artie, a teetotaller, also came in handy as a designated driver when they went out at night and Luke wanted to party. "Luke could carry on at night and go 4-for-4 the next day," Artie said. [8]

The only problem was Artie smoked Cuban cigars, which made Luke queasy.

Sporting News correspondent Ned Cronin had fun with this, reporting that Luke "grabbed little Artie by the nape of the neck and flung him into the back seat with instructions that if he didn't keep the ventilators wide open, he would find himself afoot."

Apparently, Artie decided to have his own fun with the new arrangement. He told friends that the "Buick was his and that the big guy up front was a combination chauffeur, handyman, and bodyguard" to prevent him "from being unduly molested by autograph seekers and the throngs of admiring hero worshippers."

Word got back to Big Luke what Artie was saying.

"Oh, no, you don't, Small Fry," Luke hollered at Artie the next time he tried climbing into the back seat of the Buick. [9]

Luke made Artie sit in the front seat even though the stench from his stogie made him feel ill. He would rather put up with the cigars than have folks think he was Artie's chauffeur.

Artie and Luke made a striking pair. They shared a certain sartorial splendor, and most people thought they were older than what they said. In Luke's case, they were right. He was six years older, making him 33 to start the 1949 season.

Hollywood Stars first baseman Chuck Stevens vividly recalled the first time he saw Artie play. "I said to myself, 'This guy is 10 years older than he's admitting.' The black leagues were no different than the white leagues. Everybody was knocking a year or two off because the word in baseball was age."

Luke and Artie were opposites of one another physically.

At almost 6-foot-5 and 240 pounds, Luke was a hulk, the mythical John Henry in a baseball uniform. "His shoulders are so tremendous that in his civvies he looks like he forgot to remove the coat hanger," one sportswriter said.[10]

Artie resembled Luke's coat hanger—wiry. Cronin described Artie's 5-foot-10, 162-pound frame as "spidery" with "door-knob-model knees and a pair of snowshoe-type feet that from a distance made him look as though he were kneeling."[11]

Both were left-handed hitters, but Artie was a singles hitter who faithfully executed the principle of "hitting 'em where they ain't."

"Everything he hit was to left field," said Bill Greason, a teammate with the Birmingham Black Barons. "From the middle of the diamond over to the left-field foul line, he could get that ball in there somewhere."

Suspicious teams had umpires check Artie's bat. "He's got a seeing-eye bat or something," they claimed, as Artie listened and laughed. "There's no way in the world he should be getting those balls through the infield and right by the outfielders."

Artie's unusual hitting style caused some to underestimate his abilities.

Puzzled as to why the Indians and Yankees were fighting over him, a Brooklyn Dodgers scout said, "That Wilson can't pull a ball, and he can't go to his right. Sure, he can run, but so can Harrison Dillard. If you want a runner, why not sign an Olympic champion."[12]

Dillard was an Olympic gold medalist in sprinting and hurdling.

"The longest ball I saw Artie hit was in a Negro League game at Griffith Stadium in Washington, DC," recalled Piper Davis, who played alongside Artie for five years with the Black Barons. "We had two men on, and he was going to bunt down the third-base line. The manager hollered out, 'If he come in again, hit it down his throat.' He hit the ball about two hops from the left-field fence."

No one saw the longest ball Luke hit because it landed on another planet. "I hit 'em and forget 'em," he said of his home runs.[13]

Luke's homers were unforgettable even when they were ordinary. He hit one in Portland to the opposite field after "swinging half wildly at a puzzling underhand pitch that boomed up from down under at him and was fading to the outside."[14]

What happened next lifted the *Oregonian*'s Gregory to literary heights matching one of Luke's prodigious pokes:

> In hitting it, he did just what a pitcher would ask, because he didn't catch it squarely and raised a high fly. But such was the power of his fearful swing that this ball, not even hit well, rose high into the air and soared on, against the wind and over the wall. It was a slam such as Hercules himself might have taken, or Samson, had they played baseball in the period of his struggles with the Philistines.[15]

Portland pitchers hit Luke once and low-bridged him twice. After the first knockdown, he homered; the second time, he rifled a shot right back at the pitcher's head. Luke batted .500 in the seven-game series (10-for-20) and slugged three homers, including one that "cleared the fence in deepest right center by the margin of a three-story building and, carrying on, was perceived to bounce on the roof of the gray foundry building there and carom on across it and out of sight." Gregory estimated the "mightiest homer" he'd ever witnessed "carried at least 450 feet, perhaps considerably more."[16]

Gregory's bosses got carried away themselves, jumping on the Easter bandwagon with an editorial titled "Big Luke at Bat":

> We have seen a lot of highly touted young players come up in the minors and get the publicity treatment, only to wilt under more and bigger tensions. If young Easter has the character to go along with his remarkable combination of power and agility, there is no clear reason why he couldn't be another Ruth. Ordinary men don't bingle

home runs over opposite fences and against the wind or make the ordinary infield blow too hot to handle.[17]

Artie blossomed during the summer months after being transplanted to Oakland. The spring belonged to Big Luke.

Upon arriving at the Padres spring training camp in Ontario, California, Luke got a pep talk from the team's president, Bill Starr, stressing the importance of his actions as the league's second black player. He concluded by saying the Padres wanted people to like him.

"Mr. Starr," Luke said, "everybody likes me when I hit that ball."[18]

He was soon the toast of the West Coast, the biggest gate attraction since Joe DiMaggio. Overflow crowds packed the league's ballparks.

At Seals Stadium in San Francisco, fans showed up at 4:00 in the afternoon for games that started at 8:15. "The stands were full just to watch him take batting practice," Dino Restelli said. "He hit a ball over the right-field fence and the street behind it into a park. They said it was the longest ball ever hit outside of one Ted Williams hit in San Francisco. The guy was phenomenal."

When he stepped to the plate at Seals Stadium, a "majority of the crowd rose to its feet, and hats were even thrown in the air when he hit safely." Fans were scrambling to find their hats as Luke lashed four hits in one game and 14 in the weeklong series.[19]

Opposing teams didn't share the fans' enthusiasm for Luke.

"I wish they'd get him out of here before he kills every infielder in the Coast League," complained Fred Haney, manager of the Hollywood Stars.[20]

"He put the fear of the Lord into us Seattle pitchers," veteran hurler "Kewpie" Dick Barrett said, before asking for his release from Seattle and joining the Padres and Luke.[21]

In 80 games, Luke batted .363, while racking up 25 homers and 92 RBIs. He did this playing on a broken kneecap that forced him to have surgery the first day of July. By the end of the month, there were nine blacks on four PCL teams, and the league was boasting "more Negro talent than any other circuit."

Artie, now playing for Oakland, was second to Luke in hitting, with a .358 average, and tops in the league with 22 stolen bases. "By and large," the Associated Press reported, "they've added class to the league at a time when it was sorely needed."[22]

Minnie Minoso replaced Artie in San Diego so he could learn the defensive skills needed to play the outfield in the majors. Just as he did with Luke, the Padres' Starr called Minoso into his office for a talk. This time he had a different message.

"You are a nice, young fellow," Starr said. "I don't want you hanging around with Luke Easter. I don't want you getting his bad habits."[23]

Minoso didn't always follow the advice.

In Hollywood, he went with Luke to see actor Randolph Scott making one of his cowboy movies.

"We stay up all night, and we play a doubleheader the next day," Minoso said. "Luke got 4-for-5. I am begging God, but I only get 1-for-5. I know Mr. Starr is right. I say to Luke, 'I love you. You are my friend, but I can't keep up with you.'"[24]

No one could keep up with Big Luke when he was healthy. He slugged 28 homers his first year with the Indians in 1950, one a 477-foot shot considered the longest ever hit at Cleveland's Municipal Stadium. He hit 27 in 1951, followed by 31 in 1952 to be selected the American League's Most Outstanding Player by *Sporting News*. Combined, he swatted 86 home runs and batted in 307 runs.

"Had Luke come up to the big leagues as a young man, there's no telling what numbers he would have had," said Al Rosen, an All-Star third baseman with the Indians who went on to become a highly successful baseball executive.[25]

Injuries always seemed to block his path to true greatness. Hobbled by gimpy knees, he managed only seven more homers in the majors.

In 1954, he began an 11-year odyssey through the high minors, adding 238 mighty blows to his John Henry-like legend.

In 1964, he retired, at the age of 48, finally admitting he was born in 1915, not 1921, as he told everyone. He ended up with 362 homers in white folks' ball and Lord knows how many in the Negro and Latin American leagues he terrorized.

San Francisco sports columnist James McGee was an eyewitness to Easter's parade through the Coast League in 1949. Twenty years later, he reflected on the legacy Easter left behind:

> Luke Easter was the greatest home-run hitter in the history of baseball who will never make the record books. Maybe he might have been the greatest ever, record book or not. But nobody will ever know. . . . Easter will be a legend passed down from one generation

to another by word of mouth. . . . In his brief career, he was the only man [besides Babe Ruth] who singly, and by his own prodigious feats, drew thousands into the park to see him. He was a one-man show.[26]

6

A MIGHTY OAK GROWS IN OAKLAND

They came to see Big Luke. They left talking about Artful Artie.

Three weeks after Artie Wilson joined the Oakland Oaks, Luke East-er paraded into town. The *Oakland Tribune* heralded his arrival with a banner headline fit for a king: "EASTER BRINGS BIG STICK TO OAKLAND."[1]

Luke's exploits with the bat were well known, but Oakland fans had yet to see him with their own eyes. Judging from a photo of Luke displaying his powerful hands and arms to two San Diego Padres team-mates, the question wasn't how many home runs he would hit, but whether he even needed a bat to smack the ball over the right-field fence at Oaks Park, a mere 305 feet down the foul line from home plate.

Perhaps Luke would use a walking cane as a bat and ease the pain of a fractured kneecap in desperate need of surgery. He visited a doctor in San Francisco before going to the ballpark for the opener of a seven-game series against the Oaks. "I've hit in every park in the league except Oakland, and I don't want to miss a single one," he said, like a true showman.[2]

Luke went hitless in the first game and still made headlines: "BIG LUKE DREW THRONG."

A near-capacity crowd of 10,915 showed up early for batting practice to watch Luke plaster souped-up balls over the fence. The Padres' original supply of 14 dozen was down to two dozen, and by the end of the series, they would be gone. "They're a little livelier than the official

Coast League balls, but not much," Padres trainer Les Cook said. "The pitcher grooves them for him, but Luke still hits 'em further than any-body I've ever seen."[3]

Almost everything Luke did was headline material—from his first hit, a single in the third game, to his first homer in the fourth game, to the four hits he got in a Sunday doubleheader.

Luke was getting all the headlines, but Artie was getting the most hits, stealing bases and the show. He outhit Luke in the twin bill, 5–4, and for the series, 12–8, with a triple and two doubles mixed in with his singles.

"Running Easter a close second for the affections of the fans during the series was Artie Wilson," Herman Hill wrote in the *Pittsburgh Courier*. "Wilson fielded and hit in a sensational manner all week long." He concluded, "Wilson is highly popular with Oakland fans, who regard him as their 'Luke Easter.'"[4]

Tribune sports columnist Alan Ward followed up by observing, "Per-haps over the long pull the Oaks will find they're better served with an Artie Wilson than a Luke Easter."[5]

It was Artie's coming-out party. He emerged from Big Luke's shad-ow and the cloud of uncertainty that hovered over him as the Yankees and Indians battled over his contract.

One week before he was officially handed over to the Yankees, Em-mons Byrne of the *Tribune* reported Artie was headed for the Oaks as part of a deal that would send their scrappy young second baseman Billy Martin to the Yankees the following year. "If Martin is pledged to the Yankees, we have yet to find anybody in authority who will admit it," Byrne said.

At the time of Byrne's scoop, Artie wasn't seeing much action in San Diego, and the Oaks had doubts that he was the shortstop and leadoff man they needed. "His fielding has been erratic, and he has not been impressive at the plate," Byrne said, summing up the concerns of Oaks manager Charley Dressen.[6]

Add to this the fact that the Oaks were lily-white. The roster was filled with ex-big leaguers who, the year before, had endeared them-selves to Oakland fans as the "Nine Old Men," capturing the Oaks' first Pacific Coast League pennant in 21 years.

"We were all old, and it took us six innings to warm up," explained one of the oldsters, Harold "Cookie" Lavagetto. "By that time the other team had five runs to our one. It didn't matter though, because at the end of the game we had 12 to their five."[7]

The "Nine Old Men" got their manager, Casey Stengel, a promotion to field boss of the Yankees, where he became famous as the "Old Perfessor" by guiding them to five straight World Series titles and seven overall.

How would these old-timers react to the team's first black player?

Dressen was going to find out sooner or later.

"The Negro is in professional baseball to stay," he said shortly after taking over the helm. "Any manager today would be foolish to pass up a Negro player who can pitch, catch, field, or hit the ball. I'm not foolish. I want a Negro ballplayer—if he can play Triple A baseball and if he has the right mental outlook and courage. Know any such fellow?"[8]

That fellow turned out to be Artie.

"Dressen literally welcomed Artie with open arms," John B. Old reported in the *Los Angeles Herald-Express*. "Quietly and reassuringly, Dressen began remolding a specimen that he . . . regarded as a diamond in the rough."[9]

Dressen had the black player he wanted.

"They had several players that didn't want to play," Artie said. "At least not with me."

He named only one—Les "Scar" Scarsella, a power-hitting first baseman in his eighth season with the Oaks. He was sold to a Class B team and decided to quit baseball rather than report.

One fan's reaction to the sudden departure of the popular Scarsella was a four-page letter to the *Tribune's* Ward, who deduced that he disliked almost everyone associated with the Oaks but did like, in the following order: "(1) Les Scarsella; (2) Buzz Arlett; (3) Les Scarsella; (4) Artie Wilson; (5) Les Scarsella; (6) Les Scarsella."[10]

Appearing on this list with Arlett was a positive sign for Artie, as Buzz Arlett was once declared the "Mightiest Oak of All Time" for the 251 home runs he clouted from 1918 to 1930.

Two more members of the "Nine Old Men" were soon gone. Billy Raimondi, a longtime catcher known as Mr. Acorn, was traded, and infielder Dario Lodigiani was released.

The house cleaning wasn't entirely related to Artie's arrival in the clubhouse, as the Oaks were tied for fourth place, with a 36–37 record.

"We're improving the club," Oaks owner Clarence "Brick" Laws said. "We're not satisfied with a .500 average. We're gambling for another pennant."[11]

Soon after signing Artie, Laws bet the farm on Jackie Jensen, a University of California baseball star and All-America fullback known as "the Golden Boy."

"A $50,000 gamble!" the *Tribune* called the signing bonus awarded Jensen. Laws had no qualms with the following description: "If you can call putting your money on a sure thing a gamble."

"Bonus figures of this amount are unusual in the majors," the *Tribune* pointed out. "For a minor-league club to gamble so fabulously is absolutely unprecedented."[12]

The Yankees were particularly stunned, since they had reportedly offered Jensen a $50,000 bonus and a first-year salary of $15,000.

"I can't figure a minor-league club taking a player away from the Yankees or other big-league clubs," said Del Webb, co-owner of the Yankees. "I don't think it has ever happened before in history."[13]

The big bonus put Jensen in the spotlight, while taking some of it off Artie. They quickly became best friends.

Twenty-one-year-old Billy Martin volunteered to room with Artie on the road. In 1949, this was unthinkable for most people, but not the pugnacious Martin, who grew up in nearby Berkeley and got into so many brawls as a player and manager his career statistics should include his record as a fighter.

After a night game in Portland, Artie and Billy headed for a downtown restaurant with Jensen, Lavagetto, and Oaks infielder Mel Duezabou.

"I observe," Artie said. "I got up every morning, and I walked all over and I'd watch. I'd never seen any blacks go in there."

When he visited Portland earlier in the season with the Padres, he stayed at a downtown hotel that wouldn't serve him, Luke, or John Ritchey. "They took us on through the dining room back into the kitchen and said, 'You have to eat back here.' I left and went somewhere else to eat."

The five Oaks entered the packed restaurant.

Artie recalled:

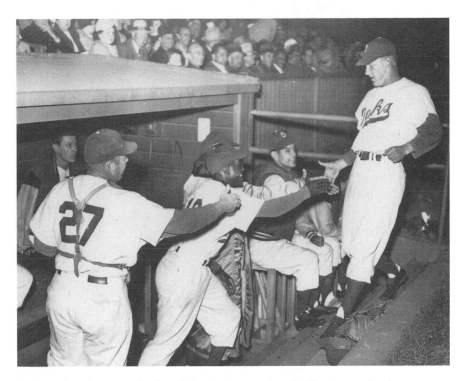

Artie Wilson is one of the first Oaks to congratulate Jackie Jensen after he slammed a home run. Artie and his wife Dorothy named their daughter Zoe Ann after Jackie's wife, an Olympic diving champion. Jensen went on to play 11 years in the majors, belting 35 homers and driving in 122 runs for the Boston Red Sox in 1958, to win the American League Most Valuable Player Award. *Doug McWilliams Collection*

When we walked in, you could hear a pin fall. I wished I had a hidden camera. I know they're not going to serve me. But I go on in with them. We found one booth in the back. Jackie sat down on the inside, I sat next to him. Billy, Mel, and Cookie sat across from us. You could see people just rising up to look back there.

The players waited 40 minutes for a waitress to appear.

"I'm sorry," she said. "Can't serve colored people here."

"Okay, let me out," Artie said.

Billy stopped him.

"What do you mean, you can't serve him?" Billy shouted at the waitress. "Why can't he eat in here?"

"I just work here," she said.

Artie pleaded with Billy to let him go. "Don't start no ruckus, Billy. I'll see you later at the hotel."

Billy insisted that Artie stay. He ordered the waitress to get the manager.

Another 25 minutes passed before the manager arrived. "I was laughing by that time," Artie said.

"I'm sorry," the manager said. "I just work here."

"Well, if he can't eat in here, we're not going to eat," Billy said loudly, as people in the restaurant stood up to get a better view. "We're going to find out about this. Let's go!"

The players walked out and went across the street to eat.

On another occasion, Artie went to McClymonds High School in Oakland with Dressen, Lavagetto, and Oaks coach George "Highpockets" Kelly. School officials didn't want Artie to sit on the auditorium stage with the others.

"What's this?" Dressen asked. "Why can't he sit up here? You all sent for him."

"Oh, no," he was told.

"Well, if he can't sit up here, we'll go," Dressen said, motioning the others to leave the building with him.

Reason prevailed, and soon Artie was speaking at schools throughout Oakland. McClymonds went on to produce an array of black sports stars, ranging from basketball great Bill Russell to sprinter Jim Hines, an Olympic gold medalist, to Frank Robinson, Curt Flood, and Vada Pinson in baseball.

By August, Artie was hitting a league-leading .370, and teams were trying to stop him with radical shifts that stacked the defense on the left side of the diamond, where he usually hit the ball. The main instigator was Francis "Lefty" O'Doul, the colorful manager of the San Francisco Seals.

"O'Doul put the shift on almost everybody," Artie explained, noting:

> He called time, took his cap off, and waved everybody around. I'd have to back out of the batter's box and laugh. "That's all right," I'd say to myself. "Put 'em all over there." I'd be just dying laughing. And the fans would be hollering, "Pull the ball! Pull the ball!" If I pulled the ball, I could walk home. 'Cause there wasn't anybody around right field.

The "Artie Wilson Shift," as seen from behind the home plate screen at Oaks Park. In this version of the shift, the right fielder is playing second base, leaving right field empty. There are three infielders on the left side, where Artie usually slapped the ball. *Artie Wilson Jr.*

O'Doul experimented with different alignments. The most unusual was Walt Judnich, a left-hander, vacating his position in right field to play second base. Artie grounded out to third.

The next two games, O'Doul bunched the three outfielders in left and made the second baseman a roving shortstop. The only defender to the right of second base was the first baseman. "The left fielder was almost on the left-field line. He could shake hands with the center fielder," Artie said.

Fans repeatedly yelled, "Bunt the ball!"

Artie batted nine times against O'Doul's revised shift, rapping six hits into left field, including two doubles. The Seals abandoned the shift the next game, and Artie laced a double and single to right field. O'Doul was ready to shift Artie to another league.

Artie continued:

Charley Dressen said, "Get on base any way you can. Stand on your head and get on base. Just get on base." No advantage in me pulling. If I pull the ball, it's going to be a single anyway, unless it gets by the outfielders. As long as I got the fat part of the bat on it, I didn't care where the ball went. They weren't going to catch all of them.

Chet Johnson, a left-handed pitcher, won 101 games in the Coast League. "It took me quite a while to even come close to pitching to Artie right. The best way to pitch him was outside because he couldn't pull the ball. He absolutely couldn't pull the ball."

Artie didn't want to either. "What good was it me pulling the ball? I'm not a home run hitter. I'm a leadoff man. I was a different type of hitter. I'd be running, and I'd be swinging. I knew they were going to push me back from the plate with a fastball and then come back with a curveball outside. That's where I wanted it. I hit the ball right off the third-base bag many a time."

"He hit everything you threw up there," Johnson said. "His body was away from the plate, but his bat was always across the plate. He just threw his arms out there and hit the ball. He was on the run."

Johnson hatched a plan for the free-swinging Artie, which he shared with his catcher. "If we get two strikes on Artie, call for the curveball. I'll throw it in the dirt. You knock it down because he'll swing at it."

Chet got the two strikes he wanted. "Here comes the curveball. I threw it low in the dirt. Artie swung and missed it. The catcher missed it, too. Artie got to first base on a passed ball."

Artie seldom struck out or walked. "My motto was, 'Thou shall not pass.' If the ball was anywhere close to the plate, I'd swing at it. I wanted to swing that bat. That's the fun of the game—swinging that bat. I didn't want a base on balls."

He was the best leadoff hitter in the league, always getting on base, stealing second, and scoring runs.

"Wear 'em down!" Dressen hollered when the Oaks faced a young fireballer.

Artie frustrated and aggravated pitchers, slapping a few balls into the third-base dugout, followed by several more inside and over the grandstand, to a fire station near Oaks Park, which he kept well stocked in baseballs. Inevitably, he ended up punching a single into left field and standing on first base, smiling at the weary and disgusted pitcher.

The O'Doul shifts didn't stop Artie, but they got national attention.

Lefty was a San Francisco landmark long before a bridge and Bloody Mary mix were named after him. He was in his 15th year managing the Seals, who were variously referred to as the O'Douls, the O'Doulies, and the O'Doulites. He was the darling of the local media, completely overshadowing Dressen.

This didn't settle well with Dressen, who prided himself on his baseball smarts and ability to outwit opposing managers. He was in his first season as Oaks manager and not getting proper credit for rebuilding the team around such newcomers as Artie and Jensen.

Dressen was certain he could get Artie to pull the ball and, in the process, one-up Lefty the next time he tried one of his shifts.

He announced an incentive plan that awarded Artie $10 for every ball hit to the right side of second base. Artie took extra batting practice to adjust his swing.

There was one more series left in the 1949 season between the Bay Bridge rivals, and Dressen had a surprise for O'Doul when he moved his right fielder to center. Artie pulled a grounder to the wide-open space in right for a double. "Truth to tell, Lefty sort of out-thunk himself," the *Tribune* reported.

Dressen got a "genius rating" for a decision he made earlier in the Oaks' victory. That's exactly what he wanted to read.[14]

But Lefty wasn't finished. He had a new version of the Wilson shift to unveil. He moved his center fielder to the infield as a second shortstop and placed his right fielder slightly to the left of center. Right field was empty. In the five-man infield, only the second and first sackers were in their normal positions. Lefty instructed the pitcher to throw nothing but high fastballs.

"Artie came to bat five times, and, sad to report, the shift worked," the *Tribune* said, noting, "If Wilson could have hit a ball into right field it would have been a home run."

Lefty had a message to deliver: "Just tell those Oakland readers that we'll play Wilson the same way in Emeryville Sunday morning."[15]

Artie got the message, too. He was at Oaks Park at 8:00 in the morning to practice pulling the ball to right field.

O'Doul kept his promise and used the same formation. This time Artie singled, doubled, and ripped a triple over the center fielder's head. The Oaks won both games of the morning–afternoon doubleheader. A photograph in the *Tribune* the next day showed a forlorn

Lefty, head drooped on a hand, staring blankly into space. The headline read, "NOBODY KNOWS THE TROUBLE I'VE SEEN."[16]

The "O'Doul Shift" took on a life of its own, with news stories referring to it by name.

At the start of spring training in 1950, Dressen had Artie drilling balls to right field in batting practice. "That ought to stop Seal manager Lefty O'Doul from pulling his right and center fielders in when Wilson comes up to the plate," a wire service quoted him as saying.[17]

What he really said probably couldn't be printed in a family newspaper.

The needling continued with a *Tribune* photo of a grinning Artie posed with a goat at a county fair. "Is that Lefty O'Doul's goat?" the caption asked.[18]

As a matter of fact, Artie got Lefty's goat early in the 1950 season.

He had already crossed up Lefty with three hits to right field in one contest. When Artie stepped to the plate in another game, the outfielders shifted. Only Les Fleming, a big, lumbering first baseman, was between Artie and a home run.

Artie ripped a line drive past Fleming. The ball was finally retrieved near the fence, but there was no chance to catch Artie flying across the dish standing up. The homer was his first in the PCL and the only one he hit in 931 plate appearances in 1950. He went the entire 1949 season without hitting a single home run.

Oaks fans didn't care because he led the league with a .348 batting average and 47 stolen bases.

"No member of the Oaks baseball team has done more to spark and inspire the club," Alan Ward wrote in endorsing an Artie Wilson Day, proposed by a poetic fan:

> Great Oaks from little Acorns grow;
> Ask Artie Wilson he should know—
> He has a lot, or at least enough,
> Of what is called "good baseball stuff."
>
> He keeps us in a dither when he hits the ball,
> With very little effort he socks it to the wall;
> Let's show him that we love him in a simple sort of way,
> By paying him a tribute of an Artie Wilson Day.[19]

The saying in Oakland was, "As Artie Wilson goes, so go the Oaks!"

No one repeated those words more than Laws, the Oaks' owner. "Wilson is more than a fine ballplayer," Laws said. "He is inspirational. He sets the team on fire when he is good—which is most of the time. When he slumps, the entire club falls off. Never saw anything quite like it."[20]

O'Doul also praised Artie: "If the Oaks had him last season, they could have won the pennant by 10 games, maybe 15."[21]

The Oaks nipped Lefty's Seals by two games in 1948. With Artie pacing their second-half resurgence in 1949, they won 104 games and finished second. He also flattened racial barriers, paving the way for two more black players—Parnell Woods and Alonzo Perry—on the team.

Billy Martin ended up hitting .286, with 12 homers and 92 runs batted in; Jackie Jensen batted .261, with nine homers and 77 RBIs.

The Yankees acquired Martin, just like the *Tribune* said they would, as part of the deal for Artie. The Oaks also sold Jensen to the Yankees.

Martin became the sparkplug of the Yankee juggernauts in the early 1950s, and Jensen eventually starred for the Boston Red Sox, winning the American League's Most Valuable Player Award in 1958.

Left behind was Artie.

Within the span of three months during the 1949 season, the Oakland Oaks added their first three black players. Artie Wilson, far right, was the first, followed by third baseman Parnell Woods, far left, and pitcher Alonzo Perry, between Artie and Oaks manager Charley Dressen. Woods was hit in the forehead by a pitched ball shortly after he joined the club and played in only 40 games, batting .275. Perry appeared in eight games, losing his only decision. *Doug McWilliams Collection*

Why?

Al Wolf, a sports columnist for the *Los Angeles Times*, quizzed several big-league scouts on Artie's chances in the majors. "The consensus: Wilson is not a good major-league prospect."

According to the scouts, Artie was a "slow swinger . . . barely able to get around on the ball." The faster pitching he'd face in the majors "would leave Artie fanning at thin air with the ball already nestling in the catcher's mitt." And, finally, he was a "flashy rather than steady infielder."[22]

The critique raised eyebrows and the question of whether the scouts were looking at the same guy who drove O'Doul bonkers with his bat. Or the ground-sweeping shortstop who had the back of pitcher Allen "Two Gun" Gettel covered like an infield tarp.

Gettel joined the Oaks late in the 1949 season and won 23 games in 1950. He recalled:

> Artie was one of the best infielders I ever had play behind me. Shoot, they couldn't get a ball by him at shortstop. He was all over the place. He had a good arm. And he always figured the hitter out before you even threw the pitch. Whether it's going to be on his side of the field or on the other side, he knew just exactly where to be.

In 1950, Artie batted .311, pilfered 31 bases, and amassed a league-best 264 hits and 168 runs, as the Oaks won 118 games and their second PCL championship in three years.

The 6-foot-3, 200-pound Gettel was called "Two Gun" because he rode a Palomino stallion, named Shutout, and walked around town in a cowboy outfit with two pearl-handled .44 Magnum revolvers strapped to his hips. He looked like the gunslinger he played in the movie *Tin Star*, starring Henry Fonda and Anthony Perkins.

In a baseball uniform, Gettel was a typical Oaks player. He was 32 and had played five seasons in the big leagues, compiling a 38–45 mark with the Yankees, Cleveland Indians, Chicago White Sox, and Washington Senators. "We had ex-major league players, and they all knew what they were doing," Gettel said, "We had a great pitching staff, two good catchers, a good infield, and a good outfield. We could've whipped any major-league club. I don't care who they were."

That's not as far-fetched as it sounds. Of the 16 teams in the majors, about six were doormats for the Yankees and Brooklyn Dodgers, perennial champions of their leagues.

After the Washington Senators lost 104 games in 1949, their manager Joe Kuhel uttered the famous line, "You can't make chicken salad out of chicken feathers."[23]

When Bill Veeck bought the St. Louis Browns in 1951, his strategy for improving the team's 52–102 won–loss record was to "get a couple of Browns on every other club and louse up the league."[24]

The 1952 Pittsburgh Pirates lost 112 games; their PCL farm club, the Hollywood Stars, won 109. Whenever the Stars' manager wanted to fire up his players, he yelled, "Hustle you guys or I'll send you back to Pittsburgh."

The 1952 Detroit Tigers were so bad (50–104) Virgil Trucks, a fine pitcher, had to throw two no-hitters to earn two of his five victories. He lost 19.

"Oakland '49 and '50 were two of the best teams I played on," Artie said. "We'd go into the last of the ninth and be four, five runs down. We came back."

The Oaks were minor league only in name.

Pitcher Clyde "Hardrock" Shoun posted a 73–59 record during his 14 years in the majors. Infielder Billy Herman was a 10-time National League All-Star for the Chicago Cubs and Dodgers, with a career batting average of .304. Outfielder Augie Galan had 16 big-league seasons under his belt; third-baseman Lavagetto, 10; catcher Don Padgett, eight; and outfielder George "Catfish" Metkovich, five.

"We had some veterans better than they had in the majors," Artie said. "They didn't want to go to the majors. They were making more money in the Coast League."

Outfielder Earl Rapp, also known as the "Earl of Rapp," batted .347 and tied Metkovich for the team high in home runs, with 24. He was batting .327 for the Browns the next year, when manager Rogers Hornsby tried changing his hitting style. "I had a little run-in with him—a real shin-bag," Rapp said in an interview years later. "I told him if I couldn't play for him, I could play someplace else. That's the way it turned out to be. It probably killed me because I got the reputation of being a clubhouse lawyer."

Artie Wilson was the talk of the town soon after he arrived in Oakland in mid-May 1949. As this cartoon makes clear, Artie liked it in Oakland and didn't want to go to the big leagues. One reason is he made more money in the Pacific Coast League. *Doug McWilliams Collection*

The "Earl of Rapp" proceeded to rule over PCL pitchers for nine years, hitting .318, with 156 homers.

"The Coast League could have been a third major league," Artie said. "Every team had four or five good starting pitchers. You saw a good pitcher every day. You saw the ace of a staff twice in a series."

Red Adams, longtime trainer for the Oaks, credited Artie with the team's success, both in 1949 and 1950. He used Ward's column in the *Tribune* as his soapbox:

> Wilson is a natural leader. He sets the pace. He is the fellow who moves faster than the others—and the others are willing to follow him.
>
> He has a fine disposition. He can make his teammates laugh, but he isn't a clown. There is a happy atmosphere when Artie is around. I haven't the fancy words to explain what I'm trying to say—but watch the Oaks perk up when that grinning, bowlegged guy is in the line-up. [25]

Artie's autograph was the most sought-after by Oaks fans, and he was just as popular with his teammates. "They loved that skinny little guy," Adams said. "They'd fight for him. There was no such thing as a racial problem with us." [26]

In 1951, Rapp got his shot with the Browns, Metkovich returned to the majors with the Pirates, and, finally, Artful Artie would get a chance to perform in the Big Show.

New York Giants manager Leo "The Lip" Durocher knew all about the scouting reports that said Artie couldn't cut it in the majors. He wasn't impressed the first time he saw him either.

In a spring exhibition game in 1949, between the Giants and the Indians, Durocher taunted Artie, then in the middle of the Tribe's battle with the Yankees regarding his contract. "What in the hell are they fighting over a guy like you for?" [27]

He found out a year later, when the Oaks embarrassed the Giants, 13–2, in an exhibition game. In his first three at-bats, Artie doubled to right, cracked an inside-the-park homer to left, and singled to center. Afterward, Durocher complained, "I don't mind veterans like Galan, Herman, or Dressen picking up signals, but I thought Wilson was supposed to be new in baseball." [28]

Durocher was in the market for a versatile infielder, a catcher, and a relief pitcher. Dressen had what he needed in Artie, Gettel, and Rafael "Ray" Noble, a catcher who hit .316 for the Oaks.

Durocher and Dressen were teammates on the Cincinnati Reds (1931–1932), and Dressen was Durocher's most trusted coach for eight years with the Dodgers. When Dressen left the Dodgers in 1947, to coach for the Yankees, Durocher was upset with his longtime friend. "This is a declaration of war," he began a byline column for the *Brooklyn Daily Eagle*, promising to "wallop" Dressen and the Yanks the next time they played the Dodgers. "I cannot help but feel bitterly. He was a valuable man."[29]

Durocher still valued Dressen's opinion on baseball matters.

The Giants boss wanted to move Hank Thompson from third base to the outfield. Dressen assured him that Artie could do the job at third, saying, "He hasn't a strong arm, but he gets the ball away so fast that I don't think he'll have any trouble making the throw. And he's so quick I don't think many balls will get past him."[30]

Gettel developed a new screwball pitch in Oakland and had the right stuff to be a reliable reliever for the Giants. Noble was another Roy Campanella, the All-Star catcher for the Dodgers. "Only thing Campy has on him now is his throwing, and Noble is improving all the time."[31]

Durocher was sold. He made the deal with Dressen for Artie, Gettel, and Noble, in exchange for $125,000 and several players.

Little did Dressen know that seven weeks later he would be the new manager of the Dodgers, the Giants' archrival. If the three players were as good as Dressen said, he had outsmarted himself and handed the Giants the pennant.

Artie was going to be playing at the Polo Grounds, the Giants ballpark, where it was only 257 feet from home plate down the right-field line and 279 feet in left. Playing for the Birmingham Black Barons, he once popped three homers into the Polo Grounds' left-field stands in a single game. Thanks to Dressen, Artie could pull the ball into the right-field stands, too. "It will surprise me if Wilson doesn't blossom out as a home-run hitter with those short lines to shoot at," Dressen said.[32]

He was serious. He wasn't playing mind games. That would come later, when he borrowed a page out of Lefty O'Doul's playbook.

7

CAUGHT IN THE MIDDLE

"Leo the Lip" was the perfect nickname for Leo Durocher. He was bellicose and brash, colorful and controversial, feisty and fiery, his teams just as daring and dangerous on the field as he was off it. He had, according to Brooklyn Dodgers boss Branch Rickey, the "most fertile talent for making a bad situation infinitely worse."[1]

On the heels of charges by a syndicated newspaper columnist that his New York City apartment was used by gamblers for a high-stakes dice game, Durocher ran off to Mexico to marry actress Laraine Day after she got a Mexican divorce. It was scandalous stuff made even worse by Leo's *Brooklyn Daily Eagle* column bashing Charley Dressen and New York Yankees president Larry MacPhail.

Baseball commissioner Albert "Happy" Chandler cited the newspaper attack on the Yankees as "conduct detrimental to baseball" and banned Leo for the entire 1947 season. This coincided with Rickey's decision to put Jackie Robinson in the Dodgers lineup and break Major League Baseball's color barrier.[2]

That was the upside of Leo's suspension.

It also was "pure accident," insisted Abe Saperstein, the self-styled white ambassador of Negro League baseball, who was in Havana, Cuba, where the Dodgers trained that spring. Saperstein recalled:

> They were going to ship him back to their Montreal farm club again. Then along came that Durocher hubbub. It stirred up such a hornet's nest of publicity that Branch Rickey had to grab something

quick to take Durocher out of the headlines. He grabbed Robinson and put him in a Dodger uniform.[3]

Durocher returned from exile in 1948. to manage the Dodgers, until resigning midseason to lead the New York Giants, a team he hated as much as the Yankees.

Meanwhile, Dressen left his coaching position with the Yankees at the end of the 1948 campaign to head the Oaks for two years. His return to Brooklyn as the Dodgers' chief made a heated rivalry hotter and set up a war of egos with Leo.

"They were oblivious to the players on the field," said Dick Williams, who broke in with the Dodgers in 1951, and went on to manage 21 years in the majors. "Charley would do something, Leo would do something else. It was like whoever made the last move won. A lot of times they'd run out of players by the sixth inning. Well, not really, but they did try to outfox the other all the time."[4]

Carl Erskine won 50 games for the Dodgers the three years Dressen and Leo went head-to-head with one another. "Dressen was a good baseball man, but he did have this paranoid thing about beating Leo."

Erskine likened it to Captain Queeg's paranoia about a missing quart of strawberries in the movie *The Caine Mutiny*, saying, "Charley felt like he had a lot to do with Leo's success, but Leo gave him no credit and the press didn't give him much either because Leo was so flamboyant and colorful. He resented that, and I think it did influence his judgment."

Five games into the 1951 season, Artie Wilson was caught in the middle of the combative managers.

Artie liked them both, saying:

> If you can play for Charley Dressen, you can play for Leo Durocher. Vice versa. Leo was the finest manager I ever played for. If there were any prejudices in him, I couldn't see them. I don't believe he had any. He was a manager you had to give respect to. He did some things I was surprised to see a manager do. I couldn't believe some of the things he let one guy do.

Hank Thompson was the Giants' hard-hitting, hard-drinking third baseman. He was playing for the Kansas City Monarchs in 1948, when an ex-sandlot teammate, Buddy Crow, whipped out a knife during a barroom argument. Hank had a gun and, in self-defense, fired three bullets into Crow's chest. The shooting was ruled justifiable and the case closed. Hank wound up hitting line-drive shots for the Giants—129 homers in eight seasons (1949–1956).

"Thompson played with a knife in his back pocket," Artie said. "I mean he was a man you didn't want to fool with. Leo always told Hank, 'Stay out all night. Don't want to see you until it's time to play.' And Hank would come in eyes all red, hardly able to stand up. But he could hit."

Dressen relied on a combination of instincts, guile, and trickery. If his team was trailing, he rallied the players by saying, "You guys hold 'em; I'll think of somethin'."[5]

He was adept at stealing the opposing catcher's signals from his position in the third-base coaching box. "He could tip a hitter off. I saw him do it time after time," Artie said. "Charley had more signals than Leo. I don't know how he remembered them. He had a little book, and every time he'd get on a plane, he'd be reading it. He could give you a signal after every pitch and never give you the same one."

Dressen didn't have any signals for Artie. He turned him loose at the plate and on the bases to use his speed and aggressiveness to rattle pitchers and produce runs. "I had signals of my own—go when I get ready," Artie said.

Leo took an immediate liking to Artie, calling him "Youngblood." His wife Laraine liked Artie so much she gave him a watch.

"Get a load of that Artie Wilson," Leo told reporters after watching him get five hits in five at-bats in an exhibition game against the Detroit Tigers. "There are a lot of clubs in this league that don't even have one guy like him to play shortstop."[6]

Before the game, Giants second baseman Eddie Stanky kidded the left-handed-hitting Artie, saying, "Crooked-arm pitching today."

Starting for the Tigers was Ted Gray, a southpaw.

"I don't care if he throws with both arms," Artie said. "He's got to get the ball over the plate. Get it up there where I can swing."

"Okay," Stanky said. "I'll bet you a Coke for my roommate."

"You're on."

Artie singled twice. The third time up, he beat out a bunt for a hit and stole second.

Another lefty came into pitch—Hal Newhouser. Artie looped a single into left field and singled to center against the future Hall of Famer to make it 5-for-5. In the dugout, Stanky took off his cap and bowed.

"All this was against good left-handers," Artie said. "They'd push me back with the fastball and then fire the curveball. I don't care what side they throw from. If a pitcher threw with both arms and two balls came up there, I'd try to hit one of them."

In his first 12 at-bats in spring games, he had eight hits.

The Giants had Alvin Dark at shortstop and Stanky at second, the best double-play combination in the National League.

"There wasn't any question I could play as good as either one of them and was faster than both of 'em," Artie said. He added:

> My record proved that I could outhit both of 'em. But I knew that it was going to be tough breaking up a combination like that. I didn't expect to sit those guys down. You can't afford to sit down a guy making $30,000 to $35,000 to play some peon—a guy just coming in. They had the experience up there; I didn't have the experience in the major leagues. They knew the hitters and the pitchers. I was willing to wait around to get a chance to play. That's how you learn— watching what's going on.

In the Negro Leagues, players had to master several positions because of the small rosters.

Jackie Robinson was a shortstop for the Monarchs. He broke in with the Dodgers at first base, shifted to second, and ended up playing mostly at third.

The Cleveland Indians converted Larry Doby and Minnie Minoso from infielders to outfielders.

Thompson played second base and some outfield for the Monarchs. Leo was tinkering with the idea of moving him to the outfield and putting Artie at third.

At the beginning of spring training, Durocher said, "Give me players like Whitey Lockman, Monte Irvin, Henry Thompson, and others of that type—players who can move around and are capable of playing good ball wherever you place them."[7]

A month later, Leo was raving about Artie:

This fellow Wilson. In my book, he has been terrific. I don't see how I'm going to keep him out of the lineup. He can play second, shortstop, or third. He can play the outfield. And don't be surprised if one of these days you see him on first base. A fellow who can field and hit the way he can is going to take somebody's job, make no mistake about that.[8]

Irvin was better in the outfield than at first base, where he was playing. "The ball would hit right in his glove, and he'd drop it. But in the outfield, he'd catch everything," Artie said.

The Giants had four blacks—Artie, Irvin, Thompson, and catcher Rafael "Ray" Noble. They were the main attraction at an exhibition game in Nashville, Tennessee, with black fans accounting for more than half the crowd of 6,196.

New York Giants manager Leo Durocher got the attention of the baseball world in 1951, when he put four black players in the infield at the same time during a spring exhibition game. This was a first for a major-league team. The four were, from left to right, catcher Rafael "Ray" Noble, second baseman Artie Wilson, first baseman Monte Irvin, and third baseman Hank Thompson. *Doug McWilliams Collection*

"Durocher never missed a chance to show in what high regard he holds the Negro players," the *New York Times* reported. "He horses around with them in the pregame workouts, to the delight of the fans, and since in the South the players must still be quartered by themselves, he never fails to make certain their food is of the best."[9]

During infield practice, Leo hit sizzling grounders so Artful Artie could put on a show at shortstop, racing in front of second base to scoop up the ball and, from behind his legs, flip it backhanded to the second baseman, who was waiting to fire it to first for a double play. The best part was the end, when Leo hit as many balls as possible at Artie, who was running toward home plate. "He hit the ball as hard as he could right at me," Artie said.

"Keep hittin'!" Artie yelled as he came up with every ball.

Finally, Leo threw up his hands and said, "I give up."

Artie laughed. The fans went wild.

During a lull in the action of one spring game, Dark, who was white and from Baton Rouge, Louisiana, asked Thompson, "See who this infield is made up of?"

Thompson was playing third, Dark was at shortstop, Wilson was at second, and Irvin was at first. As Hank surveyed the infield, a puzzled look crossed his face.

"There's a bunch of us 'darks' out here," Alvin said.

Artie didn't have trouble with any of his Giants teammates.

There was one young white player who frequently made wisecracks about Artie smoking a cigar. "It didn't bother me what he said. He was trying to make the team like I was."

One morning the player boarded the bus and said, "You can tell when they get in the big leagues. They start smoking cigars."

Artie was the only one puffing on a cigar.

"I didn't have to get into the big leagues to smoke a cigar," he replied. "I was smoking cigars before I came here, and I'll be smoking them when I leave."

Outfielder-first baseman Whitey Lockman intervened, telling the player, "He'll be here when you're gone."

Artie kept a supply of cigars in his clubhouse locker. He noticed some were missing and suspected they were the cigars his teammates were smoking.

Durocher often enjoyed a cigar with Artie. "Skip, don't take any cigars out of my coat pocket," he said. "I'm finding out who's taking them."

He planted tiny sticks inside the cigars so they would explode harmlessly a few seconds after being lit. "It wasn't dangerous or nothing. It would just go boom!" he snickered.

Artie was sitting by his locker autographing baseballs when he heard a series of loud booms.

"What happened?" Artie asked in mock surprise.

"You dirty rascal!" one player yelled.

"I don't know a thing about what you're talking about," Artie answered.

The case of the missing cigars was solved. "I didn't miss no more cigars," Artie boasted.

A sense of humor and patience was needed if Artie was going to crack the Giants lineup.

As the Giants ended a month of training in St. Petersburg, Florida, to head north on a barnstorming tour, Artie topped the club with a .480 batting average.

Durocher was brimming with praise for Artie. "He comes to play. He'll play anywhere, and he can play anywhere." He added:

> There is not a better utility man in the major leagues than Wilson. And look at the way he's been hitting. Over .400. All line drives. I asked him if he could bat against left-handers. They don't make any difference to him. "I'll mess 'em all up," he says. He thinks he can hit, and I'll bet he can hit .300 in this league. And speed! Man, he can run. [10]

Durocher coveted speedy players that rattled the opposition.

"When Wilson comes to bat," Durocher said, "the third baseman is even with the bag, the shortstop comes in three steps. The infielders just don't know where they are. And when he gets on first base, they all move up, afraid he's going to steal." [11]

The Giants closed the exhibition season against the Cleveland Indians at the Polo Grounds.

Artie had played there many times with the Black Barons, but this was his first appearance in a Giants uniform. Replacing Stanky at second base in the fifth inning, he captivated the crowd with his sparkling play in the field and a shift-defying single that he smacked off the shortstop's knee. "Everybody was pulled around to left field. I backed out of the batter's box, looked around, and laughed," Artie said.

"They know me," Artie thought to himself. "That's all right."

"Pull the ball!" fans hollered. "Pull the ball!"

"The players were yelling, too," Artie recalled. "I said to myself, 'I'm not going to pull the ball. If they're going to pitch it out there, I'll hit it out there.' That's what I did."

Leo was beginning his third full season as manager of the Giants. They had placed fifth in 1949 and rebounded from a horrible start in 1950 to end up third, five games behind the first-place Philadelphia Phillies. "If we can get away fast, the battle will be half won," Leo said. [12]

The Giants split their first four games, Artie going 1-for-2 as a pinch-hitter. Next up were the despised Dodgers.

The Dodgers were ahead, 7–3, when Artie pinch-hit in the seventh inning with one out and the bases empty. Dressen called timeout.

This was a chance for the loyal lieutenant to show who was really the general when he and Durocher were side by side in the Dodgers dugout. He could upstage Leo in their first meeting and the Giants' home opener.

When the 5-foot-5, 146-pound Dressen got excited, he bounced around like a banty rooster, issuing orders in Napoleonic fashion. He waved a surprised Carl Furillo in from right field to play second base, about 10 feet off the bag. Robinson shifted about 10 feet to the left side of second base, while shortstop Pee Wee Reese moved closer to third baseman Billy Cox, who was guarding the foul line. Don Thompson was close behind Cox in left field, and Duke Snider was located in shallow left-center field. Right field was deserted behind Gil Hodges at first base.

"He made a show of moving the players one at a time while the game was held up until he finished," Irvin said. "That kind of posturing really upset Durocher." [13]

Don Newcombe was pitching.

"Newcombe could never get me out in the Negro League," Artie said. "I just wore him out."

"Fastball, fastball," Dressen shouted repeatedly. "Don't give him a slow one."

"Pull one, pull one," Durocher countered. [14]

Artie fouled the first pitch right over the top of the Dodgers' third-base dugout. He worked the count to two balls and two strikes before tapping a one-hop grounder back to Newcombe. "Instead of trying to pull the ball, I should've hit to left field. I was trying to pull the ball because he put that shift on," Artie lamented.

"What if the switch hadda backfired?" Dressen said smugly. "Well, it didn't. And you gotta take chances like that when you know!"[15]

Shifts were rare.

The "Ted Williams Shift" had been around awhile. There also was a shift devised by Rickey that deployed six infielders in obvious bunting situations against weak-hitting pitchers.

The Dodgers' shift on Artie wasn't any different than those Lefty O'Doul tried in the Coast League and Dressen decried as "strictly bush."[16]

"It will never stop Wilson," Dressen scoffed at the time. "They tried overshifting to the right side of the diamond against Williams, and Ted got his base hits. It gives a little percentage to the defense, but not enough to justify moving your whole team around. Showboating, if you ask me."[17]

Lefty was amused by Dressen's change of heart. "I have never been so honored in baseball," he quipped. "I'm honored that Dressen is now using my idea."[18]

Dressen was right when he said O'Doul's shifts didn't stop Artie from getting his hits. But the New York media didn't know this. They made a big deal of the shift, depicting Dressen as a genius and Leo his fool. As Joe King put it in the *Sporting News*, Dressen "stole the show in the department most admired by the Lip—the sensational, the extravagant, the spectacular, the unexpected, in brief, the theatrical."[19]

Jimmy Cannon of the *New York Post* recalled an exchange between Leo and Artie at spring training.

"Can you play the outfield?" Leo asked.

"I was born in this country," Artie said. "I can play any place."[20]

Cannon described the shift as a trick—an "imprudently reckless deflation of Durocher" and his judgment was that Artie "possessed all the talents greatness demands. But hitting to right field obviously is not one of them."[21]

Durocher was fuming because Dressen ordered the shift with one out in the seventh and the Dodgers leading by four runs. "He wouldn't dare try that if it were a close game. Lemme see him try it the next time we play," Durocher barked. [22]

"If the score is tied in the ninth," Dressen said, "we'll pull the right fielder in as an infielder. That's the way to play Wilson."

"Good," Artie said of Dressen's strategy. "I'll pull the ball every time I get the pitch for it." [23]

Artie didn't play again in the series, which was swept by the Dodgers.

"Dressen played as if this were a three-game tournament to decide the pennant," Cannon observed. "I got the impression that Dressen was determined to prove he was the champion of Durocher." [24]

Irvin agreed, saying, "Dressen liked to show how smart he was. He was mainly trying to show Durocher up, but he was also trying to show Artie up." [25]

Leo wasn't deterred. "I have every confidence in Wilson. He may be able to do everything, even hit home runs to right field." [26]

He predicted Artie would eventually succeed Stanky as the Giants' regular second baseman and then benched Stanky with no explanation. "That's all I'm saying, Wilson is playing second base," he growled. "You guys can figure out why. Then if you guess wrong, you are on the spot, not me." [27]

Artie singled and walked in four at-bats and fielded flawlessly, but the Giants lost again. "He may be back on the bench at any moment," one writer said sarcastically. [28]

He was right. Artie started one more time. He was mostly used as a pinch-hitter or late-inning defensive substitute. "Skip, put me in a little earlier," he said. "Give me a chance to swing that bat. That's what I'm playing for."

The Giants couldn't break their losing streak, which was up to 11 after two more losses to the Dodgers at Ebbets Field. They were in last place, with a 2–12 record, already seven and a half games out of first. "It would take a miracle for them to win the championship now," columnist Arthur Daley wrote in the *New York Times*. [29]

Dressen felt like singing.

"He was in hog heaven," Erskine recalled. "He was flying around the clubhouse yelling, 'We killed the Giants! The Giants are dead!'"

Dressen went to the row of lockers where the pitchers dressed.

"Come on back, we're going to sing through the door," he announced.

At Ebbets Field, there was a wooden door between the clubhouse for the Dodgers and the clubhouse for the visiting team. It was always unlocked.

"Come on back," Dressen said. "We're going to sing to Leo."

Erskine didn't do it. "A couple of guys went back with Dressen, and they sang through the door, 'The Giants are dead!'"

Instead of the Giants' Waterloo, it may well have been Dressen singing his own.

"That was one of the factors that I could not get out of my head when the Giants beat us in the three-game playoff, coming from 13 games behind and giving us the most bitter loss a team could ever have," Erskine said 66 years later.

Bobby Thomson capped the miraculous comeback with a three-run homer in the bottom of the ninth inning.

"I mean, it was just fate wasn't going to let Charley off the hook," Erskine said. "He thought he buried Leo and was so happy about it and rubbing it in big time."

Leo was infuriated by Dressen's clubhouse-door serenade and used it to unleash the fury of his players.

The next day, the Giants exploded for six runs in the first inning to beat the Dodgers for the first time in six tries and end their losing streak.

Dark belted two grand slams in four days, Noble swatted a pair of homers in a 17–3 bashing of the St. Louis Cardinals, and Artie stroked a run-scoring single to right field as the Giants returned to the Polo Grounds to win 10 of 13 games. They were back in the pennant race, but neither Artie nor Leo was satisfied.

"The other guys don't get kicked out of the game early enough," Artie kidded Leo after Stanky was ejected in the sixth inning and in his only at bat walked and scored a run on the front end of a double steal.

Artie got his wish two days later. The usually mild-mannered Dark was thrown out in the second inning, Artie replacing him and going hitless in three at-bats—his last in the majors.

"There's no joy in sitting on the bench," Artie said. "Leo knew me. He knew I liked to play . . . that I liked to swing the bat. I felt if they couldn't use me, they could sell me to somebody else."

He wanted to go where he could play every day. "I know Pittsburgh was trying to get me," Artie recalled. "There were a couple of other clubs that tried to buy my contract, but the Giants had the price so high."

"He's my handyman," Leo told the Pirates.

He said the same thing in a heated argument with Giants owner Horace Stoneham.

The Giants had a 20-year-old hotshot in the minors he wanted to bring up.

Leo had been down this road before with the Dodgers in 1948. They had a kid pitcher in the Texas League with 15 wins in half a season.

"Durocher needed pitching real bad," Erskine said. "He wanted Mr. Rickey to bring me up. But I had only one full season in the minors, and I was barely 21 years old. He objected: 'He's too young, too green.'"

Erskine wound up joining the Dodgers right after Leo left to manage the Giants.

The issue with the Giants wasn't whether Willie Howard Mays Jr. was ready for prime time. It was who would go to make room on the roster for the budding superstar.

Would it be Clint Hartung, a weak-hitting outfielder with a glove of steel?

Allen Gettel or Jack Kramer, seldom-used pitchers?

Bill Rigney, a good-field, no-hit infielder?

Noble, a backup catcher?

Artie?

The addition of Willie meant the Giants could field a lineup with more blacks than whites. The potential controversy excited Durocher. Stoneham wanted to maintain the status quo by getting rid of Artie. There was an unwritten quota of three blacks on a team, and the Giants already had four.

In the book *The Miracle at Coogan's Bluff*, author Thomas Kiernan gives the following account of the argument:

> "Then you agree to drop Wilson?" Stoneham prodded Durocher after he outlined plans for four black players—Willie in center field, Irvin in right, Thompson at third, and Noble catching.
>
> "Like hell I agree," Leo snapped. "We keep Wilson to spell Stanky and get rid of Hartung. Or Gettel. Or Kramer. They ain't doin' me no good."

"Rigney can spell Stanky."

"Wilson'll hit rings around Rigney."[30]

The debate continued for three days.

Artie was wise to the ways of big-league teams. He knew that if Willie was coming, either he or Noble was going.

"Let me go, keep Noble," Artie pleaded with Leo. "I'm a singles hitter, and I've got to play every day to keep my timing."

Artie asked to return to Oakland, where he made more money than he was earning with the Giants.

Reluctantly, Durocher agreed. "But I'll recall you," he assured Artie.

When Artie and Willie traded places, the Giants were in fifth, with a 17–19 record, four and a half games behind the league-leading Dodgers. They trailed by 13 as late as August 11, finishing the regular season by winning seven straight and 37 of their last 44 to force a best-of-three playoff with the Dodgers for the National League title.

Erskine was warming up in the Dodgers bullpen when Bobby Thomson hit his pennant-winning homer off Ralph Branca in the third game—the famous "shot heard round the world."

Thomson's blast is the sports equivalent of man landing on the moon. People remembered where they were when it happened.

Bob Mercer was a salesman for the Goodyear Tire & Rubber Company at the time. He was driving on a highway in Iowa, listening to a Liberty Radio Network broadcast of the game by Gordon McLendon, self-nicknamed "the Old Scotsman."

Bob grew up in Roselle Park, New Jersey, a small town near Newark, and went to Giants games at the Polo Grounds as often as his father had time to take him.

They saw Jackie Robinson play his first game at the Polo Grounds in 1948.

"It was a beautiful sunny day, and the Giants' white uniforms and all of the white faces stood out," Bob recalled.

So did Jackie, the only black player on the field.

"Which one is Jackie Robinson?" he wisecracked.

"He's number 42," his father said tersely.

"Dad really put me in my place. He judged people by their character, not by the color of their skin. And he wanted me to know that: 'Jackie Robinson is forty-two.'"

Bob played baseball at Yale University in 1945 and 1946. His manager was Red Rolfe, a four-time American League All-Star at third base during his 10 years with the New York Yankees.

Bob played third base until Rolfe pulled him aside and said, "I'm moving you to left field."

"Why is that?" Bob asked.

"The way you played third base, that's where most of those balls wind up."

Bob went on to become chairman and chief executive officer of Goodyear and to meet the guy he replaced on the Yale baseball team—President George H. W. Bush. "You left, and they had to get somebody as good as you," he said to President Bush.

But one of Bob's fondest memories is listening to the radio the afternoon of October 3, 1951, while driving through the cornfields of Iowa from Ottumwa to Cedar Rapids.

Bob could imagine being there with his father George, who used to stand on Coogan's Bluff, overlooking the Polo Grounds, and watch the Giants' legendary Christy Mathewson pitch. "He could see him from the waist up." Bob said, "And he could see second base, shortstop, and the outfield. That's how he watched a Giants game."

It was going to take a miracle at Coogan's Bluff for the Giants to win this game, Bob thought to himself. They trailed by three runs going into bottom half of the ninth inning.

Alvin Dark and Don Mueller hit back-to-back singles. Monte Irvin fouled out, and Whitey Lockman doubled to score Dark. There were runners on second and third with Thomson coming to bat.

Dressen called the bullpen, where Erskine and Branca were throwing side by side.

Erskine listened as coach Clyde Sukeforth said, "They're both ready."

Dressen asked how they looked.

"Erskine is okay, but he's bouncing his curveball," Sukeforth replied.

Carl threw a hard-overhand curve that often wound up in the dirt.

"Let me have Branca," Dressen said.

"I've always said that the best pitch I ever threw in baseball was a curveball I bounced in the bullpen," Erskine joked.

In the first playoff game, Branca had given up a game-winning home run to Thomson.

"Boy, I'm telling you," McClendon said on the radio. "What they're going to say about this one I don't know."

Bob gripped the car steering wheel tightly.

The first pitch from Branca was a called strike on the inside corner. Thomson lined the next pitch toward the left-field wall.

"Going, going, gone!" McClendon exclaimed. "The Giants win the pennant!"

Bob was overcome with emotion. "I couldn't drive anymore. It was too exciting. I had to stop."

He pulled off the road and parked so he could hear McClendon describe the pandemonium at the Polo Grounds.

"Lo and behold, the guy in the car in front of me pulled over and parked."

Both men got out of their cars.

"Did you hear that?" Bob asked.

"I sure did."

They talked about the game for about 10 minutes and then Bob drove off. "Never saw the guy before or since."

When Bob got to his hotel in Cedar Rapids, he called his dad in New Jersey.

George Mercer answered: "The New York Giants, champions of the world."

Father and son were one bundle of joy. "To be able to talk to him about it was just great." Bob said. "It was really a big moment in my life and in his life."

For the Dodgers players and their fans, it was the worst moment.

Dressen was widely blamed for the Dodgers' collapse. One writer compared him to a bookmaker "who always hedged his bets" and Durocher to a "gambler who knew when to take a chance."[31]

Charley took at least two chances that were careless and came back to haunt him.

Singing to Leo through the clubhouse door helped raise the Giants from the dead.

Pulling the shift against Artie in the dramatic way he did made headlines nationally but needlessly showed up Leo and one of his favorite players. "People made quite a to-do out of that play," Charley chuckled.[32]

Dressen made the biggest deal of all.

In 1966, Dressen put the shift back in the news with a byline story for the Associated Press wire service.

"Did you ever hear of a left-handed batter who couldn't pull the ball to right field?" Dressen began.

He discussed managing Artie in the PCL and becoming manager of the Dodgers after selling him to the Giants. "That meant that someday I'd get to see how Artie progressed under Leo."

He described the shift, concluding, "We had no right fielder, because Wilson couldn't pull Newcombe to save his life."[33]

Artie got one crack at beating Dressen's shift, and it defined his big-league career.

"You know what he said to me about the Giant experience?" Artie Jr. asked. He continued:

> During spring training, he was performing, but once it came time for the real deal, they decided to try and make him a utility guy. He wasn't comfortable. That wasn't his cup of tea. "If you're not going to play me, let me go back to Oakland because I need to play." He was proud enough that he wanted to play.

A standout basketball player in high school and college, young Artie recalled the time he was frustrated with a coach about his lack of playing time.

"I understand," Artie said to his son, "especially if you know you're better."

"He didn't go into detail," Artie Jr. said, adding:

> But I got the impression he was talking about that '51 season. He knew how good he was. He always felt like with a bat in his hands, he could answer any of the critics, any of the criticisms, any of the negative taunts—that type of thing. He could slap a double somewhere, make a play, that would be the end of it. That was his mindset. If he had a bat in his hands, he had the opportunity to win.

The Giants took the bat out of his hands. But Artie would never say that.

"I had a shot at the majors," Artie acknowleged. "If I had another opportunity to go back, I would have taken it. That's the tops. That's where you go. Every kid works for the majors if he's going to play any sport. Go to the top. I would've taken another shot at it."

But one shot is all he got.

8

TRADING PLACES

The kid phenom was watching a movie at a theater in Sioux City, Iowa, where his team, the Minneapolis Millers, had an exhibition game that night. Suddenly, the movie stopped, the lights came on, and a man walked on stage to announce, "If Willie Mays is in the audience, would he please report immediately to his manager at the hotel." [1]

Willie rushed to the hotel, hoping for the best but thinking the worst.

When the season started, Millers manager Tommy Heath told Willie, "It's only a matter of time before the Giants call you up." [2]

That time had arrived.

Only 339 days earlier, Willie had graduated from Fairfield High School in Fairfield, Alabama. He was barely 20, with less than a year of experience in white folks' ball.

"No minor-league player in a generation has created so great a stir as has Mays at Minneapolis," the New York Giants enthused in a press release.

Willie was making the pitchers in one of the best minor leagues, the American Association, look like kids half his age. In 35 games, he had 71 hits in 149 at-bats for a batting average of .477—more than 100 points higher than his nearest competitor. The rest of his numbers were equally amazing: 18 doubles, three triples, eight homers, 38 runs scored, and 30 runs batted in.

Willie's exploits in center field were being talked about in such glowing terms that one sportswriter found it necessary to point out that "experienced and trusted eyes report stories of his brilliance in the outfield are based on fact."[3]

At the hotel, Heath informed Willie that Giants manager Leo Durocher had called and wanted him to join the team immediately.

"Tell him I don't want to go to New York," Willie said, explaining he wasn't ready for the majors.[4]

Heath tried reasoning with Willie, but when that failed, he called Leo and put Willie on the line to get an earful of obscenities.

Finally, Leo asked Willie what he was hitting. Then he inquired whether Willie could hit .250 for him, sarcastically cramming an expletive between "two" and "fifty" for shock effect.

Willie was on his way to the majors and superstardom.

Artie was a superstar himself in the Negro Leagues. He was headed back to the relative obscurity of the minors. His most enduring claim to fame would be that he's the answer to the trivia question, Who went down to the minors when Willie Mays came up?

But the careers of Artie and Willie were linked long before that.

Artie played in the Birmingham Industrial League against Willie's father—William Howard "Cat" Mays Sr.

"You think Willie could play outfield?" Artie asked. "You should've seen his dad." He continued:

> Oh, he could play. Played a shallow center field. That's where Willie got that. He'd stand sideways towards home plate. When the ball was hit, he'd turn to see if it was going out of the park. If he took off after it, I guarantee you he'd catch it. He wasn't as strong as Willie. Not as big as Willie. But he could hit. And he could run. That's why we nicknamed him Cat.

When Willie made his pro debut with the Birmingham Black Barons in 1948, Artie was the team's biggest star. Piper Davis was player-manager.

One day at practice Piper heard someone say Willie's name and made a beeline for him.

"Boy, don't you know that if they catch you out here playing ball for money, you can't play no high school sports the next year?" Piper said.

"I don't care," Willie replied.

"Well, you go home and talk with your daddy," Piper said. "And if he let you play, have him to call me."

A longtime teammate of Artie's with the **ACIPCO** Pipemen and Birmingham
Black Barons, Piper Davis traded places with Artie when he returned to Oakland
in 1951. Piper was back with the Oaks in 1952, after Artie was sold to the Seattle
Rainiers. Piper once played all nine positions for the Oaks, prompting someone to
suggest he also work an extra inning as a beer vendor. *Doug McWilliams Collection*

Cat called Piper and said, "If he wants to play, let him play."

"Well, have him out at the ballpark," Piper said.[5]

That's how Willie wound up with the Black Barons.

Piper was a fountain of baseball knowledge and Willie the perfect sponge.

He focused on things like the fastest way to throw the ball to home plate from the outfield. "Bounce it," Piper said. "When the ball skips off the ground it picks up speed."[6]

Piper reduced the intricacies of hitting to the basics, squaring Willie's shoulders toward the pitcher so he could pull inside pitches to left and shoot outside pitches to right.

"Willie was gifted," said pitcher Bill Greason, another Black Barons rookie. "He had the talent and the abilities. And we believed that he was going to go higher once he had the opportunity to play. We saw all of that in him."

Some of the older players also saw him as a threat to their careers.

Piper knew there would be grumbling when he penciled Willie's name into the lineup for the second game of a Fourth of July doubleheader at Birmingham's Rickwood Field. He recalled the situation in a video documentary on the Black Barons.

"Here's the lineup today, men. Willie Mays is playing in center field."

"What the hell is wrong with Piper?" one of the players complained. "He's gone crazy puttin' that damn little ol' boy out there in center field."

"Anybody that don't like it, you know what you can do," Piper shot back.

Actually, Willie played left field for the Black Barons until center fielder Norman "Bobby" Robinson broke his leg. He soon had Jim Zapp in left and Ed "Stainless" Steel in right cheering him on.

"They were so happy, they didn't know what to do," Greason said. "Anything hit between them and Mays, they would just stand and watch to see if Mays would catch up with it. Most often he would."

Piper, pitcher Alonzo Perry, and Greason did most of the talking to Willie.

"Artie was very quiet," Willie said. "He just did his job. Every year 200 hits. Every year he played every day without any problem."

Willie was amazed how Artie could get so many hits, always hitting the ball to left field.

"When Willie started, and didn't do much hitting, he became down," Greason said. "Artie encouraged him."

"You're a big, young buck," Artie reminded Willie. "Get up there and hit the ball."

Artie called Willie "Buck."

"They'd knock him down; he'd get up and hit the next pitch—BOOM!" Artie said.

Soon after joining the Oakland Oaks in 1949, Artie tried persuading the Oaks to sign Willie.

"Oakland couldn't sign him because he was in high school," he said. "But I could've signed him to come play on the same team with me in the Coast League."

Artie pitched the idea of becoming Willie's legal guardian to Oaks manager Charley Dressen and the team's owner, Clarence "Brick" Laws.

"The kid's got it," Artie told Dressen. "He can play."

The Oaks had just shelled out $50,000 for Jackie Jensen, a strong-armed outfielder. "You know how Jackie can throw the ball from the outfield," Artie said. "Willie can outthrow Jackie. He can outthrow every player on the team. He's a better player. You keep him one year and you'll sell him for more money than anybody who ever played in the Coast League."

On Artie's recommendation, the Oaks signed Perry in 1949, and Piper in 1951. But not Willie.

The following spring, Cat Mays huddled with Artie the night before he left his home in Birmingham for training camp. Cat wanted Artie to sign Willie so he could take him to Oakland.

"When I get to camp, I'll tell them," Artie assured his friend.

Artie cornered Laws at camp and repeated what he'd been saying for almost a year. "He can't miss. Just give me the word and we've got him."

"Okay, we're looking into it now," Laws said.

Soon after the 1950 season started, Artie was walking into the clubhouse at Oaks Park in Emeryville when he heard Laws holler, "I see where the Giants got our boy!"

"Who?" Artie asked.

"Mays!" Laws said.

Replaying the clubhouse scene, Artie chuckled, saying, "Every time I'd see Mr. Laws after that, he would have a fit. 'I just let a million dollars slip through my hands,' he'd moan. 'You sure did!' I'd say."

Artie wasn't going to let a pennant slip through the Giants' hands.

"Durocher kept telling me he needed a center fielder. So I told him, 'Why don't you bring Mays up? Let me go.'"

Leo had seen Willie play once.

"I had to play what they called a simulation game, where Leo wanted to see what I could do," Willie said. "They made me come out in the morning and play a whole game for them. Leo said, 'You might be able to play.'"

Artie knew more about Willie than Leo and all the Giants scouts combined. He saw Willie hit Negro League pitchers as talented as any in the majors and knew what would happen if he got knocked down. Willie could run rings around anyone the Giants had in the outfield.

"Bring Mays up, let me go," Artie told Leo several times. "I'd rather be in the Coast League playing and making more money than sitting on the bench in the majors."

Leo wanted to move Monte Irvin back to the outfield where he belonged and put Whitey Lockman at first base. With Willie in center, Bobby Thomson could play left field or third base, where he finished the season.

Durocher figured if Willie was half as good a center fielder as everyone said and could hit two-blanketly-blank-fifty, the Giants might just win the pennant.

"The Giants' front office thumps the tub with the advice that 'he could make New York fans forget Mickey Mantle,'" the *Brooklyn Daily Eagle* reported. "But his real mission is to make New York fans forget the Giants' 11-game losing streak last month."

Mantle was a rookie with the Yankees.

"The Yankees' precocious kid is being asked to make his club," the *Daily Eagle* added. "Mays is being asked to lead his."[7]

Willie got only one hit in 21 at-bats his first week in the majors, the decimal point in his batting average moving from .477 to .0477. "I must be in a slump," he said. "They're throwing me the same pitches I was hitting at Minneapolis only I'm not hitting 'em here."[8]

Minneapolis fans were still upset about losing Willie so early in the season. One sports columnist referred to it as a "kidnapping."[9]

To soothe the fans, Giants owner Horace Stoneham wrote a letter that appeared as an advertisement in the *Minneapolis Star Tribune*. It read:

> We feel that the Minneapolis fans, who have so enthusiastically supported the Minneapolis club, are entitled to an explanation for the player deal that on Friday transferred outfielder Willie Mays from the Millers to the New York Giants.
>
> We appreciate his worth to the Millers, but in all fairness, Mays himself must be a factor in these considerations. Merit must be recognized. On the record of his performance since the American Association season started, Mays is entitled to his promotion and the chance to prove he can play Major League Baseball. It would be most unfair to deprive him of the opportunity he earned with his play.
>
> We honestly admit too, that this player's exceptional talents are the exact answer to the Giants' most critical need.
>
> Please be assured that the New York Giants will continue in our efforts to provide Minneapolis with a winning team. The Millers won the pennant in 1950, and another in 1951 is our objective. [10]

The newspaper credited Stoneham in an editorial for being "gentleman enough to spread a little epistolary balm and ointments on the wounds" caused by Mays's departure. [11]

The Giants didn't send Artie directly to Oakland, as he requested. Instead, he went to Ottawa and played the outfield for two games and was then loaned to Minneapolis as a replacement for injured shortstop Rudy Rufer.

Artie arrived in Minneapolis with his own message of hope for the struggling Mays and Giants, and a compliment for Dressen, his former boss with the Oaks, who was now managing the Brooklyn Dodgers.

"You know I was with the Barons when Mays started, and I figure he's got a great chance, a really great chance," he reminded reporters, adding, "He's a great player, a great prospect." [12]

He predicted the Giants would win the pennant. "The Giant pitching will make the difference."

Of Dressen, he said, "I would have loved to have been sold to Brooklyn, where chances to play regular would have been very good." [13]

Minneapolis fans got a preview of the greatness Mays would achieve and a three-week glimpse of what Artie was like as a young player for the Black Barons.

"Artie Wilson made his debut, and it was a peach," veteran sportswriter Halsey Hall raved. "He was sure in the field at all times, brilliant twice. You wondered where this left-field tradition was when he hit two balls to right field his first two trips, one a single. Then he doubled to left and wound up with no strict partiality as to fields."[14]

In 17 games at Minneapolis, Artie batted. 390. In his last game, he had four hits, including a triple and rare home run, stole a base, scored three times, and batted in four runs.

"In one way of looking at it, the withdrawal of Artie Wilson from the Millers was a rougher deal than the withdrawal of Willie Mays," bemoaned *Minneapolis Tribune* columnist Dick Cullum.[15]

For Artie to return to Oakland, the Oaks had to give up Piper, who they had signed earlier in the year. Piper went to Ottawa.

On June 21, Artie was back in Oakland, his trademark smile as big as ever. "It's good to be back, and I hope my traveling around is over," he said.

"The spark to light the fires of enthusiasm of Oakland baseball fans is home," the *Oakland Tribune* announced.[16]

There was joy in Emeryville.

Friends showered Artie with flowers and gifts, and, in turn, he put on a homecoming show that "couldn't have been more impressive if Hollywood had written the script."[17]

The San Francisco Seals were even there to welcome Artie with one of Lefty O'Doul's shifts. Artie responded by hitting two singles and a long fly out that produced one of five runs the Oaks scored in the ninth inning to win, 5–4.

"ACORNS 'RE-WILSONIZED' BY ARTIE," one newspaper headline read.[18]

"Agile Artie Wilson hasn't put the Oaks in first place yet," the *Tribune* reported. "But give him time."[19]

Artie was credited with attracting the biggest crowds of the season—23,000 in three days. "Artie's name was on the lips of virtually all the spectators," wrote *Tribune* columnist Alan Ward. "The audience was on fire, and it was Wilson who struck the match."[20]

In a Sunday doubleheader against the Seals, he made seemingly impossible plays at shortstop and started three lightning-fast double plays that left Lefty in awe. "You don't see shortstop played better by anybody than you saw it today," he said. "I spent a few years in the majors, but I never saw anything like the exhibition Wilson staged."[21]

Lefty sounded like the president of Artie's fan club. "I'm not saying that he'll transform the club into a pennant winner, but he'll turn this league upside-down."[22]

Artie had paced the Oaks to a second-place finish in 1949, followed by the Pacific Coast League crown in 1950. He was expected to do it again, as they were only three games behind the league-leading Seattle Rainiers.

The Oaks won four of five games as Artie started out with a nine-game hitting streak. Then the hits stopped falling. By the end of July, his batting average hovered around .230, and he could hear some Oakland fans hollering for a pinch-hitter when he stepped to the plate.

"My timing was way off," he lamented. "The pitches they were giving me, I was fouling and popping up. Usually I didn't pop up too many."

Artie ended up hitting a career-low .255.

Making matters worse, the Oaks sold their top two hitters, Earl Rapp and Bert Haas, to big-league teams. They lost 20 of 29 games during one stretch and finished fifth, with an 80–88 record.

"The Oaks, who were nifty in '50, are done with '51, and everybody seems to be glad of it," concluded *Tribune* columnist Emmons Byrne.[23]

Whatever chances Artie had of making it back to the majors were also done.

The Giants recalled Artie and 10 other players in early September, with instructions to report the following spring. Artie never made it. During the winter, he was traded to Seattle.

Piper replaced his longtime friend and teammate in Oakland. They became role models for such future black major leaguers as Charlie Beamon, a pitcher for the Baltimore Orioles from 1956 to 1958, and Elijah "Pumpsie" Green, the infielder who finally succeeded in breaking the Boston Red Sox' color barrier in 1959. They were students at Oakland's McClymonds High School in 1951, when Piper and Artie played for the Oaks.

"It was a respect thing that I had for them," Beamon said of the two Black Barons stars. "I used to talk to them, and I asked, 'Do you think I could've played in the Negro Leagues?' I always thought that if I could play there, I could play in the big leagues."

Artie, Piper, and the other 1948 Black Barons shared a special bond with Willie Mays.

"All those guys in Birmingham took care of me—made sure I didn't get in any trouble," Willie said.

Artie and Piper knew Willie was a boy wonder and wanted to make sure he got the opportunities they were denied. He was their personal representative on baseball's biggest stage, an extraordinary athlete-showman who captivated fans with his speed, power, grace, daring, and passion for the game.

Willie fueled the Giants' amazing comeback to win the pennant, covering center field like a tent and batting .274, with 20 homers and 68 runs batted in. He was selected National League Rookie of the Year, the first of many honors in a Hall of Fame career.

"Willie Mays, he played for the fans," Piper said. "Artie played for the fans."

It's a pity more fans didn't see Artie play in the Big Show.

9

LI'L ARTHUR REIGNS IN SEATTLE

In the spring of 1952, Artie Wilson was supposed to be at the New York Giants training camp in Phoenix, Arizona. He wound up on the other side of the Mojave Desert, in Palm Springs, California, at the spring training facilities of the Seattle Rainiers.

Instead of being back in the majors, he was with another Pacific Coast League team—the last one to integrate.

The Rainiers acquired Artie from the Giants a week after they signed two black players—George Walker, a right-handed pitcher, and Jess Williams, a shortstop, both former Kansas City Monarchs.

Walker showed up in Palm Springs with a gimpy knee that made him appear several years older than his listed age of 31.

It was Walker's first shot at white folks' ball, and Artie wanted to put him at ease.

"Where you been eating?" Artie asked Walker upon arriving in camp.

"Oh, there's one eatin' place here," he said.

"What do you mean only one eatin' place?" Artie asked.

"Across the tracks," Walker replied.

"What about all these other places up the canyon here? What's the matter with them?" Artie inquired.

"You can't eat in them," said Walker matter-of-factly.

In the Negro Leagues, most of the restaurants willing to serve black players were across the railroad tracks in the black section of town.

Artie accompanied Walker to the place he'd been eating. He walked inside, looked around, and declared, "Man, I wouldn't eat in here for any man."

He returned to their hotel and had dinner.

The next morning Artie invited Walker to breakfast.

"Where are you going?" Walker questioned.

"Let's go right here, man—this exclusive restaurant," Artie said.

"They aren't going to serve you," Walker said.

"You stay right here," Artie ordered.

Artie went into the restaurant and requested a table by a window so he could be seen by people passing by on the sidewalk. He did this until Walker started eating with him.

Walker explained he had gone into the restaurant and read on the menu that the restaurant had the right to refuse service to anyone.

"That don't mean you," Artie said. "That doesn't say black person. If it did, I'd still come in here."

Artie had some black friends living in Palm Springs who had never been to an exclusive nightclub there.

"Go in there," he said. "They have good shows."

He decided to take them.

"Artie, where do you want to sit?" the owner of the club asked.

"Close to the bandstand," Artie replied.

"Can we buy you a drink?" Artie was asked.

"No thanks, I don't drink. Just give me a glass of milk. I just want to see the show."

Artie might have bought a round of drinks for friends, but that was it. "It's the way you carry yourself," he said. "I was usually the only black player. On the road, I had a room by myself. The guys wouldn't go nowhere unless they'd come by and tell me. Never had any problems."

Walker didn't make it to Seattle. His bad knee got him a bus ticket home to Waco, Texas.

Artie was the first black player to wear a Rainiers uniform. He was closely followed by Bob Boyd, a first baseman dubbed the "Rope" because of the line drives he specialized in hitting.

Just as Artie did in 1949, Boyd led the PCL in stolen bases (41) his first year in the loop. He also hit .342.

The first black signed by the Chicago White Sox, Boyd played at Sacramento in 1951, before being assigned to Seattle in 1952.

Seattle was managed by Bill Sweeney, beginning his first year with the Rainiers and his 13th in the league. He had the unusual nickname of "Tomato Face."

"You knew by just looking at him that he was probably pretty busy drinking when the games were over," said Ed Mickelson, a first baseman for the Portland Beavers during Sweeney's third and last go-around there in 1956–1957.

Sweeney piloted the Los Angeles Angels the first month of the 1955 season before health problems forced him out.

"One of the great winos of all time," pitcher Jim Brosnan said.

One of his Angels teammates was "Stout" Steve Bilko, a prolific home-run slugger. At 6-foot-1 and 240-something pounds, he was hard to confuse with other players, especially the professorial Brosnan, who wore glasses.

"We knew Sweeney was on his last leg, mostly because he could barely walk," Brosnan said. He continued:

> We're up in Oakland. Bilko and I are standing at the top of the dugout. Now there are two steps down in the dugout. We're 10 feet away from Sweeney. Some guy comes over and asks Bill for the starting lineup. He pointed at Bilko and said, "He's pitching." And he pointed to me and said, "He's hitting fourth."

It didn't matter if Artie and Boyd were mistaken for one another. They were almost identical bookends. Boyd was born and raised in Mississippi, and at 5-foot-10 and 170 pounds, he was about the same size as Artie.

"LIGHTNING STRIKES TWICE," declared a *Seattle Times* cartoon depicting the pair. "The elements have changed for storm-tossed Bill Sweeney . . . two of the PCL sky's flashiest bolts have landed right in his lap."[1]

Both peppered the field with hits and raced around the bases with a sprinter's speed. Sweeney was so ebullient he called the 1952 Rainiers his dream team and predicted they would deliver his fourth PCL pennant in 14 years. He had a new three-year contract and the best job in Minor League Baseball—"one that is a lot better than some major-league managerships."[2]

"Managing is overrated," Sweeney often said. "There's nothing to it."[3]

The Seattle Rainiers were the last Pacific Coast League team to integrate but they did it with a bang as Bob Boyd and Artie Wilson finished the 1952 season one-two in hitting. *Illustration by Jack Winter, Dave Eskenazi Collection*

"Just play between the lines," he told his players. "Do the job you're supposed to do. I have no curfews, but don't try to fool me. I'll know by the way you perform. You can't fool an old fooler."

Mess with Sweeney and it was run for cover.

After one of his teams blew an 11–1 lead in Oakland, the Irishman stormed into the clubhouse. He picked up a fungo bat, got within striking distance of a big mirror on the wall, and yelled, "Guys, stand aside!"

He smashed the mirror to smithereens.

Sweeney managed Portland the three seasons Artie wreaked havoc in Oakland, so he knew what Artie could do between the lines. His biggest concern was that his skinny shortstop might vaporize from the energy he burned up constantly moving around.

"Go in the clubhouse and sit down," Artie recalled Sweeney telling him upon arriving at training camp. "You're already in shape."

Artie kept going, running and shagging fly balls in the outfield. "I can't sit down," he said. "I got to keep moving."

"You can't go all the time," Sweeney said. "You don't have any weight to lose."

"Don't worry, I'm solid," Artie assured him. "I'm not going to lose any weight."

"If you do, you'll fly away," Sweeney joked.

Artie's weight was on cruise control, never varying from 162 pounds.

Artie and Boyd made a pledge to one another that one of them would win the batting crown.

Boyd was immediately hampered in his pursuit by an ulcer condition that sidelined him for three weeks. Injuries caused Artie to miss about the same amount of time.

Without his two best hitters, Sweeney's dreams became nightmarish. The Rainiers were in seventh place and making mental mistakes that got his dander up.

"You are the highest-paid club in the league," he ranted in a team meeting. "The fans pay to see you play heads-up ball, and you're not doing it."[4]

The Rainiers hit bottom before winning 11 straight in June to move up to fourth place.

By the end of July, Boyd and Artie were one–two in the chase for the league batting title.

Artie went on a .432 tear against Lefty O'Doul's San Diego Padres the last week of August, with 16 hits in 37 at-bats. One of the hits was his first out-of-the-park homer in four years in the league.

The pitcher was Al Olsen, a left-hander who won 114 games for the Padres in 12 seasons.

"He got the ball between me and the plate, and I hit it over the right-field fence," Artie said. "I never was so surprised. I was running hard all the way. They asked me, 'How come you didn't Cadillac?' I said, 'I didn't know the ball was out.'"

The outburst came against an overshifted defense first used by Lefty in 1949, when he managed the San Francisco Seals. In addition to the homer, Artie fooled Lefty in another game by poking three singles into a vacant right field.

"The shifts didn't work," said Chuck Stevens, first baseman for the Hollywood Stars. "We tried them. He had the natural ability to make you honest. No matter how you shifted on him, he still found some place to hit that little parachute shot between the outfielder, third baseman, and shortstop. I'll bet I saw him hit a hundred like that."

Artie was leading Boyd in their battle for the league batting title going into a doubleheader against Hollywood the last day of the season. Boyd got five hits in eight at-bats; Artie went 3-for-9. This put Boyd on top, .320 to .316. They were also one–two in hits, Artie ending up with a 216-to-205 edge.

The Rainiers' third-place finish wasn't the dream Sweeney had in mind, but it was good enough for him to hang onto his job.

The big question at spring training in 1953 was whether Li'l Arthur would stick around.

Seattle sportswriters now referred to him affectionately as Li'l Arthur. Fans loved him.

He'd walk into a department store wearing one of his signature berets with a tassel.

"Where did you get that cap?" someone would ask.

"Frederick and Nelson gave it to me," Artie would say.

"Well, here, take one of ours."

"I had it made in Seattle," Artie said.

He didn't want to leave town. But the Rainiers' new general manager, Leo Miller, had him boxed in on upcoming contract negotiations. At least that's what he thought.

Artie Wilson was a "great in-between guy," according to Eddie Basinski, a team-mate in Portland, "because he got along with the white guys as well as he did with the black guys." Artie is shown here celebrating with Seattle Rainiers teammates, left to right, Merrill Combs, Gordon Goldsberry, Clarence Maddern, and Bob Hall. *David Eskenazi Collection*

Sweeney had been "bitterly disappointed" in Artie's play at short-stop—"not enough arm, too much juggling in clutch situations."[5]

Artie committed six errors the first week of the 1952 season and 53 overall, second highest in the league at that position. His fielding per-centage of .937 was the worst.

During the offseason, the Rainiers made a deal with the Cleveland Indians for Merrill Combs, a seasoned shortstop who was one of Casey Stengel's "Nine Old Men" that won the pennant for Oakland in 1948.

This would allow Sweeney to move Artie to second base and Miller to bad-mouth the excellent year he had and slash one of the higher salaries on the team.

"If I can't get a raise every year, I might as well quit," Artie said publicly.[6]

Artie had no problem switching to second base, but he refused Miller's contract offer in their first face-to-face meeting in Palm Springs.

Miller headed for Los Angeles to sign Combs and unload Artie. But first he had to find Combs.

"Seattle may have had better shortstops over the years, but it never has had a more elusive one," the *Seattle Times* reported. "Miller intends to try to track down the phantom, who reportedly lives in the outskirts of Los Angeles, and have him ghostwrite his name on a contract."[7]

Miller and Artie met again the final week of spring training. Neither of them budged.

Artie decided to quit baseball rather than play for what the Rainiers were offering.

"Let him go," Miller said smugly. "We'll get all the infield-hitting punch we need from Bob Boyd, due any day from the White Sox."[8]

Artie was barely out the door when Miller was handed a Western Union telegram from the White Sox notifying him that they were keeping Boyd in Chicago.

Miller immediately sent out an "Artie Alert" to stop him from leaving town.

The next day, Artie was back in uniform, flashing a million-dollar smile at second base.

Artie got the best of management in an era when few players were able to do so. There were no agents, no free agency, nowhere to go except home if you didn't take what was offered. Artie called Miller's bluff in an act of true brinkmanship, a side of Artful Artie never before witnessed.

"We used to grill him periodically about his technique, but his only reply was the enigmatic smile of the Sphinx," *Seattle Times* columnist Lenny Anderson wrote three years later.[9]

"He had a great poker face," Artie Jr. said of his father.

He also had a steely eyed look that Miller probably saw but didn't know what it meant.

"It was one of those looks," young Artie explained, "where you go, 'Okay, this is a quiet, happy, nice guy. Let's just leave it alone and walk away.'" Artie Jr. added, "My Dad recognized his value. He didn't want to go backward. He always felt like he was going to give a team his hundred percent, and he wanted to be compensated for it, especially in the latter part of his career. He thought he'd paid his dues."

"I always got top dollar wherever I played," Artie said.

He gave this elevator speech:

> I was there every day. They could count on me. Never kicked out of a ballgame in my life. Why? I never argued with an umpire. What's the use in arguing? Can't do no good. Can't help the club sitting in the clubhouse. I went out there to play. When I put that uniform on, I'm ready. If they play in mud, I'll play in mud, too.

In baseball and later selling cars, Artie Jr. said his father "was always trying to make the deal versus trying to make the extra dollar. He seemed to always get agreement. Everybody shook hands, walked away, and smiled."

Sweeney had the biggest smile, calling Artie's performance at second base his "happiest surprise" of spring training.[10]

The Rainiers' chief was in for more surprises.

Aside from the ball he popped over the fence in 1952, Artie's only other PCL homer was an inside-the-park drive off Seals pitcher Elmer Singleton in 1950.

Singleton pitched parts of eight seasons in the majors. The rest of his career was spent in the PCL, compiling a 101–94 won–loss record and beaning hitters whenever he felt like it.

"He hit me in the head, the sonofabitch," Ed Mickelson said.

"I must have been about 1-for-40 against Singleton through the years, so why he threw at me was a mystery," Mickelson wrote in his memoir, *Out of the Park*. "He should have sent a cab to the hotel to make sure I got to the ballpark on the day he was pitching."[11]

Singleton also was known for throwing a spitball and verbally harassing Artie from the bench. "He rode Artie to death," Mickelson said. "He called him every name in the book."

Singleton was pitching when Artie led off the seventh inning of a game at San Francisco's Seals Stadium—the scene of Artie's first PCL homer.

The right-hander reared back and fired a pitch that Artie lined into the right-field seats—a "whistling cruncher" against the wind that "carried about 365 feet before hitting the seats some 20 feet above the ground and rebounding into the playing field."[12]

"Saw it go into right field and thought, 'I got a triple anyway.'" Artie recalled. "When I rounded second base, I saw the umpire doing this."

The umpire was motioning home run, but Artie didn't recognize the sign. He kept racing for third. Artie continued:

> When I got to third base, I could see the ball was in the stands. If I'd
> known that ball was in the stands, talk about a showboat. I'd put on a
> show. I'd crawled around the bases. I lived for the day I hit a home
> run when I knew the ball was over the fence. I was going to put a
> show on for the folks.

Two weeks earlier, Mickey Mantle of the New York Yankees had blasted a 565-foot homer over the left-field wall at Griffith Stadium in Washington, DC. "The shot that shook the records," *Sporting News* called it. The 21-year-old Mantle posed for a picture with the ball, pointing at the stitching torn apart from the cover.[13]

Artie figured his homer was historic, too.

After the game, he requested a measurement and then asked for the ball so he could sign and send it to Mantle to let him know he had competition on the West Coast. He was informed that the flight of the ball made it difficult to estimate the distance it had traveled. Besides, the Seals' right-fielder tossed the ball back into the stands after it ricocheted onto the field.

Sweeney moved Artie from the leadoff spot to sixth in the batting order, and it seemed to bring out the slugger in him.

Seven weeks later, at Wrigley Field in Los Angeles, where the original Home Run Derby was filmed for television, Artie cranked another ball over the fence for his second homer of the season and sixth in Organized Baseball.

"The Seattle dugout was a riotous place when Artie Wilson returned after homering," the *Los Angeles Times* noted. "Artie flexed his biceps and doffed his cap toward pitcher Cal McLish."[14]

The few homers Artie hit were off quality pitchers. McLish returned to the majors in 1956, to win 84 games in the next nine years.

The Rainiers led the league until midseason when a six-game losing streak dropped them into second. That's where they finished, eight games behind first-place Hollywood.

Artie was solid defensively at second base and, for the second consecutive year, runner-up for the league batting title, with a .332 average.

Success on the field, however, didn't pay off at the box office for the Rainiers. Attendance tumbled almost 22 percent. The last week of the season, four games attracted less than 1,000 fans.

Miller was replaced as general manager by Dewey Soriano, a hometown boy who once was a peanuts vendor at the Rainiers' ballpark, Sicks' Stadium. "We need some new blood in our organization," said the team's president, Emil Sick.[15]

At 33, Soriano was three months younger than Jerry Priddy, the player-manager he hired to succeed the fired Sweeney. Priddy had 11 years of big-league experience playing second base but none guiding a team at any level.

Soriano made sure Artie was signed before he got to training camp. They agreed to contract terms by telephone.

Artie preferred the Coast League over the majors because he could play every day. "So I can produce. So I can ask for more money."

He was always on a baseball field somewhere.

In mid-October 1953, Artie and Willie Mays hooked up with Jackie Robinson's All-Stars for a game in Birmingham. They treated hometown fans to vintage Black Barons baseball, Artie getting four singles in five at-bats and Willie two hits, plus a delayed steal of home.

Artie spent seven winters playing baseball in Puerto Rico. "Winter months, what are you going to do? Spend what you made in the summer months, if you don't get a job. Well, there was no job that paid that kind of money. Why not play ball? That's what I like to do."

Artie didn't care what position he was at so long as he played.

A few weeks into the 1954 season, Priddy shifted Artie from second base to first. "He's found a home," the manager proudly announced.[16]

Home was wherever he was assigned on a given day. He played 72 games at first, 49 at second, and 45 at shortstop.

During one game, the Rainiers ran out of catchers because Priddy pinch-hit for the only one he had available. Recognizing his manager's dilemma, Artie popped out of the dugout wearing the chest protector and shin guards used by the regular catchers.

The protector "hung on Li'l Arthur's meager frame as loose as a bathrobe," the *Times'* Anderson observed. "The shin guards could have gone a time and a half around the pipe-stem legs."

"I'll stop 'em running, Skip," Artie said.

This was no laughing matter, but Priddy couldn't help but chuckle at what he saw.

"I know you would," Priddy said, "but I'm saving you for the real jam, when we are really up against it."[17]

There was no saving the explosive Priddy. He was in one tight spot after another, starting with the Rainiers' season-opening series against the Padres, described as "one of the most eventful and turbulent" in the 16-year history of Sicks' Stadium.[18]

In one game, Priddy got into a fistfight with Padres catcher Red Mathis, triggering a free-for-all. Priddy's punches sent Mathis to the hospital with a fractured right arm that required five hours of surgery to repair. Priddy took a blow on the back of the neck that forced him to sit out a game.

At the end of the seven-game series, nine Rainiers were hobbled by injuries. "When the season started," Priddy said, "I was trying to put together a pennant winner. Now I have my hands full just trying to find a full nine."[19]

Through 50 games, the Rainiers had lost as many as they won and were floundering in fifth place. "We have too many complacent players," Soriano charged. "As far as I'm concerned, everybody on the club, with a few obvious exceptions, is subject to be sold or traded."[20]

The Rainiers could never dig themselves out of their fifth-place hole, ending up with a 77–85 record.

Artie was no longer one of the exceptions.

He had the kind of numbers Soriano needed to get the most out of him in a trade—a league-leading 16 triples and 182 singles, and the third-best batting average in the circuit, with .336.

"Wilson has been above .310 in every full season he has been in the league," Soriano said in promoting his star in early December. "We will get the kind of players we need in exchange for him or there won't be any deal."[21]

Four PCL clubs wanted Artie—Los Angeles, San Francisco, San Diego, and Portland. One would get him. But they'd have to wait until after Christmas.

Artie Wilson was more like a Molotov cocktail than TNT as he peppered the left side of the diamond with singles that fell between bunched-up defenders. His batting averages of .316 in 1952 and .332 in 1953 were second best in the league and in 1954 he placed third with a .336 mark. *Illustration by Jack Winter, Dave Eskenazi Collection*

10

PREJUDICE IN PORTLAND

The Mississippi-born gentleman spelled his name "Clay Hopper," but the way he said it with a thick Southern accent was "Clayhoppeh."

Hopper managed 15 teams in 14 leagues in 25 seasons, all in the minors. He was in his fourth year as boss of the Portland Beavers when Artie Wilson joined the team in 1955.

The Beavers were coming off a last-place finish that Hopper pretty much had predicted in a pep talk to his players at the start of the season.

"Well, I ain't got much of a club this year," first baseman Herm Reich recalled Hopper saying as he puffed on a cigarette. "My outfield can't run, and there's not goin' to be much hittin'. My infield is like a sieve. I don't know about my pitchin'. It's v-e-r-y, v-e-r-y meed-ee-oh-cree . . . v-e-r-y meed-ee-oh-cree. I don't know where we're gonna finish. It looks like we're gonna be a miracle club."

The miracle didn't happen, and Hopper decided to rebuild the team, beginning with the sieve-like infield he talked about.

Using the number-one minor-league draft pick, which they got for finishing last, the Beavers grabbed a new first baseman, Ed Mickelson, a reliable line-drive hitter and sure-handed fielder.

"Give me a player like that and you'll never hear a complaint from me," Hopper said. "That's the type of player we're always looking for and so seldom get."[1]

After several months of pestering by Hopper, the Beavers' front office made a deal for Artie shortly after Christmas, giving the Seattle Rainiers two players and an undisclosed amount of cash. He wanted a holler guy to liven up the team and admired Artie's hustling and scrappy all-around play. It reminded him of the first black player he managed—Jackie Robinson at Montreal in 1946.

Hopper worked for the Brooklyn Dodgers at the time. He managed teams for Branch Rickey for almost 20 years, long before Rickey became president of the Dodgers.

He wasn't happy to hear Jackie was going to play for his Montreal team as part of Rickey's great experiment to integrate Organized Baseball.

"Please don't do this to me," he said to Rickey. "I'm white, and I've lived in Mississippi all my life. If you're going to do this, you're going to force me to move my family and my home out of Mississippi."[2]

Hopper lived in Greenwood, Mississippi, and was a successful cotton broker in the offseason.

In the 1950 movie *The Jackie Robinson Story*, there's a scene showing Hopper and Rickey sitting side by side, watching an intrasquad game during spring training. After Jackie made an acrobatic play at second base, Rickey said, "No other human being could've made that play."

"Mr. Rickey," Hopper said, "do you really think he is a human being?"[3]

The comment was a watered-down version of what Hopper really said.

A shocked Rickey didn't answer Hopper's question in the movie or real life.

Montreal went on to win 100 games, capture the International League pennant by 18 1/2 games, and beat Louisville, the American Association champion, in the Little World Series. Jackie was selected the International League's Most Valuable Player, and Hopper was named Minor League Manager of the Year by *Sporting News*.

Hopper walked into Rickey's office after the season.

"I want to take back what I said to you last spring," he said. "I'm ashamed of it." He added, "Now you may have plans for him to be on your club, but if you don't have plans to have him on the Brooklyn club, I would like to have him back at Montreal."

Hopper concluded by saying Jackie "was not only a great ballplayer good enough for Brooklyn," but also a "fine gentleman."[4]

In Hopper's eyes, Artie was just like Jackie—a gentleman in the clubhouse and off the field, and a one-man riot with a bat in his hands and running the basepaths.

"Never fear, Artie's here," he constantly told teammates at spring training in Glendale, California.

"He was very positive," Mickelson said. "He had a great deal of self-confidence. It was contagious. I fed off it . . . so did the other players. We're good. We're fine. We'll do all right. 'Never fear, Artie's here.' He said it so often it was really uplifting."

The new Beavers also responded favorably to Hopper's firm but entertaining leadership style.

Mickelson was ready to ask for an interpreter after one of the team's early meetings left him and catcher Sam Calderone wondering what Hopper had said.

"Boys, ya'll gonna git rail soah thcsc fust few daies—specially yo ahms, yo laeggs, and yo ahss."

Sitting next to one another in the front row are Ed Mickelson and Artie Wilson, third and second from right and the top two hitters for the 1955 Portland Beavers, with batting averages of .308 and .307, respectively. Standing in the back row, third from left, is Joe Taylor, the slugging outfielder Artie tried to keep sober, with little success. *David Eskenazi Collection*

Mickelson wrote in his book *Out of the Park* that whenever things got dull during the season, Calderone reminded him to take good care of "yo ahms, yo laeggs, and yo ahss!"[5]

Soon Artie was covering for the "ahss" of teammate Joe Taylor, or "Old Taylor," as the players referred to the hard-hitting (and hard-drinking) outfielder.

Taylor was 28 in 1954, and hitting .325, with 16 homers and 24 doubles for Ottawa, when Rickey, then vice president and general manager of the Pittsburgh Pirates, filed the following report:

> A tall, rough, sea-going Negro who allegedly plays a great game when sober. He has a reputation for being a complete rounder—a fence-screeching tomcat with not enough females in sight. 'Tis said he even plays a good game with a snoot full. This fellow can run and he can throw and he can hit the ball a "fur piece." I don't know how old he is. So far as I can find out, no one does. My guess is somewhere between 20 and 40. Age doesn't matter because he is fast, agile, and obviously full of confidence . . . Taylor bears such a vile reputation that I guess I couldn't have the remotest interest in him, but he impressed me very much as a player.[6]

Artie knew all about Taylor, playing with and against him in Puerto Rico.

Taylor began the 1955 season in the majors with the Kansas City Athletics. Near the end of spring training, they sent him to their International League farm club in Columbus, Ohio. The Beavers had a chance to get him.

"You think he'll help us?" Artie was asked.

"He'll help the club. He's a good ballplayer," Artie replied.

"We heard he drank a lot."

"Well, I guess that's why they shipped him out of the majors."

The Beavers obtained Taylor in mid-May and assigned Artie to be his roommate on the road.

Taylor landed in Portland at 6:00 on a Sunday morning after an overnight flight from Columbus. Artie met him at the airport.

The Beavers had a doubleheader against the Oakland Oaks that afternoon, but Artie told him to forget about playing, go to his hotel, and get some rest.

"No, I feel like playing," Joe insisted.

He led off the second inning by belting the first pitch over the center-field wall for a 400-foot homer.

With a runner on base in the fourth inning, he swatted the ball over the left-field wall for a two-run homer.

In the sixth inning, Joe drilled another shot to deep center. "The ball would've gone out if the center fielder hadn't jumped so high to catch it," Mickelson said.

Taylor strolled to the plate in the eighth inning with the crowd yelling for him to hit another homer. On the first pitch, he bashed the ball into the center-field seats.

In four at-bats, Taylor blasted three home runs and came within inches of a fourth. L. H. Gregory of the *Oregonian*, called it the "most sensational debut any player ever made" in the 52-year history of Portland's Vaughn Street Stadium.[7]

"They were three of the longest home runs ever hit in that park," said Eddie Basinski, the Beavers' third baseman. "All of a sudden, this guy is going to be the black Babe Ruth."

"He did the same thing to us in Puerto Rico—beat us single-handedly," Artie said. "He'd be half high, but it'd make no difference. He could still hit that ball."

By July, Taylor was hitting at a .345 clip.

"You shouldn't be down here," Artie told him. "You ought to be in the majors."

"He had major-league talent," Artie explained. "He could play the outfield, he could hit the long ball, and he could run for a big man. He should've never been in the minors. But that bottle! He couldn't play sober. I saw him try."

Several times after a road game Artie ushered Taylor directly back to the hotel. "Next day he couldn't hit the side of a building. So, I told him, 'Don't come in tonight.'"

Taylor stayed out until 5:00 in the morning and slept until Artie woke him up to go to the ballpark. "He'd get out there and hit and catch everything," Artie said.

Sometimes fly balls hit to Taylor in right field could be an adventure. Fans offered encouragement. "Stay with it, Joe," they would holler, "stay with it!"

In late July, Taylor was in a prolonged batting slump. His average was down 45 points, to .300.

"Whenever he was singing in a loud voice or whistling coming into the dugout, Clay would run and take his name off the starting lineup," Mickelson said.

Hopper decided Taylor was unfit to play the first game of a double-header against the San Diego Padres.

"He knew Joe was drunk as a skunk," Mickelson said. "He told him to get his uniform on but sit in the bullpen with the pitchers."

In the fourth inning of the first game, Basinski slashed a line drive into left field and toward the bullpen. Everybody got out of the way except the groggy Taylor.

"Joe jumped up out of a fog and fielded the ball and threw it back into play," Mickelson said.

Basinski recalled coasting into second base thinking he had a run-scoring double. Umpire Vinnie Smith, an ex-player, informed him otherwise: "Ed, I hate to tell you, but you're out."

Basinski couldn't believe it. "You've got to be kidding. Hell, there wasn't even a play on me."

"Taylor was sleeping on the bench down there in the bullpen," Smith said, "and the ball came rolling by him and he picked it up and tossed it to the outfielder."

That's interference.

Basinski stormed off the field, passing a puzzled Hopper in the third-base coaching box.

"Eddie, where the hell you going? Get back! Get back!" Hopper yelled.

Basinski gave him the bad news.

Mickelson watched from the dugout with mixed amusement and amazement. "I could hear Basinski calling Joe names from second base, and Hopper was running down the left-field line as hard as he could with the reddest face I ever saw."

Looking on was a crowd of almost 5,000, which turned out to honor Frank Austin, the team's popular black shortstop, for playing in 600 consecutive games.

They could hear Hopper call Taylor the "N" word and drop the "F" bomb to vent his anger.

"Get your goddamn black ass out of here," he screamed. "Get it in the clubhouse where you can't hurt our ball club anymore."

"He called him all kinds of names," Basinski said. "And he did that in front of all these people."

The *Oregonian's* Gregory called Taylor's one-handed stab an "old-fashioned, country-fair type of pure bonehead play" and a "freak of baseball stupidity." Taylor, he added, will "never make a bonier one if he plays 100 years."[8]

Taylor played in the second game of the doubleheader, going hitless in four at-bats and committing an error in right field. He quietly disappeared from the lineup, not playing another inning for the Beavers. Ten days later, he was shunted back to the International League, this time to the Toronto Maple Leafs.

Mickelson said the Beavers players were upset with Taylor at first, and then it became a laughing matter. "We would be sipping an old brew after a game and someone would say, 'Hey, I really thought Taylor showed a great pair of hands that day in the bullpen.' And we would all crack up."[9]

Artie had his own struggle early in the season. He was benched for three games after a string of 20 hitless plate appearances plunged his batting average below .200.

"One day they suddenly find they've lost it," Bill Sweeney said to a sportswriter, referring to Artie and several other ex-Rainiers. "There comes a day."[10]

Sweeney was Artie's first manager in Seattle (1952–1953) and tried buying him from the Rainiers to play third base for the Los Angeles Angels, the team he led at the beginning of the 1955 season.

Artie was Seattle's top hitter in 1954—the only starter to bat over .300. Management justified his trade to Portland by saying "his weak arm prevented him from playing third base or shortstop, and handicapped him at the other two positions."[11]

His arm had nothing to do with the throwing problems he had in Portland.

"He was missing the top part of his thumb on his throwing hand," Mickelson said. "It was cut off right at the knuckle. One or two of his throws went up in the stands because of the nub he had there."

Hopper was just as unflappable as the time Mickelson complained about being taken out of the starting lineup because of a 0-for-19 slump.

"Yaw'll mean yaw'll wanna plaigh?" Hopper asked.

"You're damned right I do," Mickelson replied.

"Okay, yaw'll in thayer ta-day."[12]

Mickelson wound up with a team-high .308 batting average. Artie was second, at .307.

The Beavers finished fifth, with an 86–86 won–loss mark, nine games behind the pennant-winning Rainiers.

In 1956, the Beavers went from operating independently to being a farm club of the Brooklyn Dodgers. It was out with the old and in with the new.

Out was the 53-year-old Hopper. In was Brooklyn-born Tommy Holmes, age 39. A consistent .300 hitter for 11 seasons with the Boston Braves, Holmes had limited experience as a manager, guiding the Braves briefly in 1951 and 1952.

The Beavers moved out of ancient Vaughn Street Stadium and into Multnomah Stadium, an old dog and car racing track transformed into a baseball park. "It was a short porch in left field," said Sacramento pitcher Bud Watkins. "You stand at home plate and spit over the left-field fence. Right field was seven miles. You could run for two or three weeks."

Playing at an old dog track was a sign of the dog days ahead for Artie.

As vivid as his memories are of Artie in 1955, Mickelson can't remember him playing for the Beavers in 1956.

That's because Artie didn't play much in spring exhibition games or the first six weeks of the regular season.

Why?

Tommy Holmes.

One mention of Holmes to Artie and his light-up-the-room smile was replaced by a steely eyed look rarely seen.

"He was prejudiced. I'll tell you like it is—he didn't like blacks," said Artie.

Holmes was a stranger to the Pacific Coast League and its players, as he had never seen a game.

"Everybody's starting from scratch on the Portland team this year, along with myself," he said at the start of spring drills. "For example, I've heard plenty about the double-play combination of Artie Wilson and Frankie Austin. But they will have to show me they're better than Young and Littrell."[13]

Artie Wilson quickly became a fan favorite after joining the Portland Beavers in 1955. He started selling cars in Portland and soon relocated to the city from Birmingham, Alabama. Under a new manager in 1956, Artie saw little action and was traded back to Seattle, where he finished the season. *Doug McWilliams Collection*

Jack Littrell, age 27, took over at shortstop, and Dick Young, 28, stepped in at second base. "In spring training, Holmes didn't play us," Artie said.

When Artie did see action, it was as a late-inning substitute for Mickelson at first base or a brief trial in right field. "He looked out of place in judging flies and got no hits," the *Oregonian* reported.[14]

The 39-year-old Austin was a fixture at shortstop for the Beavers, playing in 659 consecutive games since he and outfielder Luis Marquez broke the team's color barrier in 1949. He was released a week before the season opener.

The Beavers also had a promising young black catcher who would go on to star for the Dodgers—John Roseboro. "He sent Roseboro out of camp," Artie said.

Through 41 regular-season games, Artie had two hits in eight at-bats, for a .250 average. "Tommy Holmes had me pulling the ball. I pulled down from .307," Artie said.

The Beavers' other blacks, Marquez and pitcher Rene Valdez, were the team's biggest stars, along with Mickelson.

Marquez made his big-league debut with the Boston Braves the same day Artie broke in with the New York Giants—April 18, 1951. He started only 13 games after Holmes became Braves manager in June.

"When Luis went up, I told him, 'You're not going to make it up there with that club. You're going to have to go somewhere else. Wrong manager,'" Artie said.

Artie played against Marquez in the Negro Leagues and again in the PCL.

"Another Willie Mays," Artie said. "He could go back like Mays and catch the ball and throw you out. Get up at the plate and hit the ball downtown. He could run . . . steal bases. Smart. He could do it all."

The Rainiers came to Artie's rescue in late May. Lenny Anderson of the *Seattle Times* celebrated the news with a sports column titled "Mr. Automation Is Back with Rainiers; Heed the Warning, Tommy Holmes."

"Tommy Holmes, poor misguided soul, was unable to find a place for Li'l Arthur on the Portland varsity," Anderson wrote. He continued:

This is not uncommon. The Rainiers thought they couldn't find a place for him either, and he came back to haunt them; now they have bought him back.

The years pass, but Wilson seemingly goes on forever. If he gets back into regular action, he is little short of a mortal cinch to hurt at least a few clubs before the season is finished. One of them might just be Portland. Brother Holmes, don't say we didn't warn you.[15]

What Brother Holmes needed most was prayers, and it's doubtful they would've done much good. He tried everything. To ensure his players stayed focused, he had them stand in the dugout throughout a game.

Perhaps it was fatigue from all the standing that led to an 11-game losing streak and a fifth-place record of 44–49. He resigned after 93 games—"one of the shortest managerial tenures in Coast League history," according to the *Oregonian*.[16]

"I felt sorry for him," Mickelson said. "He was a helluva nice guy and a pretty good hitting instructor. He helped me a lot."

Sweeney replaced Holmes and spread a little cheer.

"I love you," he told Mickelson. "I love your bat."

Mickelson hit .309, belted 21 homers, and batted in 101 runs.

Marquez did even better—a .344 batting average, 25 homers, and 110 runs batted in.

Valdez led the league with 22 victories.

The Beavers placed third, close behind Artie and the Rainiers in second.

Artie picked up where he left off with the Rainiers to end up hitting .293—seven points shy of reaching the magic mark of .300 for the fifth-straight year.

Austin found a new home in Vancouver, batting .285 in 120 games.

Roseboro slugged 25 homers for Montreal in the International League, earning a promotion to the majors the next year.

"Maybe someone else can perk up the club," Holmes said on his way out the door.[17]

In 1955, the Beavers handpicked Artie to be the holler guy to fire up his teammates. If Holmes had played Artie more, he might've heard him chattering, "Never fear, Artie's here."

Holmes had the guy needed to perk up the team sitting on the Beavers bench. He didn't know it. That's why he didn't last long in Portland.

11

SAY HEY, IT'S MR. HEY HEY!

Mr. Hey Hey made it to California the year before Willie Mays, the Say Hey Kid, and the Giants arrived in San Francisco in 1958.

Upon joining the Sacramento Solons two months into the 1957 season, Artie Wilson was given a new nickname by a Sacramento sportswriter—Mr. Hey Hey.

It was fitting because Artie and Willie had a shared history, and they played the game with the same fervor and flair that electrified fans and had them shouting their names.

The Solons were the bottom-feeders of the Pacific Coast League. From 1950 to 1956, they finished at the bottom of the eight-team standings four times, next to last twice, and fifth once.

One sportswriter couldn't understand how Richie Myers, the Solons' star shortstop from 1952 to 1955, remained so easygoing and calm during all the losing.

"I never see you show any emotion," Solons pitcher Roger Osenbaugh recalled the writer saying to Myers. "If you have a bad game or the team has a bad streak, I never see you throwing your glove around or screaming, yelling, or throwing any tantrums in the clubhouse. Do you ever do anything?"

Osenbaugh and the other Solons listened as Myers responded to the question.

"Yeah, there's one thing that I do," he said. "When I get home after a real bad game, I don't use the key to get in the house. I knock on the front door. When my wife Loretta answers the door, I punch her right in the nose."

"The funny thing is Richie was the kindest, gentlest man in the whole world," explained Osenbaugh. "His wife was the sweetest in the whole world. That was Richie's sense of humor."

Myers used it to deal with the losing situation in Sacramento.

The manager who pulled off the miraculous fifth-place finish in 1956 was Tommy Heath, a good-humored fellow frequently referred to as a jolly round man.

He once went to the mound to settle down a pitcher for an opposing team.

In the 1956 season opener against the Portland Beavers, he protested the candy-striped sleeves worn by Portland pitchers as part of their uniforms, claiming they might distract batters. The umpires backed him up, but they were overruled by the league president. This prompted Heath to announce that his pitchers would start wearing blue sweatshirts with big white polka dots the size of a baseball. Pitcher "Chesty" Chet Johnson posed in one for a wire-service photo. He added a Mickey Mouse cap and a giant gag thumb for extra impact. "If the intent is to dress up the league," Heath said, "far be it for us to be left behind in the style parade."[1]

Somehow Heath guided a group of misfits and unfits to a surprising 84–84 record. Many of the players were claimed off waivers from other PCL teams. "Why, when we claim anybody, we're scared to death— afraid we might get 'em," he joked.[2]

One player Heath picked up was Hal "Hoot" Rice, a veteran outfielder.

"Hoot liked to partake of the grape—a lot," said Solons pitcher Bud Watkins. "Every time he'd partake a little too much, he would get hives. Big, red blotches would appear all over his body."

After a Sunday twin bill in Vancouver, British Columbia, Hoot loaded up.

Heath took one look at the red blotches covering Hoot and decided to teach him a lesson by playing him the next day in both games of a doubleheader at Portland's Multnomah Stadium.

"It could be 85 degrees at Multnomah, but you'd think it was a hundred and twenty-eight because you were playing down in a hole," Watkins explained. "The air was dead, and you could hardly breathe."

Uniforms were made of wool, and they itched in hot weather.

"Hoot was going through contortions," Watkins said.

"Please, get me out of here," Hoot pleaded. "Get me out of here."

"I hope you die in right field," Heath said. "Don't ever get another drink in Vancouver or I'll do it again."

"Please, get me out of here," Hoot continued to beg.

The 1956 season was Hoot's last in baseball.

Heath shared PCL Manager of the Year honors with Bob Scheffing, the pilot of the pennant-winning Los Angeles Angels.

In 1957, Sacramento was the only independent team in the PCL. The others were affiliated with big-league teams, ensuring a steady supply of talent. The cash-starved Solons relied heavily on players picked up for the league's waiver price of $5,000. "If your till is lean," Heath asked, "what do you use for money to buy 'em—if and when you can find 'em?"[3]

A former big-league catcher, Heath managed both Artie and Willie Mays during their brief stops at Minneapolis in 1951.

Heath piloted the San Francisco Seals from 1952 to 1955. He was relieved of his duties by the Boston Red Sox after they took over the Seals and made it a farm club. "A new order," Red Sox general manager Joe Cronin announced. "A new broom sweeps clean."

"I don't want to be the janitor," Heath quipped. "I just want to manage the club."[4]

Heath moved up the road 90 miles to Sacramento.

Artie was a castoff himself in 1957, sold by the Seattle Rainiers to Tulsa in January. Tulsa was a member of the Class AA Texas League, a demotion from the PCL, the only open-classification league in the minors and generally considered the strongest.

Lenny Anderson, sports columnist for the *Seattle Times*, couldn't believe the "senior active inhabitant of the Pacific Coast League" was being treated this way.

"Long ago, students of antiquity had ceased to expect the day would ever come," Anderson wrote. "Studying the fine old specimen, these observers began to report, as long ago as 1951, the first signs of erosion."[5]

This was the second time the Rainiers had given up on Artie.

Anderson acknowledged Artie's listed age of 36 was possibly a "mathematical miscalculation of major proportions" and there were times "his range around second base suffered from too-great maturity," but he was one of the true believers that expected Artie to go on forever.

"The Coast League won't seem the same," Anderson concluded. "But who would be reckless enough to bet that he won't be back?"[6]

Artie figured there was nothing to gain from going down one level in the minors and taking a pay cut, too. He stayed home in Portland until the Solons beckoned in late May.

Artie was sort of a mystery to Sacramento fans prior to joining the Solons.

He was playing for the Rainiers in 1952, when Bill Conlin, sports editor for the *Sacramento Union*, spotted him downtown one afternoon.

"Very dapper, well-dressed fellow," Conlin said. "He had a big Shriners pin on—one of the biggest I've ever seen."

This surprised Conlin because there was a rumor circulating throughout the league that Artie grew up in a Catholic orphanage near Birmingham, Alabama. Catholics aren't supposed to be Shriners, as they are part of a men's fraternal organization, the Freemasons, which is considered incompatible with Catholicism.

That night at the ballpark, Conlin told Vinnie Smith, a catcher for the Solons and a devout Catholic.

"I'll ask him about it tonight," Smith said.

Smith was behind the plate as Artie stepped into the batter's box to start the game. Conlin watched from the press box.

"Before a pitch is even thrown, Artie backed out of the batter's box," Conlin said. "He was laughing. And, then, he talked to Smith."

Conlin made a beeline for Smith after the game.

"Vinnie, what went on out there?" Conlin queried.

"I said to him: 'You grew up in a Catholic orphanage and now you're a Shriner.' He backed out of the batter's box and said, 'Well now, Vinnie, I'll tell you about that. I play both sides of the street.'"

Artie was a Shriner.

"But I didn't come out of no orphan home," he said with a chuckle. "They used to get on me about a little bit of everything. I went along with them."

Sometimes Smith picked up dirt and threw it in Artie's shoes to slow him down.

"Kick him out of the game," Artie would tell the umpire jokingly.

"I had to call time and pull my shoe off and get the dirt out of it. He'd throw some more dirt in there. It was all in fun."

When Artie arrived in Sacramento in 1957, Heath had a mess on his hands and needed a cleanup crew. The Solons had an 8–26 record and were in last place, 14 games behind the league-leading Hollywood Stars. Heath also added first baseman Jimmy Westlake and shortstop Leo Righetti, a teammate of Artie's the previous year in Seattle.

Artie always believed he could fall out of bed and get his singles. This was a chance to prove it. The Rainiers suspended him after he refused to report to Tulsa, so he missed spring training and the first six weeks of the season.

No problem. In a seven-game series against the Stars, Artie singled in each of the first two games, slashed three in the next, and, overall, had 11 hits in 32 at-bats for a .343 average. The Solons won two straight games for the first time all season and captured the series, four games to three.

Success vanished as quickly as it appeared.

The good-natured Heath was ejected from three games in as many days.

Catcher Cuno Barragan suffered through a 0-for-46 batting slump.

In a game against the Angels, Osenbaugh was bludgeoned for 18 hits, including nine homers and 22 earned runs, 11 of them in the seventh inning, when Heath finally removed him from the game. "Osenbaugh was ill recently and hasn't been getting enough work to regain his early season form," Heath explained the slow hook. "I figured a stiff workout would sharpen him up."[7]

The Solons lost 21 of their last 25 games in June to fall 10 games behind the seventh-place Portland Beavers, before rebounding in July to win 13 of their first 18 games and tie the Beavers by the end of the month.

In 10 years of managing, Heath never had a club finish last, and it looked like the Solons might spare him that embarrassment. Artie was batting .263 and, paired with Righetti at shortstop, tightened the defense up the middle. And then disaster struck the duo on back-to-back plays in a game against the Angels at Sacramento.

"Got hit in the eye," Artie said, continuing:

Photographer Doug McWilliams was 19 years old in 1957, when he took this photo of Artie Wilson in the Sacramento Solons' dugout at Edmonds Field in Sacramento. Artie incurred an eye injury at Sacramento that ended his career. *Doug McWilliams Collection*

> It was a freak accident. Something you'll probably never see. I was on deck. We had a man on first base. Pitcher was up. He bunted the ball. The runner went to third when they overthrew the ball to first. Anyway, they retrieved the ball and threw it to third. Ball got by the third baseman. I'm the next man up, and the runner is coming home.

Angels pitcher Bob Darnell was at first base to field the bunt. The team's bulky first baseman, Steve Bilko, lumbered toward home plate to back up the play there as the baserunner, Barragan, headed for home.

"I'm standing behind the plate," Artie said, "signaling the runner to hit the dirt because it's going to be a close play. The pitcher finally got back there to cover in case of an overthrow. The ball bounced over the pitcher's head and hit me in the right eye."

The ball actually deflected off Darnell's glove.

"Bilko caught me because he thought I was going to fall. He'd seen the ball hit me," Artie said.

Some fans jumped up from their seats in the stands and started toward the field.

"They thought Bilko had hit me," Artie said. "I told them, 'No, no, he didn't hit me. He caught me. The ball hit me.'"

Bilko gently laid Artie back on the ground. His right eye was closed and bleeding. He was carried off the field on a stretcher.

Righetti was the next hitter.

Darnell's fastball had been sailing in on batters throughout the game. One struck Righetti in the head on the right side behind the ear, just below his protective helmet. He never saw the ball and crumbled to the ground.

"They took both of us to the hospital in the same ambulance," Artie said.

Righetti was released the following day. Artie stayed one week, as doctors were concerned the retina was damaged.

"It didn't affect me too much," Artie explained. "If it had hit me any other way but just flush, I probably would've been blind in that eye."

The season was over for Artie and perhaps his career.

But, first, Sacramento fans wanted to pay tribute to him with an appreciation night.

"SOLON FANS WILL HONOR MR. HEY HEY," a headline in the *Sacramento Bee* announced.[8]

The accompanying photo showed Artie blowing a bubble with the bubble gum he chewed and popped loudly during games, while continually shouting, "Hey hey!"

Ironically, the fan who organized the event was the same one who had heckled Artie unmercifully when he entered the league in 1949.

"I'd kneel down in the batter's circle, and he'd call me some names I'd never heard. He'd holler at the pitchers, 'Knock that nigger down!'"

Artie responded with a big smile and a single.

Artie elaborated:

> My mother always told me, "Names don't hurt you; nothing hurts you but a lick." I was brought up to pay no attention to names. As long as they're paying their money, they're paying my salary. They can go out and holler, say whatever they want. Never got mad at a fan. I just laughed and smiled at them.

One reason Artie was grinning was the plate umpire telling him, "Don't pay that fan no mind. Let him just holler."

"Did you hear that guy telling me to throw at you?" a Sacramento pitcher asked after one game. "I wouldn't have thrown at you then anyway even if I'd had any intention to."

The acid-tongued fan ended up Artie's most avid rooter.

"You going to get me a hit this time, Artie?'" he would yell when Artie came to bat.

"I'll be swinging," Artie answered. "I'll be trying."

Artie signed an autograph for the man to give his daughter. "He became my best friend in Sacramento," Artie said.

Solon fans showered Artie with cash and gifts, including two boxes of bubble gum.

A 10-year-old Little Leaguer presented the gum to Artie. "I'll teach you how to play second base if you teach me how to blow the bubble gum," he said.[9]

"I certainly appreciate this," Artie told the fans. "May the Lord bless each of you."[10]

It was the first appreciation night he had received in 14 years of pro baseball.

The Solons rewarded Heath with a seventh-place finish, keeping intact his record of never managing a last-place team.

"He let us play," Osenbaugh said. "And we played our hearts out for him." [11]

Osenbaugh almost pitched his arm off for Heath the time he was bombarded for 22 runs in a game. He toughed it out until the seventh because, as Heath said, "Our other pitchers are pretty well used up." [12]

He didn't know it at the time but the shellacking earned him a badge of courage with a future Hall of Fame manager—George "Sparky" Anderson.

One of the nine home runs hit off Osenbaugh that game was by Sparky, the Angels' second baseman. He went on to manage 26 years in the majors, leading the Cincinnati Reds to World Series titles in 1975 and 1976, and the Detroit Tigers to the 1984 crown.

Every year at spring training, Sparky told the Osenbaugh story to his players as an example of selflessness and toughness—taking a bullet for the team.

"That was the greatest act of courage I had ever seen on the athletic field, let alone baseball," Sparky said. "He showed guts. He didn't want to be taken out of the game."

"In that era, it was a dishonor to come out of a game," Osenbaugh said. "You didn't ask to come out. You didn't want to come out."

Artie missed the last 59 games of the 1957 season because of the eye injury. Worse yet, he was carted off the field on a stretcher his last game. That's not how he wanted his illustrious baseball career to end.

He reported to the Solons' spring training camp in 1958, smiling and yelling, "Hey hey!"

He even looked like the Say Hey Kid in an exhibition game when he raced around the bases for an inside-the-park homer against Portland and his old boss, Tommy Heath.

Heath left the Solons to manage Portland to a 78–76 record and a fourth-place finish in 1958. He should've taken Artie with him.

Sacramento tried selling Artie to Tulsa, but he nixed the deal. "I didn't think I should have to go to the Texas League," he said. "They didn't have anything to offer me. I wasn't gaining nothing by going back there."

The Solons released him the day after their season opener against the Beavers in Portland was rained out. "It rained and rained and rained," said Sacramento pitcher Bud Watkins.

Six games were rained out. It was almost as if they were tears from heaven, sorrowful about how Artie's Coast League career was ending.

In nine seasons, he accumulated 1,566 hits (1,328 of them singles), scored 758 runs, stole 159 bases, and batted .314. He topped the league in hitting once. Twice he was runner-up. Five times he had more than 200 hits in a season. He also led the league at least once in such categories as hits, runs scored, singles, triples, stolen bases, and times at bat. Amazingly, he struck out only 313 times in 5,518 plate appearances (once in about every 18 at bats).

Artie did all this without the tip of his right thumb, cut off in an accident when he worked for the American Cast Iron Pipe Company in Birmingham.

"I always told him he would've hit .350 if he'd had his thumb," said George Freese, who played against Artie in the PCL and was a golf partner in Portland, where they both lived after retiring from baseball.

By the spring of 1958, the Dodgers were in Los Angeles and playing their home games in a football stadium with a 40-foot-high left-field fence a mere 250 feet down the foul line, an easy target for Artie's slap shots to left. He hit just six homers in the Coast League, but that didn't stop someone from kiddingly suggesting that the Dodgers sign Artie and let him take aim at the barrier and Babe Ruth's home-run record.

The Dodgers never called.

Heath eventually called. But that's another story.

12

THE COMEBACK

Artie Wilson Jr. was nine years old. He was in the garage under a car, following instructions from his grandfather on how to change the oil. They were listening to the Portland Beavers game on the radio.

Dorothy Wilson was tuned in to the same broadcast in the house. She heard a familiar voice.

"Big Pop, don't that sound like Artie?" she hollered to her father, David Frank Daniels.

Daniels and his wife Annie lived with the Wilson family—Artie and Dorothy and their two children, Zoe Ann and Artie Jr. He also recognized the background chatter coming from the radio.

"It sure does!" he said.

Artie Wilson was so soft-spoken in casual conversation that people often leaned closer to hear what he had to say. On the baseball diamond, his voice was easy to pick out from the crowd noise. He was the ultimate chatterbox, encouraging the pitcher, always trying to keep everyone alert.

But what was Artie doing at Portland's Multnomah Stadium the evening of July 3, 1962?

He was almost 42 (some said 43), out of pro baseball four years, and a successful used car salesman for a dealership in nearby Gladstone, Oregon.

When he left for work that morning, he didn't say anything about going to the game, let alone playing in one. "Not one thought," young Artie said. "Not one inkling."

Soon the Beavers announcers were talking about Artie coming out of retirement to help the beat-up Beavers. Third baseman Ron Debus had been sidelined for a month with a fractured thumb. Second baseman Chet Boak had a sprained knee. First baseman Tony Bartirome was playing with an eye injury. Player-manager Les Peden, normally a catcher, was doing his best to knock down hard-hit balls to the hot corner at third base with his 240-pound body.

When Artie got home that night, Dorothy found out he had signed a short-term contract to play with the Beavers until the injured players returned to action.

"Mom loved it," Artie Jr. said. "She wanted him to play as much and as often and long as he wanted to play. For me, it was the coolest thing because I got to go in the clubhouse at the ballpark, hit in the batting cage, and field fly balls in the outfield. I always wanted to be a center fielder after doing that."

Every now and then Artie went to the ballpark to pitch batting practice to the Beavers or visiting teams.

On this occasion, he told a colleague at work, "I'll be back in a couple of hours. I'm not staying for the game."

He took the essentials with him: a pair of shoes, sweat socks, a jockstrap, and his baseball glove. Everything else he borrowed.

The Beavers had a doubleheader against the Salt Lake City Bees that night and another the next day. The 38-year-old Peden had just survived one twin bill at third base, but two more in as many days was pushing his luck.

He played for the Los Angeles Angels in the Pacific Coast League when Artie was running catchers ragged, stealing signs and bases pretty much at will. Artie looked the same, willowy and peppery as he was in his heyday.

Artie walked onto the field, ready to throw batting practice.

"Where's the balls?" he asked Peden.

"Don't worry about the balls," Peden said. "Somebody else will bring them. Come on."

They went to the office of the Beavers' general manager, Bill Sayles.

"I've got my man," Peden announced.

"Who?" Sayles said.

The Beavers planned to bring up Dick Green, a promising young third baseman in the lower minors, who would go on to play 12 years in

Artie Wilson and Dorothy Daniels met at a record shop in Birmingham, Alabama, got married in February 1949, and made beautiful music together for 61 years. At their 40th wedding anniversary celebration in 1989, jazz legend Lionel Hampton was Artie's best man and performed with his band at the reception in a Portland, Oregon, hotel. *Doug McWilliams Collection*

the majors for the Athletics, first in Kansas City and then Oakland. But Green had fractured a thumb, and the Beavers didn't have a backup plan until Artie appeared on the scene.

Peden gestured toward a puzzled Artie.

"What do you mean you've got your man?" Artie said to Peden.

"You've got to play ball tonight."

"You've got to be kidding."

"I can't play no three doubleheaders in a row. Got too many games here. All my infielders are hurt."

Artie took batting and infield practice, before calling his boss at work to tell him he'd signed to play temporarily for the Beavers.

"I knew I could count on Artie," Peden said. "I knew he could still play."

In all the excitement, Artie neglected to phone Dorothy.

She listened on the radio as Artie played all seven innings of the first game and part of the second. He played second base and, in the opener, batted in the number-one spot for the Beavers.

Ferd Borsch, a sports columnist for the *Honolulu Star-Advertiser*, noticed the name of A. Wilson in the box score.

"This A. Wilson played second base, and he was batting leadoff, the customary spot in the lineup for Artie Wilson," he wrote. "Of course, it had to be another Wilson. After all, age does take its toll. But, as news finally trickled across the Pacific, it was the same and seemingly ageless Artie Wilson."[1]

The Beavers dropped both games of the doubleheader but rebounded the next day to beat the Bees twice. Artie played the entire nine innings in the first game and the tail end of the nightcap.

"He always had been a leadoff hitter," Peden said. "He really wasn't a good leadoff hitter because he swung at the first pitch all the time. But he was a fiery ballplayer. He inspired a team."

Going into his seventh game, Artie was hitless in six at-bats. He slapped two singles to left field. In his first game at San Diego, where he had broken into the PCL in 1949, he lashed three singles for old time's sake.

"My timing was off," Artie said. "I fouled a lot of pitches that normally I would've hit fair. I stayed right in there. They knew I was there because I was swinging."

"There wasn't anything wrong with him in the field," Peden said. "His reflexes were slower, but he had a strong arm and his instincts were as good as ever."

"One of the wonders of Pacific Coast League baseball has been the comeback of Artie Wilson," wrote L. H. Gregory, sports editor of the *Oregonian*, two weeks after he came to the rescue of the Beavers.

"On the fielding side, he covers ground as agilely as he ever did, he has both started and pivoted on half a dozen double plays, still has those 'good hands,' and if there's any difference in his running on the bases, we haven't noticed it," Gregory continued. "He doesn't hit with quite the old-time zip, almost always to left, his off-field, but his eye is coming back!"

Gregory pointed out Artie had "batted in a couple of runs and kept rallies going, several of his hits being of the line-drive type . . . We'd hardly believe it if we hadn't seen him, but his legs and arm actually seem as good as ever."[2]

In 25 games, Artie had nine hits in 55 at-bats for a batting average almost identical to his weight—.164. He was perfect at second base, making no errors in 19 games, for a fielding percentage of 1,000.

After one month, the Beavers released Artie with a "certificate of appreciation . . . for his fine services" in an emergency role.

"He did an almost unbelievable job," the Beavers' Sayles marveled. "I wouldn't have thought it possible."[3]

Artie played in a Beavers' old-timers game and then was back selling cars.

Three weeks later, he got a telephone call from his old boss, Tommy Heath, manager of the Tri-City Braves, an independent team representing the Washington cities of Kennewick, Richland, and Pasco in the Class B Northwest League.

The Braves' casualty list sounded like something from a war zone. The team's second baseman, the best in the league, had a broken nose and fractured cheekbone after being struck in the face by a pitch. An outfielder also was the victim of a beanball, suffering fractures in the front of his right temple that impaired his vision. The shortstop had bursitis in his throwing arm.

"We tried unsuccessfully to get an infielder from one of the major-league organizations, but none of them wanted to shift a player from one minor-league team to another with only two weeks left in the season," explained Al Daniels, the Braves' general manager.[4]

Heath had been Artie's manager at Sacramento in 1957 and Minneapolis in 1951. Of course he would help an old friend.

Artie was now the baseball equivalent of calling 911.

He met his new Tri-City teammates, several of them half his age, in Salem, Oregon, where the Braves were beginning a four-game series. "Ancient Artie Wilson," the *Salem Statesman-Journal* called him.[5]

The Northwest League was quite a contrast from the Negro Leagues where Artie had gotten his start 18 years earlier, making $300 a month. The circuit featured 14 players who had received signing bonuses ranging from $25,000 to $100,000, the amount the Chicago Cubs paid 17-year-old outfielder Danny Murphy. He wound up playing 49 games for the Cubs, batting only .171.

Artie played for the love of the game, not the money. He fired up those around him, and the young Braves were no different. They won their last seven games to capture the second-half Northwest League title and advance to a best-of-seven championship series against Murphy's Wenatchee Chiefs, the first-half winners.

Back in Portland, the Beavers were planning something special on the last day of the season to honor Artie. He could attend the event or keep on playing with the Braves.

"Artie Wilson was the kind of guy that you just throw him the ball and say, 'Let's play ball!'" said Herm Reich, a former teammate. "He'd play anywhere to get into the ballgame."

He continued with the Braves. They lost in six games, but it was a hit by Artie in the third contest that got the attention of *Tri-City Herald* sportswriter Charlie Van Sickel.

He hailed Artie as the "greatest 43-year-old infielder in the nation," pointed out he was a "notorious left-field hitter," and said everyone in the ballpark was surprised "when he pulled a double down the line in right field."[6]

In 20 games at Tri-City, including the playoffs, Artie had 13 hits in 63 at-bats, for a .213 batting average. All of the hits were singles except that double. It was his next to last hit in pro baseball and, in effect, gave him the last word on whether he could pull the ball.

"It was an opportunity for him to get back and do something that he absolutely had a love affair with," said Artie Jr. "It's crazy to say it, but 20 years after that experience, he honestly believed he could go up to the plate and get a hit."

In fact, Artie was 63 in 1984, when he played with his son's team, the Columbia Inn Roundtable All-Stars, against Tom Selleck, star of the television show *Mangum, P.I.*, and other celebrities in a softball game in Honolulu.

"Dad got more hits in the game than I did, and we turned a double play with him playing second base. I was at shortstop and started it. He's the one who turned it. I got the ball to him coming across the second-base bag, and he made that little underhanded throw of his to first base."

Telling the story in 2017, Artie Jr. was still incredulous. "We turned a double play in softball!"

For the record, Artie never went back to Multnomah Stadium to pitch batting practice. He had already come out of retirement twice in a single season. He had plenty of baseball stories to tell and cars to sell.

13

TALKING BASEBALL (SELLING CARS)

People came from all over to talk baseball with Artie Wilson.

He was easy to find because he was a fixture at the Gary-Worth dealership in Gladstone, Oregon, for nearly a half century.

It didn't matter what kind of cars Artie was selling. His specialty was talking baseball.

"He was always extremely humble and quiet," Artie Jr. said of his father. "But you start talking baseball and there was a switch that went on. He was very proud of what he did."

Artie started mixing baseball and cars while he was playing for the Portland Beavers in 1955.

"The man who knows baseball also knows cars," Ralph-Hoyt Pontiac of Portland introduced Artie as its new salesman in a newspaper advertisement. "Come in and talk over baseball and cars with Artie."[1]

Artie got the job after a two-hour interview with the sales manager that ended like this:

> "Gee, we were just talking baseball here. I forgot what you came over for. You want to sell cars?"
>
> "Yes, I'd like to try."
>
> "What makes you think you can sell cars?"
>
> "I don't know whether I can. But people are buying them. Someone is selling them."
>
> "Okay, when do you want to start?"
>
> "Whenever you want me to start."

Artie reported to work the next morning and immediately asked the sales manager a question that nagged him overnight: "You aren't hiring me to sell only to blacks, are you? If so, I don't want the job."

"You sell to everybody that walks in the showroom," he was told.

"If I was only going to sell to blacks, I'd starve," Artie explained. "There wasn't that many here."

Artie sold a car that first day and kept going after he left baseball in 1958.

Worth McManus took over the Ralph-Hoyt dealership and renamed it Gary-Worth. "You stay with us," McManus said to Artie. "We eat, you eat. I got three sons—Gary, Worth, and you."

He was at Gary-Worth until he retired in 2005.

"You got to keep going," he said as he approached his 69th birthday in 1989. "No use getting in the rocking chair."

Later he joked, "I'm retired when I'm not selling cars."

Would you buy a used car from this man? Roger Kahn, author of the baseball classic *The Boys of Summer*, said he would purchase one from Artie Wilson. A lot of people did. After retiring from baseball, Artie was a fixture at the Gary-Worth car dealership in Gladstone, Oregon, for nearly a half-century. This picture was taken in 1995. *Courtesy of the author*

He loved talking baseball almost as much as playing it. Of course, talking baseball was the same as selling cars. They were intertwined like the yards of string wrapped around the cork center of a baseball.

"Best business there is other than baseball," Artie declared. "If I could go back into baseball, I'd go. But I'd have to have something concrete and know which way I'm going."

That opportunity never came.

In a conversation with Roger Kahn for his book *A Season in the Sun*, initially published in 1978, Artie asked the author if there was any chance Leo Durocher might become manager of the Seattle Mariners. Leo was Artie's man, even though he didn't get much of a chance with the New York Giants in 1951.

"I know a lot about the game," Artie said. "I can teach good. I'm fine selling cars, but I was just thinking that maybe if Leo got the managing job he might just happen to remember me."[2]

Durocher didn't get the job, and Artie never got an offer of any kind from big-league baseball.

"He had a following second to none," said Chuck Christiansen, a Beavers fan as a kid who became part of Artie's legion of friends. "Our scenario was baseball. He never tried to sell me a car. It's like they didn't exist. When I was there, we talked baseball."

This was the key to Artie's success as a salesman.

"He sold used cars, but you'd never describe him as a used car salesman—one of those hustlers that would run out to people and try to sell them anything and everything," explained Artie Jr., a realtor in Hawaii since 1979, and a pretty good salesman himself. "That was not his style. He was so laid-back, so low key that people called him and said, 'Can you meet me at the dealership because I want to come out and look at cars.' He was never a hard salesperson, but he was successful at selling. That's because people liked him and trusted him."

Sometimes Artie received calls from customers while he was in Honolulu on extended stays with his son.

"When are you coming back?" they inquired. "I want to get a car, but I'm not going to do it until you're back in town."

Sometimes they waited three months for Artie to return to Portland. "Most of my business is repeat business. I try to take care of them," he said.

Artie started selling Pontiacs, switched to Chryslers and Plymouths, and then started selling Mercurys and Lincolns. "If a customer wants to buy a bicycle, I will sell him a bicycle. But I am going to tell him the truth about the bicycle."

One day, he sold five cars. "Should've sold six."

For every car sold, Gary-Worth made a donation to Artie's church, Allen Temple.

"I'll only drive a black car on a clear, sunny day," he explained. "If it's a rainy day, you'll never see me in a black car."

It was raining the day he drove a white Chrysler Cordoba to a customer who was buying a black one.

Nearly every morning around 6:30, Artie stopped on his way to work for breakfast at the Bomber Inn restaurant and gas station. Customers got their gas pumped under a World War II vintage B-17 bomber nicknamed the "Flying Fortress."

"When they see me drive up, they get ready to bring it out," Artie said.

He usually had a cup of coffee; toast; and a bowl of oatmeal with brown sugar and milk, which he stirred until it was to his liking.

"I called it mush," said Christiansen, who frequently met Artie at the Bomber Inn.

"How do you know it will stay on your spoon?" Christiansen once asked.

"I've eaten enough of this. It will stay on my spoon until it gets in my mouth," Artie responded.

Sometimes Artie switched to eggs and bacon, which he wanted so crisp it popped apart when he touched it. "Breakfast is my main meal. I can go all day on breakfast. I like grits. Eat grits every day. Grits are good for you."

The owner of the Bomber Inn, Art Lacey, called Artie "Dude."

"He was a very cool dresser," Christiansen said. "Always wore silk shirts. Do you know why? He didn't have to iron them."

As finicky as Artie was about his bacon and his shirts, he swung at almost everything when he stepped into the batter's box. "If they got the ball close to the plate, I was swinging," he said.

Artie usually had company at the Bomber Inn in the form of old-timers who remembered the Pacific Coast League before the Dodgers and Giants forced it out of Los Angeles and San Francisco in 1958.

"There was a bunch of guys in the Coast League who would've burned them up in the majors if they'd had a chance," he said one morning. "The Coast League could've been a third major league."

Someone asked who was the toughest PCL pitcher for him to hit.

"Bob Malloy. Pitched in the Coast League, and he pitched up in the majors. He'd just throw that ball and say, 'Hit it.' Did the same thing down in Puerto Rico. He got me out. Everybody—even the pitchers—hit him except me."

The right-handed Malloy had a 4–7 won–loss record in five big-league seasons and was 11–11 in the three years (1951–1953) he pitched in the PCL, mostly as a reliever for the San Diego Padres.

Artie continued:

> We're in Puerto Rico fighting for the championship. We've got to beat Ponce two out of three. They sent back to the States and got Bob Malloy. I looked in the paper and everybody was talking about Bob Malloy. I wondered if it was Bob Malloy, the pitcher. Sure enough, it was. We go to Ponce to play. I'm taking batting practice. Bob Malloy is walking around.
>
> I said, "Bob, what in the world are you doing down here?"
> He said, "I come down here to stop you."
> I said, "You know how you dog me in the States."
> He said, "I'm going to dog you the same way down here."
> I'm leading the league in hitting. He pitched against us. I got one hit. One hit! And the other players were hitting him all over the park.
> The fans say, "Artie, why can't you hit Malloy?"
> I said, "I don't know why I can't hit Malloy."
> I still don't understand how he did it. He had my number for some reason. I'd like to catch him now. Try it again.

Artie was asked if Malloy was still living.

"I don't know. If he isn't, I'd like to bring him back. I wish I was playing against him now. Maybe I could hit him."

Artie found some solace in discussing the troubles the great Satchel Paige had with two unheralded Birmingham Black Barons teammates—Leroy "Lee" Moody and James "Shifty" West, both first basemen.

"They'd stand back in the batter's box and walk up when Satchel was pitching," he said. "They hit 'em all over the lot. Satchel couldn't get them two guys out. And that's something when Satchel can't get you out. I didn't think anybody could hit Satchel like that, but they could."

The conversation moved to the Gary-Worth showroom and back to the Bomber Inn for lunch, but it never strayed from baseball.

"If they don't put Pete Rose in the Hall of Fame, they ought to close the door. He deserves to be there," Artie said.

Rose was a singles hitter like Artie. Of the record 4,256 hits in his career, 3,215 were singles. They played the game with the same energy and passion. In 1989, Rose was banned from baseball for gambling on games, while playing for and managing the Cincinnati Reds.

Artie added:

> There's a guy I considered a superstar. He could play any position and play it well. Played it like he'd been playing it all the time. It just makes my heart ache to think that Pete wasn't smart enough to get by some of those things. When it first came up, I said, "Oh, no, not Pete. I don't think he'd ever do a thing like that."

Artie was also upset by the steroid scandals that shocked baseball in the 1990s. It got him to thinking about the man who was his role model—Robert Hollman, superintendent of the Sunday school at the church he attended growing up in Birmingham.

"I always wanted to be like him. There was something about him that inspired me," Artie said, noting:

> I knew nothing about him other than his being a gentleman. He liked kids. He played baseball . . . started kids off playing baseball. I just wanted to be like him. I tried to conduct myself in a way that some kid might be looking at me like I looked at him and want to be like me. I wanted to have a *clean* spot.

Artie loved sharing his baseball experiences with kids.

"My dad would never miss an opportunity to go and talk to a coach, give batting tips to any 10-, 12-, 14-year-old," said Artie Jr. "He'd come to Hawaii and spend all day at the ballpark with kids. And he was 75 years old."

Artie went wherever he was needed in the Portland area as well.

"I go out and help them—high school, Little League, Babe Ruth League," he said. "I won't go unless the coach calls me. Don't want them to be thinking I'm trying to take their job, or interfering."

Artie regularly gave talks at high schools.

"What's your thing?" they often asked.

"I tell them that I like to know what their thing is. I listen because I want to know."

He'd let them talk and then respond.

"The road that you're trying to travel now, I must've passed by it. I missed something along the line. If your thing is better than mine, let me know what it is."

Artie spoke softly, but his voice had a toughness to it.

"Don't tell me about your broken home," he told students, continuing:

> That doesn't make you bad because your mother and father separated or divorced. You be bad because you want to be. You get with the wrong group and you want to do what they do. They are doing wrong, you do that, too. Don't put that on your parents. You're looking at a fella who wouldn't know his dad if he walked into the room.
>
> My mother raised me. She was a father, mother, sister, and brother to me. I've never been in jail. Never been searched by a policeman. I've been all over the world. You name it, I've played baseball there. Got along with everybody. A kid isn't bad because of his parents. That doesn't make it. You have to tell me something else. I'm a witness to that. I know about that.

That was Artie's stump speech, one he gave time and again to young blacks.

"I enjoy it," he said, smiling. "If I change one life, it's worth my efforts."

Most days Artie was at the car dealership talking baseball.

"The past was good," he mused one day. "The Coast League days were good. I have a lot of good memories."

Oh, by the way, he sold a car that day.

14

THE BALLPLAYER, THE BOY, AND THE CIGAR

Once upon a time there was a boy, a ballplayer, and his cigar.

Kids adored the ballplayer because he happily signed autographs for them. They surrounded him outside the Oakland Oaks clubhouse after home games, waiting their turn.

The ballplayer smoked cigars. He always had one with him.

One night he asked an 11-year-old boy to hold his cigar while he signed a piece of paper.

The boy never forgot the cigar. It connected him to the ballplayer for the rest of his life, as it symbolized first his respect and admiration for him, and then the bond they developed in later years.

Artie Wilson was the ballplayer and Doug McWilliams the boy.

Doug grew up to be a professional photographer—the Rembrandt of baseball card photographers. "When I smell cigars any time, I think of back then and Artie."

Doug was 79 years old when he said that.

He doesn't need a black-and-white newspaper photograph to jog his memory, but Doug has one of him and seven other kids crowded around Artie, looking straight at the camera, the stub of a lit cigar accentuating Artie's signature smile like an exclamation point. "He had the cigar in his mouth in that picture. But I can remember holding it."

Artie signed autographs with the same flair that characterized his play on the field. He wrote "Artie" on the ball and then circled the logo of the sporting goods company that made it—Wilson.

Surrounded by young admirers, Artie Wilson flashed his signature smile for the camera while signing autographs outside the Oakland Oaks clubhouse. Doug McWilliams is the boy in the dark shirt with his back to the camera. He grew up to be a Topps baseball card photographer and Artie's biggest fan. *Doug McWilliams Collection*

Most baseball players willingly sign autographs—but not all.

Ralph Mauriello pitched eight years in the minors and briefly for the Los Angeles Dodgers near the end of the 1958 season.

Ralph was 12 years old in 1946, when he took a train from his home in Brooklyn to the Hotel New Yorker in Manhattan, where the Boston Red Sox were staying. He positioned himself near the revolving door leading into the hotel lobby so he could ask the players for autographs as they came out.

Ted Williams appeared.

"Don't have time kids," muttered the Red Sox great sometimes called "the Kid" as he walked briskly past Ralph and several other youngsters.

Ralph caught up with Williams at a busy intersection and asked if he'd sign his autograph book while waiting for the traffic light to turn green.

"Go away kid," Williams muttered.[1]

The story gets better *and* worse.

Ralph stuck around the hotel until a bus came to take the players to Yankee Stadium. Dom DiMaggio, brother of Joe, was one of the first to emerge. He signed Ralph's book and then thumbed through the pages to see who else had signed.

"Wow, you haven't done very well. Let me take your book with me on the bus and I'll get all the guys to sign it," he offered.

As the bus left the hotel, DiMaggio leaned out the window and tossed Ralph his book and pen.

"I started flipping through the pages anxiously looking for Ted Williams's autograph," Ralph wrote in his book, *Tales Beyond the Dugout*. "The jerk refused to sign . . . even while sitting on the bus waiting for it to take the team to Yankee Stadium."[2]

Artie would've invited Ralph on the bus and made sure he got everyone's autograph.

"You didn't have to tell him to do it," said Bill Laws, the Oaks' radio announcer and son of team owner Clarence "Brick" Laws. "He enjoyed doing it."[3]

Artie was the Oaks' first black player, and with the New York Giants in 1951, he was one of four blacks on the field at the same time, unprecedented for a big-league club. Monte Irvin was at first base, Artie at second, Hank Thompson at third, and Rafael "Ray" Noble catching.

"Wonder how many people noticed it?" asked Billy Rowe, a columnist for the *Pittsburgh Courier*, a black-owned newspaper.

It didn't matter to Rowe that it was an exhibition game. It was progress.

He recalled the accomplishments of Jackie Robinson in baseball and Joe Louis and Sugar Ray Robinson in boxing. Rowe wrote that in the new order of things, "Joe Louis was the wedge, Jackie Robinson the open door, Ray Robinson the trimmings."[4]

Rowe could've gone on to say Artie was the dessert.

He was the ice cream sandwich, the candy bar, the box of Cracker Jack that kids could buy at Oaks Park in Emeryville.

"Artie became the most popular player we ever had," Laws said. "He did it because he performed. He made the plays. The fans loved to see him come to bat."

Laws estimated Artie fouled off 20 to 25 pitches every game, spreading souvenir baseballs like they were Hershey's Kisses.

"He was fast, and he hustled, and you could hear him hollering out at shortstop on defense," Laws continued. "He just had it."[5]

It was a long walk from the clubhouse to the gate where the kids waited for Artie after a game.

Dorothy Wilson knew the moment her husband walked through the door. "She could smell his cologne," Artie Jr. said. "Her eyes could be closed and she could tell."

Artie loved his Tabu cologne. He bought it in quantities in Tijuana, Mexico, when the Oaks played in nearby San Diego. He splashed it all over. "Pooh-pooh water," Giants manager Leo Durocher kidded Artie.

Doug McWilliams knew Artie was approaching the gate from the smell of his cigar. "He lit it up in the clubhouse and here he came. Kids all clamored after him."

For Doug, it wasn't just the aroma of the cigars. He also was impressed by the fancy clothes and Kangol® caps Artie wore.

"Artie was the first black person I ever knew. He really opened my eyes. What a wonderful person he was. And how friendly he was. It was amazing," Doug recalled.

Black players would play a major role in Doug's future success as a baseball photographer. Of course, he didn't know that at the time.

There was a sizeable black population in Oakland, but not in the part of Berkeley where Doug lived. One of the neighbors—a couple that owned a popular vaudeville nightclub in San Francisco—had a black cook named Beulah. She often slipped Doug chocolate chip cookies out the back door. But that was his only contact with blacks. "I never went to school with a black person until 10th grade. Artie came along when I was in the sixth grade."

Doug was 10 years old when he discovered baseball in 1948.

He attended a birthday party and received a pack of Bowman baseball cards as a prize. His parents gave him a subscription to *Sport*, a monthly magazine that featured full-page color photographs of baseball players and other star athletes. He covered one entire wall in his bed-

Where there was cigar smoke, there was usually Artie Wilson. Wearing a hat borrowed from a policeman, Artie lights the cigars of two Oakland teammates, pitcher Earl Harrist, center, and catcher Rafael "Ray" Noble. *Courtesy Artie Wilson Jr.*

room with them. That got him thinking about taking pictures like that someday.

It so happened that his best friend, Dick Dobbins, also loved baseball and photography. Dick was three years older than Doug and a "surrogate father" of sorts, teaching him photography and talking baseball and how to treat people. "It was a good friendship for our entire life."

While listening to an Oaks game on the radio one night, he heard about a Signal Oil baseball card promotion—go to one of its gas stations and get a free card.

He talked his father into taking him to a station for a card and then to a game at Oaks Park in Emeryville. "He wasn't a sports fan at all," Doug said.

Doug's new, prized possession was a full-color card featuring Ray Hamrick, the Oaks' shortstop. "It was evening. Got up to the top of the walkway at the ballpark and looked down on the field and it was all lit up. It looked like it was magic."

He spotted Hamrick signing autographs, hurriedly grabbed a pen from his father, and rushed to where his new hero was standing. "I was hooked," Doug said, adding, "hooked more on baseball cards than the game."

The Oaks won the pennant in 1948. Artie arrived in May 1949, replacing Hamrick at shortstop. Now, he was hooked on Artie. "I was totally blown away as a little kid about how friendly he was. He respected the kids. He paid attention to you, which most adults don't when you're a kid. He was very patient and kind, and took his time."

There was a 14-year-old black boy, Charlie Beamon, who felt the same way. He would go on to pitch in the majors, facing Artie in the Pacific Coast League on his way up. "We admired him so much," Beamon said. "He was polite, very respectful, and always had time to talk, even if you were a kid. He was the same when I played against him."

A clothing company produced baseball cards one year, and Remar Bakery offered a set that kids referred to as "Sunbeams" because the delivery trucks had the Sunbeam bread logo on the side. "If you met the driver, you could get a stack of them," Doug said. "They didn't have any monetary value. That came much later."

Doug and Dick continued collecting cards and getting them signed at the ballpark. Doug began taking a camera with him and snapping shots of Artie and other players from a distance. "I didn't approach anybody. I was still a little kid."

The Oaks and two other PCL teams in the area, the San Francisco Seals and Sacramento Solons, issued cards of their teams from 1946 until 1953, when they stopped.

Dick suggested they make their own baseball cards. Visiting teams were in town a week. That gave them plenty of time to photograph the players, process and print the negatives in a darkroom at Dick's house, and return to the ballpark to get them signed. "After a while the players started buying them from us," Doug said.

Doug started selling photos to the Portland Beavers for their annual yearbook.

When Artie played for the Seattle Rainiers in 1956, Doug and Dick photographed him at Sicks' Stadium. Artie started the season with the Beavers. "He was still wearing his Portland sleeves, which had stripes on them," Doug said. "They looked out of place but kind of neat with the red uniform."

Artie posed as the two friends took pictures. "I shot at the same time, but Dick's photo is the one that went national and reproduced a lot."

Doug got one of the few pictures of Artie in a Sacramento uniform. He played two months for the Solons in 1957, before the eye injury ended his career. "I got a wonderful picture of him in the dugout."

Meanwhile, Doug drifted away from baseball. He went to college, got married, started a family, and became a scientific industrial photographer at the Lawrence Berkeley National Laboratory.

The A's moved to Oakland from Kansas City in 1968. The next year, he attended a "Picture Day" and went on the field with other fans to snap shots of the players. "It reminded me of when I was a kid," he said. "I thought, 'This is kind of fun.'"

He began going to games and taking pictures from his seat in the stands. "I got to know some of the players, and they wanted to buy my pictures."

One of them was Jim "Mudcat" Grant, a black pitcher who won 145 games in 14 big-league seasons. He joined the A's in 1970, and remembered Doug photographing him 13 years earlier when he pitched in the PCL for the San Diego Padres. "I was totally shocked," Doug said.

Mudcat connected Doug with Vida Blue, another black pitcher who moved into Grant's downtown Oakland apartment when he was traded to Pittsburgh near the end of the 1970 season. "Get Doug to take some pictures for your folks back home," Mudcat said.

Upon returning to Oakland in August 1971, Mudcat was told to contact the team's photographer and get some new publicity shots.

"Doug is going to do them," Mudcat said.

"Who?" he was asked.

The shots of Mudcat were as big a hit as the pictures Vida sent to his mother in Louisiana. She loved them. Vida did, too.

In 1971, Vida was the American League's Most Valuable Player and Cy Young Award winner, notching a 24–8 record, 8 shutouts, and a 1.82 earned run average. "Everybody loved Vida—everybody!" Doug said.

"He was like Artie. He was friendly. He stopped and talked to everybody. He was fun to know."

Vida needed postcards to send to a rapidly growing fan club.

"How many you want?" Doug asked. "A hundred . . . two hundred?"

"I get a hundred letters a day," Vida said. "And I need color."

Doug had 15,000 color postcards printed for Vida with his name and contact information displayed prominently on the back. One of them landed on the desk of Sy Berger, a Topps executive and the father of modern-day baseball cards.

Berger called Doug and said, "I like the way you shoot. Would you like to work for Topps?"

Doug was a Topps photographer for 23 years, combining it with his work at the Lawrence Berkeley Lab.

In his second year with Topps, Doug invited his father to tag along with him to the Cleveland Indians spring training camp in Tucson, Arizona.

James McWilliams grew up in Kansas, moved to Berkeley to get his master's degree at the University of California, and became a tax specialist for Pacific Telephone and Telegraph until he retired to Sun City, Arizona.

"You can be an engineer or a dentist," he said to young Doug, images of baseball players flashing in his head.

"My father's only experience with photography as a profession was he had a cousin in a small town in Kansas who was a portrait photographer. Apparently, he didn't have two nickels to rub together."

The Indians had a black outfielder, George Hendrick, newly acquired from the A's. He had a reputation among photographers and sportswriters for being prickly and uncooperative. At one point during his stellar 18-year career, he stopped talking to reporters, earning the nickname "Silent George."

"I sold my first images to Topps in the fall of 1971," Doug said. "It was a picture of Hendrick when he was with the A's. And then he got traded to Cleveland. I got along with Hendrick famously, and took some beautiful pictures of him."

Doug's father was on the field with him as he took the six posed shots of Hendrick required by Topps.

Upon seeing the older man, Hendrick asked Doug, "Is that your dad?"

He acknowledged that it was.

"That's kind of neat," Hendrick replied.

Doug introduced Hendrick to his father and went on to photograph the other players. Finally, he looked around for his dad, wondering where he went.

Then he spotted him in the stands. He was sitting next to Hendrick, and they were talking. "I just couldn't believe it. They'd been talking for about a half-hour."

It was the first time Doug's father had talked at length to a black man.

"That guy was really interesting," he told Doug on the drive back to Sun City. "You've got an interesting job. It's amazing."

"He was jacked up," Doug said. "I had been a professional photographer for 11 years, and he never said anything like that before. I'm forever grateful to George Hendrick for talking with my dad and changing his life a little bit, and having him realize that the career I chose was an excellent one."

Proximity was one of the keys to changing racial views, Branch Rickey believed.

The Brooklyn Dodgers president credited proximity for the transformation of Mississippi-born Clay Hopper, Jackie Robinson's first manager in Montreal and one of Artie's managers in Portland.

Proximity to Artie (and his cigar) shaped Doug's attitude toward blacks. "I had no views on race because I had no experience with anybody. To my family, blacks were mysterious because they didn't know them. Once you get to know them, they're people just like you and me. They jump into their pants two legs at a time just like I do."

Doug had good relationships with black stars others considered difficult.

"I've known Doug since I had hair and he didn't have a beard," Doug recalled Reggie Jackson saying to a friend.

Doug met the outspoken slugger—the self-described "straw that stirs the drink"—when he was with the A's in 1969. "Reggie was extremely nice and always took time to talk to me."

Rickey Henderson, baseball's all-time stolen base king, sent Doug Christmas cards to commemorate the holiday, as well as his birth on Christmas Day. "I was there when he first came to the majors. I always tried to be there the first day players came so they knew who I was."

Frank Robinson belted 586 homers in 21 seasons in the majors, most of them with the Cincinnati Reds and Baltimore Orioles. He played for the California Angels in 1973. Robinson could be impatient and blunt with photographers and sportswriters.

"It's hard to photograph every player just how you want. You have to get them when you can," Doug said of his profession.

Doug ran to the right-field foul line, where Frank was standing, and asked if he could take his picture.

"Sure, but I'd like to have a bat in my hand," Frank said. "I'm a hitter."

Doug hurried to the dugout, grabbed a bat and delivered it to Robinson. He took a couple of swings and said, "Mighty fine bat, except the company I have a contract with isn't this company. And they wouldn't like me to pose with it."

Doug rushed to the Angels clubhouse and returned to Frank with one of his customized bats.

"You're all right," Frank said. "Now, what would you like?"

Dick Williams was a fiery, no-nonsense manager who led the Oakland A's to back-to-back World Series titles in 1972 and 1973.

Williams would stop what he was doing to round up players Doug needed to photograph. "He'd call them in off the field and he'd stand right beside me while I shot them."

Doug photographed Vida Blue's wedding on the pitcher's mound at San Francisco's Candlestick Park after the A's traded him to the Giants in 1978.

"I wasn't pushy . . . I was polite," Doug explained his popularity among the players. "I treated them like I wanted to be treated, and they seemed to act that way back at me. It got to the point where I was doing their family pictures, their weddings, and bar mitzvahs."

In 1976, with free agency looming over the head of tightwad owner Charles Finley, the A's traded Reggie and pitcher Ken Holtzman to the Baltimore Orioles. Finley tried selling Vida to the Yankees and relief pitcher Rollie Fingers and outfielder Joe Rudi to the Boston Red Sox, but the deals were blocked by baseball commissioner Bowie Kuhn.

That didn't stop Doug from getting the only pictures that exist of Fingers and Rudi in Red Sox uniforms.

He heard about the trade on his way to the Oakland Coliseum, where the A's and Red Sox had a game that evening. Doug always arrived at 5:30 p.m. sharp. The light was perfect for the shots he wanted of Rollie and Joe. He went directly to the Red Sox dugout and waited. "And here they came in their Boston uniforms. I got posed pictures of them in color."

Fingers never pitched for the Red Sox. Rudi wound up playing for them five years later.

Timing and lighting were everything to Doug.

In 2010, he donated 11,000 color negatives to the National Baseball Hall of Fame in Cooperstown. The images are estimated to be 12 percent of everyone who has played baseball.

"It looks like everybody in the pictures knows you," a Hall of Fame representative said after reviewing the treasure trove.

"Some of 'em did, a lot of 'em didn't," Doug replied.

"Why do they look like they know you?"

"I think it's because I shoot fast."

Doug didn't keep the players waiting.

"This is the reason I shoot fast," he said, showing examples of first shots taken of various players and managers with their eyes half open or closed. "I get their attention and then I get better shots—second, third, fourth, fifth, and sixth."

Doug's father may not have understood his son's desire to be a photographer, but he was highly supportive, sending him to Brooks Institute, a school that specialized in photography.

When Doug started working for Topps, he was instructed to photograph players facing the sun with the shadow of the cap bill across the face to show ruggedness and character. He said:

> I thought to myself: "All it shows is poor lighting." Why not turn them around? And then you've got light coming from behind to separate them from the background. And you flash-fill at the same exposure of your sunshine. It's a matter of being aware where you are and where the light is.

One of his projects at Brooks was to take a picture of white Lux soap on a black cloth that's folded. "You had to show detail in both the black cloth and the white soap. I've seen pictures of black players that were just terrible. They're just a black hole. Mine aren't that way."

Maybe that's why he was well liked by black players. They made each other look good.

It's no coincidence that Doug's all-time favorite Topps card features a black player—Harold Reynolds.

Reynolds was a second baseman, the position Artie played the last part of his career.

He played 10 of his 12 years in the majors with the Seattle Mariners. Artie spent three and a half seasons with the Seattle Rainiers, the longest he played for any team in Organized Baseball.

Reynolds grew up in Corvallis, Oregon, a short jaunt from Portland, where Artie lived for 55 years. They are both members of the Oregon Sports Hall of Fame.

At 5-foot-11, 165 pounds, Reynolds is almost a spitting image of Artie.

"Harold came out early one day at spring training in Tempe, and we talked about all kinds of things," Doug said. "He had a great smile and a sweet personality."

Just like Artie.

Of all the players Doug photographed through the years, Artie is still number one—in his heart and the memories preserved in five large albums.

There are photographs of Artie in the uniforms of almost every professional team he played for in his storied career.

There is a preprinted card with the names of players for the 1951 New York Giants that showed how they were doing against right-handed pitchers. The name "Wilson" was blacked out and "Mays" scribbled next to it.

There are newspaper articles and a *Sports Illustrated* story, published in 1989, about Lucille and Chester Willis.

In 1949, the doors of a resort hotel in Tucson, Arizona, were closed to the Cleveland Indians' black players. So, the Willises welcomed into their home a downsized version of the Satchel Paige All-Stars—Artie, Satchel, Larry Doby, Luke Easter, Minnie Minoso, and Jose Santiago. "They practically turned the house over to us," Artie said. "I'd rather have been there than at the hotel."[6]

He went back to see Lucille and Chester in 1989. "It was a homecoming," he said. "I was like a lost child coming home after 40 years."[7]

After taking shots of Artie in the dugout at Sacramento in 1957, Doug didn't see him again until 1994, when he attended an event in Oakland celebrating the history of the old PCL. They posed together

After taking thousands of pictures of baseball players, Doug McWilliams gladly posed for one with his boyhood hero, Artie Wilson, prior to a turn-back-the-clock game in 1994, between the San Francisco Giants and Oakland A's. Artie is wearing the uniform of the Oakland Oaks, the Pacific Coast League team he played for from 1949 to 1951. *Photo by Barry Colla*

for a photo at a Giants–A's turn-back-the-clock game, Artie wearing an Oakland Oaks jersey and cap. There was no cigar.

That would come later, after Chuck Christiansen entered the picture.

Chuck and Doug are longtime friends. Chuck grew up in Portland and saw Artie slap singles to left field both for and against the Beavers. He knew how much Artie meant to Doug. He offered to be Doug's eyes and ears, and meet Artie for breakfast at the Bomber Inn in Gladstone, Oregon. "He was my conduit," Doug said.

During the last 10 years of Artie's life, Chuck had breakfast with him regularly. Afterward, he would call Doug to share tidbits of their conversation. "I might as well have been sitting there," Doug said.

Every now and then Artie gave Chuck something to pass on to Doug.

Artie hoarded "K dollars"—$1 bills with the letter "K" in the Federal Reserve symbol on the left side with Dallas, Texas, underneath the "K."

"I don't know if he read it somewhere or whether someone told him, but in his mind the K dollars were going to be valuable someday because of the assassinations of John F. Kennedy, Martin Luther King, and Robert Kennedy," explained Artie Jr.

Artie never talked about the "K dollars." He just held on to them.

"Hey, Dad," young Artie might say, "give me five bucks."

"I don't have five dollars. I only got my K dollars," Artie would answer.

Artie Jr. knew what that meant. "It would have to be a dire emergency for him to part with his K dollars. They were almost untouchable."

When Artie died, more than 1,000 "K dollars" were found stashed in suit jackets, in pants pockets, in between shirts, in envelopes, and even in a cigar box.

But there was one "K dollar" that his family didn't find. That's because he autographed the bill and gave it to Doug to save in an album.

There was another memento Doug wanted—one of Artie's bats, either a blond-colored Louisville Slugger from his time with the Oaks or a black one he used later in his career.

Doug arranged to pay for the bats, with Artie's signature to be produced by manufacturer Hillerich & Bradsby. But first he needed Artie's permission.

Artie wanted to think about it.

Months passed, and then one day he asked Chuck, "Does Doug still want a bat?"

"Absolutely!" Chuck said.

"I'm going to get you two bats, Chuck. You keep one."

The next morning, Artie showed up at the Bomber Inn with the blond and black bats he used in the Coast League. "Enjoy them," he said.

Artie wanted to give Doug something else to remember him by.

One day, Doug received a padded envelope in the mail. Inside was a cigar in a metal tube signed, "To Doug . . . from Artie Wilson." There also was a 40-page pamphlet of Coast League trivia. Artie was pictured on the cover in an Oaks uniform. On the inside front cover was a note in Artie's handwriting. It read:

> To Doug,
>
> A diehard Oaks fan and a true fan of myself during my two years in Emeryville, and thereafter. I understand you still think of those great years whenever you smell cigar smoke, since you held mine while I autographed your item.
>
> Yours in sport, Artie Wilson

Doug couldn't believe his eyes.

He picked up the cigar and held it in his hand like he had done nearly a half-century earlier.

The cigar was unlit, but he could still smell the aroma of it burning.

He was 11 years old again.

15

THE LAST .400 HITTER

Artie Wilson was the last .400 hitter in the Negro Leagues, Ted Williams the last in Organized Baseball.

Artie did it in 1948, Williams in 1941, when the pitchers he faced were as white as the balls he laced.

It's black and white. Artie was baseball's last .400 hitter.

Still, Major League Baseball records show Williams was the last to scale the mountaintop of hitting, even though he batted .406 for the Boston Red Sox seven years before Artie of the Birmingham Black Barons in the Negro American League poked, punched, and popped the ball for a .402 average.

The Negro Leagues weren't part of the baseball establishment. What happened there didn't amount to a hill of black beans to the white folks running Organized Baseball or the media reporting on it. The accomplishments of Artie and other Negro League stars were either ignored or relegated to the back of the sports section, next to the cotton and grain price reports. That's where the hometown newspaper, the *Birmingham News*, placed a four-paragraph story about the Black Barons beating the Kansas City Monarchs to capture the Negro American League title in 1948.

The *News* devoted a little more space to a wire-service story about another hometown star, Willie Mays, when he was called up by the New York Giants in 1951. It also appeared on the last sports page. There was no reference to Artie, the Birmingham-reared player Willie replaced on the roster.

Artie's feat of hitting .402 got scant attention when he was playing. The only people who remember nowadays are baseball historians like Eric Enders.

In 2000, Enders wrote, "The names of those who have batted .400 in the majors—Ty Cobb, Joe Jackson, Rogers Hornsby—roll off the tongue with ease, but those who might have done it in the Negro Leagues—Artie Wilson, Oscar Charleston, Spotswood Poles—are less familiar."[1]

Enders interviewed Artie during the 2000 season, when Todd Helton of the Colorado Rockies flirted with .400 for a while. He ended up hitting .372.

"Some might say it doesn't count because I did it in the Negro Leagues," Artie said. "Well, if I hit .400 in the Negro Leagues, I probably would have hit more in the majors, because I'd have gotten better pitches to hit."[2]

That may sound boastful, but it's not.

"In his mind, it was just a fact," said Artie Wilson Jr., adding:

> If a pitcher threw a ball within two inches of the plate, he had the ability to do what he wanted with the bat, and he would put the ball wherever he needed to hit it.
>
> The one thing I can remember my dad saying is that when you have the bat in your hand, you control the outcome. You can foul off as many pitches as you want, and then the pitcher will give you what you want and you hit it. He was a master at that.

Fouling off pitches was one of many reasons he was nicknamed Artful Artie. "It's just like bunting," he said. "You don't swing hard. Just flick it off."

When a hotshot pitcher entered the Pacific Coast League, Artie's assignment was to run up the pitch count and wear him down. "I'd watch him warm up. Pick up on his delivery," Artie said.

The victim in one game was Bob Gillespie, a right-handed pitcher for the Sacramento Solons. "First pitch, I fouled off. He kept pumping them in there, and I kept fouling. Fouled off 13 pitches. He finally walked me. Threw a pitch behind me."

As Gillespie found out, Artie was annoying and "pestiferous," a term one sportswriter used to describe him.[3]

Artie Wilson had a habit of turning pitchers into basket cases, intentionally fouling off pitches to wear them down and out. One time he fouled off 13 pitches in a single at-bat. He wound up walking, the pitcher throwing the last ball behind him. *Doug McWilliams Collection*

He frustrated pitchers and played a cat-and-mouse game, with infielders and outfielders shifted out of position in a mostly futile effort to stop him.

"Rinky-dink in front of you, rinky-dink in back of you, rinky-dink," said Bob Dillinger, an outfielder for the Sacramento Solons.

"No matter what he did, he got a base hit or beat the ball out, or we blew the play," said Jack Graham, a first baseman for the San Diego Padres.[4]

"He always had a smile on his face," said Dino Restelli, an outfielder who played both with and against Artie. "You'd run into him, you'd knock him off the basepath or something. He was always smiling."

That was how Artie hit .402—singles and smiles.

He downplayed the accomplishment, telling Enders, "I still say it doesn't mean that much. I never worried about my batting average, and nobody ever mentioned it to me. I never looked at the newspaper to keep up with my batting average; all I worried about was playing and getting on base."[5]

One Black Barons teammate never forgot what Artie did in 1948, and wanted to make sure others didn't either. "Artie Wilson of Birmingham led everyone, black and white, with a .402 batting average," Willie Mays wrote in his 1988 autobiography.[6]

Artie seldom talked about it.

Even when the 1994 television documentary series on baseball by Ken Burns created a groundswell of interest in the Negro League players still living, Artie preferred to stay in the background. He loved talking baseball with customers at the car dealership and friends at the Bomber Inn, and he graciously granted interviews to writers interested in telling the Negro League story. But he paid little attention to baseball card show invitations and requests from different organizations wanting to know about his baseball career.

"Honey, you keepin' yourself from being in the Hall of Fame just because you don't respond to anybody," Dorothy Wilson told her husband.

"That's something my mother used to always say to him," Artie Jr. said. "I even found a letter from Major League Baseball asking for information on his time in baseball. He would open a letter, read it, and just put it on the side. My mother would come around, look at it, and say, 'Honey, why don't you complete this?'"

Artie Jr. couldn't understand his father's reluctance to follow up. At one point, he asked, "Is there something you don't like to talk about?"

"I don't need to talk about it all the time now," Artie said. "I played the game. My playing spoke for itself."

Artie Jr. was born in 1952—too late to enjoy seeing his dad play. Other players filled in the blanks.

Mays recalled the time Artie fouled off 15-straight pitches.

Orlando Cepeda, another superstar, related how huge Artie was to him and other kids growing up in Puerto Rico. Artie won two Puerto Rican League batting titles and was selected to the All-Star team five times.

"People around him have told me how special he was," Artie Jr. said. "There were good baseball players, and then there were guys like my dad who were in a totally different category. If he had played in the big leagues two, three, four years earlier than he did and given a legitimate shot, Lord knows what would've happened."

Twice Artie went to spring training with major-league teams, and both times he batted more than .400 in exhibition games—.417 for the Cleveland Indians in 1949, and a team-high .480 for the Giants in 1951.

Herm Reich, a first baseman, was at the Indians' training camp with Artie. In 1954, they were teammates at Seattle in the PCL.

"It was a big disappointment of mine that he never got a chance with the Indians because they had two shortstops: Lou Boudreau and Ray Boone," Reich said. "Artie could've led the league in hitting just about anywhere he went."

Allen "Two Gun" Gettel was the pitcher acquired by the Giants from the Oakland Oaks, along with Artie and catcher Rafael "Ray" Noble. Like Artie, he finished the 1951 season with the Oaks.

"Artie didn't really get the chance that a lot of ballplayers would get," Gettel said, noting:

> They wouldn't put him in a ballgame and let him stay in there to find out whether he could make the grade. They were changing him from one position to another all the time.
>
> When he was in Oakland with me, shoot, they couldn't get a ball by him at shortstop. He was all over the place. He was a good little ballplayer. The Giants just figured they had these other guys—Alvin Dark and all that bunch—and they would just let him go.

These were things beyond Artie's control.

"Like everything, there's a time for all things," Artie said. "It just wasn't the time for it."[7]

Eventually, the time came for Artie to get the recognition he deserved when he was playing. He didn't have to fill out any forms for the accolades. They came to him.

He was inducted into the Oregon Sports Hall of Fame in 1989, and the Puerto Rican Baseball Hall of Fame in 1994.

The next year, he was among the 216 Negro League players saluted by the Negro Leagues Baseball Museum in Kansas City.

At about the same time, the Giants and Los Angeles Dodgers paid tribute to him and other Negro League players prior to a game at San Francisco's Candlestick Park.

Dodgers manager Tommy Lasorda gave Artie a big hug, as if he was his old pal, Frank Sinatra.

Fred Claire, the Dodgers' vice president and general manager, remembered seeing Artie play in the PCL and quickly introduced him to one of the team's young prospects so he could share some of his hitting wisdom. "I told him, 'Listen to this guy. You learn to hit like he did, and you'll be in the major leagues for a long, long time.'"

Mays praised Artie in a pregame ceremony: "Artie broke me in, when I was 15 years old. I wish I could somehow pay him back. I wish I could buy him a house or something—but I'm not Barry Bonds."[8]

The tributes kept coming.

The city of Portland declared November 15 "Artie Wilson Day" and the date to honor him annually.

The city of Gladstone, where Artie worked for a car dealership, named him "Citizen of the Year."

He got invitations to play in old-timers' games with other PCL and Negro League players. As much as he loved the three-inning games, he wanted to go nine. Someone estimated his batting average for these games was .750. "I love to hit," Artie said.

Afterward, the players gathered at the hotel and reminisced about the good old days. "We'll be in the lobby, and people will just show up, some of them even in their pajamas, to listen. A caterer will arrive with food, and we'll all eat and just keep talking. It usually goes all night. I'm so lucky. If I had 10,000 tongues, I couldn't thank the Lord enough for being alive."[9]

He was 73 at the time.

In 1997, Artie got a letter from Major League Baseball informing him that he and about two dozen other Negro League players would begin receiving a yearly pension. "They said I'd be getting between $7,000 and $10,000 a year," Artie said. "I don't care if it's a dollar; it's more than I had. Whatever it is, I'm grateful. They didn't have to do it."[10]

In 2002, he was among 12 players to attend a reunion of the 1951 Giants at San Francisco's Pacific Bell Park. The main man in the team's miracle comeback, Bobby Thomson, relived for the umpteenth time his game-winning homer and being mobbed by teammates as he neared

Willie Mays was 17 when he put on a Birmingham Black Barons uniform for the first time in 1948. Artie Wilson was on his way to becoming baseball's last .400 hitter, posting a .402 batting average, which was tops in baseball—black and white. Here, they embrace at Willie's 75th birthday celebration at San Francisco's Pacific Bell Park in 2006. *Courtesy Artie Wilson Jr.*

home plate. "And Bobby Thomson has never touched home plate yet," Artie said.

In 2003, Artie was elected to the Pacific Coast League Hall of Fame.

In 2004, at age 83, Artie was on the field for a Portland Beavers–Iowa Cubs game at Portland's PGE Park. Wearing a replica Black Barons uniform, he threw out the ceremonial first pitch and coached first base.

But that's not what had fans buzzing. Before the game, he took batting practice and blistered one line drive after another to left field.

"That may have been the coolest thing I ever shot," raved photographer Craig Mitchelldyer.[11]

In February 2007, Artie attended a reunion of five Black Barons at a baseball event in Beverly Hills. Pitchers Bill Greason and Sammy Williams were there, as well as outfielder Jim Zapp and Mays. "These guys," Mays said, "made it possible for me to come to the majors."[12]

Three months later, Artie was in Seattle to throw out the ceremonial first pitch at a Mariners game.

In 2007, Artie Wilson wowed the crowd at a sold-out Safeco Field in Seattle, shaking off the catcher's signs and then huddling with him to discuss the signals before throwing out the ceremonial first pitch prior to a Seattle Mariners–New York Yankees game. *Doug McWilliams Collection*

Artie Jr. was in the Mariners dugout at Safeco Field with a video camera. What he saw through the lens was vintage Artie Wilson putting on a show for fans who had never heard of him.

Artie walked onto the field, stopped halfway between the pitcher's mound and home plate, and pretended to toss the ball. Then he strolled back to the mound and slowly removed his jacket. He toed the rubber and looked for the sign from the catcher, Mariners outfielder Jason Ellison. He shook off Ellison and trotted to the plate for a chat. Finally, he reared back and bounced a three-hopper that more closely resembled one of his infield singles. The crowd of 46,153 roared.

"He worked the crowd," Artie Jr. said. "It was hilarious."

It was the last time Artie would appear at a professional baseball game.

Father Time was finally catching up with the elusive Artie.

As a player, one manager wouldn't let him run sprints against others on the team because he didn't want to discourage them.

Artie was still leaving people in the dust at 40-something, outrunning his teenage son and several of his buddies in races from left field to center. "It would be close, and then at the end, he'd blow right by us and win by five to seven yards," Artie Jr. said.

He stopped selling cars and began using a cane to get around. Signs of dementia appeared.

In late October 2010, Artie Jr. traveled to Portland from his home in Honolulu to be inducted into the halls of fame for the Portland Interscholastic League and Grant High School. He excelled in both basketball and baseball at Grant, batting a then-record .521 as a senior. He went on to star in basketball for the University of Hawaii, leading the Rainbows to postseason tournaments three of the four years he played.

"The one thing my father instilled in me more than anything else is if I'm going to compete, I need to compete a hundred percent and not talk about it," said Artie. "Just compete. Let your performance speak for itself."

The senior Artie taught young Artie something else—how to put his pants on without getting the bottoms wet on a moist locker-room floor.

As it turned out, Artie Jr. got drenched the last time he saw his father at an assisted living facility in Portland.

Artie had lost what little weight he had to lose and was too weak to attend his son's Hall of Fame induction ceremonies. His beard was unusually long.

"I've got to trim that beard, Dad."

He shaved his father in his hospital bed and walked him to the shower to wash off the loose hair. "I stepped into the shower with my clothes on and ended up holding him to make sure he got clean and didn't fall. I got completely soaked."

Artie Jr. returned to Honolulu the next day for a business meeting.

Arthur Lee Wilson died on October 31, 2010, three days after he turned 90 and two days before his beloved Giants beat the Texas Rangers in the fifth game of the 2010 World Series. He watched the first three games on television, never losing the ability to understand and enjoy the game he loved.

"He had a television, and he'd watch the games," Dorothy said. "That was his whole life."

Zoe Ann Wilson Price described how her father was the "Birmingham Gentleman" until the very end. "He was walking on a cane and would still open the door for ladies, pull my chair out, and take his hat off before getting in and out of an elevator."[13]

"He went to sleep and never woke up," Artie Jr. said. "That moment in the shower just stands out in my mind. It was like a good-bye to my dad."

About half the people at Artie's funeral were customers who had bought a used car from him. There were as many white people as there were blacks.

Chuck Christiansen, Artie's breakfast buddy, was there. "Artie was the kind of guy that everybody liked. Race was not a problem with him. Perfect gentleman. Just a nice, sweet guy—a jewel of a person."

The color of a man's skin didn't matter to Artie.

"You would've thought that he lived in an integrated world, baseball being played equally by everybody and everybody loved everybody," Artie Jr. explained.

He was thinking of his father in December 2016, when he visited the Negro Southern League Museum in Birmingham. It's located next to Regions Field, the city's new downtown ballpark.

The museum tells the story of black baseball through the eyes of a city that once had a law called the "Checkers Ordinance," which made it a crime for blacks and whites to "play together or in company with each other in any game of cards, dice, dominoes, checkers, baseball, softball, basketball, or similar games."[14]

The first thing visitors see is a replica of the Black Barons batting lineup as it appeared in the dugout for their first game against the Homestead Grays in the 1948 Negro League World Series.

Leading off was P. Davis, followed by A. Wilson. W. Mays was in the eighth spot.

"Wow!" Artie Jr. thought to himself. "Amazing! My dad batted second and the great Willie Mays eighth."

Elsewhere in the museum, there's a quote from Ted Williams that reads, "They invented the All-Star Game for Willie Mays."

One of the bats Artie used in 1948 is on display, along with a wire-service photo taken of him in a Cleveland Indians uniform the following spring. There's a ball signed by Artie with "402 in 48" inscribed under his name.

The last exhibit features the Birmingham Industrial League, a proving ground for young players striving to move up to the Black Barons and other Negro League teams, and veterans trying to hang on.

Artie worked in machine shop number three at the American Cast Iron Pipe Company (ACIPCO) and played shortstop for its "colored" team, the Pipemen. Piper Davis was a teammate there, as well as catcher Sam Hairston, who played in the majors about as long as Artie did. Artie topped .400 in five of his seven seasons with the Pipemen and batted .438 overall.

There's a framed painting of Artie on the wall near the exit. He's wearing an ACIPCO uniform and swinging a bat. "Artie Wilson," the caption reads. "Birmingham Industrial League's Greatest Hitter of All-Time."

As he admired the painting, Artie Jr. was filled with pride. And then he tried to imagine his father standing next to him and what his reaction might be.

He would be proud, but he wouldn't make a big to-do about it. That's not the way he was.

He wouldn't say much, perhaps something like, "Nice."

Artie Jr. thought about it a little more before realizing the answer was as obvious as the look on his father's face in almost every photograph taken of him.

He would just smile.

Visitors to the Negro Southern League Museum in Birmingham, Alabama, can step back in time to the first game of the 1948 Negro League World Series, between the Birmingham Black Barons and Homestead Grays. The lineups show Artie batting second and Willie Mays eighth for the Black Barons. Luke Easter is the leadoff hitter for the Grays. *Courtesy of the author*

16

EXTRA INNINGS: A LOT OF HISTORY

Writing a book like this is bittersweet. Bitter because almost all the Negro League players are gone—and their stories as well. Sweet because I got to spend time with some of them and share their amazing tales with others.

Still, I have many regrets.

My biggest was missing an opportunity to interview Satchel Paige in 1970, when I was editor of a magazine in Kansas City, Missouri. I had spoken with Satch on the phone, and everything was set until my publisher refused to pay him $50 to go to a nearby photo studio and pose for a cover shot. I didn't even think about paying him out of my own pocket.

In the late 1970s, I lived in the Akron–Cleveland area of Ohio. I worked for the same corporation as Harry "Suitcase" Simpson, a Negro League player who played eight years in the majors for the Cleveland Indians, Kansas City Athletics, New York Yankees, Chicago White Sox, and Pittsburgh Pirates. A colleague in the company's public relations department did a story on Suitcase for the employee newspaper, but I never sought him out.

Luke Easter was one of my childhood heroes. He played with and against Artie Wilson, who I first interviewed in 1975. Luke worked as a security guard for a Cleveland company until he was killed by armed robbers in 1979. I had plenty of reasons to interview Luke but never got around to it.

In the 1970s, I interviewed by telephone Lorenzo "Piper" Davis, James "Buzz" Clarkson, and Sam Hairston, Negro Leaguers all. The conversations were far too short.

I could go on, but one thing impressed upon me by Artie Wilson, Rev. Bill Greason, and the other Negro Leaguers I interviewed at length, was to count my blessings and be grateful for those I did have the privilege of meeting or talking baseball with on the phone.

One of those players was Clint "Butch" McCord Jr., of Nashville, Tennessee.

Butch followed the same path as Jackie Robinson into Organized Baseball: He served in the military during World War II (two years in the U.S. Marines); played college football (Tennessee A&I, now Tennessee State); and played in the Negro Leagues from 1947 to 1950 (Nashville Cubs and Black Vols, Baltimore Elite Giants, and Chicago American Giants).

Unlike Jackie, Butch didn't make it to the majors. The closest he came was the Triple A level, the highest in the minors. In 11 seasons from 1951 to 1961, he hit .306 and was almost flawless at first base, leading the minors in 1958, with a .996 fielding percentage.

"I call myself a backup singer," Butch said. "You sing good, but nobody watches you."

Despite winning back-to-back Class D Mississippi–Ohio Valley League batting titles in 1951–1952, he didn't make it to Class AAA with the Richmond Virginians until 1955, when he was almost 30.

At Richmond, he played against Al Pinkston, another black player and the "greatest hitter you never heard of," according to Bob Hoie, a minor-league historian. Pinkston spent his entire career in either the Negro Leagues or the minors. He won a record-tying six minor-league batting titles and was runner-up four times. His career batting average of .352 ranks eighth all time in the minors.

I called to talk about Pinkston, but we wound up talking mostly about Butch. I'm glad we did.

"I've got a lot of history, and you're bringing it out," Butch said at one point. "I haven't even thought about all this."

I listened as Butch told one fascinating story after another.

He was playing for the Chicago American Giants in 1950, when the team signed three white players, the first to appear in the Negro

Leagues. One of them was 19-year-old pitcher Lou Chirban, who Butch befriended and shared a room with on the road.

A crowd of 8,579, the Giants' largest of the season, showed up at Chicago's Comiskey Park to see the novelty of whites on a black team. Chirban was roughed up for five runs and four hits in the first two innings.

Chirban and his mates were treated even more rudely a month later in Birmingham, when they arrived at Rickwood Field to play the Birmingham Black Barons and their star center fielder, Willie Mays.

"The police got on the bus before we could get off, and one of them said, 'I hear you got some white players on the team? If you put those white players in uniform today, I'll close this stadium down. People are already in the stadium. There will be no ballgame here today.'"

When Chirban asked if he could sit on the bench, he was told he had to sit in the grandstand area restricted to white people.

"It wasn't until 1963," Butch continued, "when I saw on television that guy putting those dogs, fire hoses, and pipes on the civil rights protestors in Birmingham, that it dawned on me who that was that got on the bus. Do you have an idea? It was Bull Connor! George Wallace's right-hand man."

Eugene "Bull" Connor was Birmingham's public safety director in the 1960s and the face of racial bigotry in the South, along with Alabama governor George Wallace, a staunch segregationist.

"I was the first black to play Triple A ball in Richmond," Butch said. "All of the stands were segregated. We had a reunion in '80 of all the ballplayers that played at Richmond. The white wives asked my wife, 'Where were you in '55?' She showed them where she sat in the black section on the first-base side. They didn't even know she was there."

Richmond was part of the International League, along with the Havana Sugar Kings.

"They'd come there (Richmond), and they didn't have but two white players to stay in the white hotel. All the other players looked like me and stayed in the black hotel. Bo Diddley was in Richmond at that time and just getting his start."

A singer and guitarist, Diddley is considered one of the founders of rock 'n' roll, in addition to Chuck Berry, Little Richard, Jerry Lee Lewis, and a few others.

Prior to Richmond, Butch played two seasons (1953–1954) for the Denver Bears in the Class A Western League. The second baseman in 1953 was Curt Roberts, the first black to play for the Pittsburgh Pirates. "Somebody hollered out of the stands, 'Who we playin', the Kansas City Monarchs?'" Butch said.

In Western League cities like Des Moines, Omaha, and Wichita, Butch stayed in the same hotel as his white teammates. "I quit sitting in the lobby because some white would come up to me and we'd have a great conversation, but before leaving, he'd say, 'Are you with the band?'"

Butch laughed. "He couldn't believe it."

He got in a cab in Omaha and told the driver to take him to his hotel. "He took me to the side entrance. I said, 'I want to get out in front of the hotel. I stay here.' He couldn't believe it."

To better cope with the racial conditions, which varied from city to city, blacks on visiting teams met their counterparts locally to discuss "where to go, where to eat, and all that kind of stuff."

Two future major-league stars, Bill White and Maury Wills, played in the Western League in 1954, White for Sioux City, Iowa, and Wills for Pueblo, Colorado. "They always came to my house, and my wife would cook breakfast for us. We'd eat together after games. We were like that. We were friends off the field. That's the way we got along. We'd talk about the situations that we'd come into. We understood the hardships."

After three years at the Triple A level, Butch moved to the Class A Sally League in 1958, five years after Hank Aaron and several others integrated the loop.

"I asked Hank Aaron, 'What was the worst city in that Sally League?' Do you know who it was?"

I guessed Macon.

"Go again. Where's the Masters played?" Butch asked.

"Augusta," I said.

Butch continued:

> Yes, sir, I've never seen anything like that in my life. These farmers coming in and chewing that tobacco, and they would sit there strictly to harass teams that had black players. I thought I had heard all of the derogatory stuff, but I heard stuff that I never heard. They were so nasty that the white women wouldn't sit near them. It got funny to

me. I said, "Well, every time I come in here I'm going to get me a few base hits. Y'all encouraging me to hit."

Augusta was a Detroit Tigers farm club.

"They had a black pitcher. He wouldn't warm up in the bullpen. He'd loosen up but he'd do his warmin' up on the mound because of the situation."

Butch played for the Macon Dodgers.

He recalled:

> You had to go through a city park to get to the Macon ballpark. As I got near the end one night, there were the boys in robes having a meeting. They didn't have their hoods on, but they had their robes on. They looked at me and I looked at them and I said, "I hope to hell you be gone when I come back."

Butch had another good laugh.

At the Sally League All-Star Game in Savannah, Georgia, Butch singled and was standing next to the white first baseman when a fan hollered, "Don't stand by him! He wants to go to school with you!"

"I got tickled," Butch said, as he continued down memory lane.

"I had the opportunity to play with the first black that played in the Texas League—Dave Hoskins," Butch said. "And I had the opportunity to play with Marvin Williams, who went to Boston with Sam Jethroe and Jackie Robinson."

The Boston Red Sox and Braves were pressured by a local politician into giving the trio a tryout in April 1945.

Butch related:

> I said, "'Marvin, did they treat you all right when you tried out with Boston or did they go through the motions because they were put on the spot to get a Negro League ballplayer?"
>
> He said, "No, the Red Sox had to catch a train out of town. And we were supposed to try out with the Boston Braves when they came in. And then President Roosevelt (Franklin D. Roosevelt) died."

"Just think how history would've changed," Butch added. "I'm going to say this: Clark Griffith could've integrated baseball before Branch Rickey because he had Josh Gibson and all them people playing for him."

The mightiest home-run hitter in black baseball, Gibson played for the Homestead Grays, the New York Yankees of the Negro Leagues. The Grays played half their home games at Griffith Stadium in Washington, DC, operated by Clark Griffith, owner of the Washington Senators.

"Clark Griffith was making money off both, and he wasn't going to integrate and break up that situation because he made more off the Grays than the Senators. It's a lot of history, I tell you."

Butch paused, before continuing:

> If you looked at me, starting in the white minor leagues, I tried to do everything Jackie did. My first year, I stole 22 bases and hit .363. I almost won the Triple Crown. I missed out on the RBIs. One guy had 119, and I had one less. The next year, I stole 20 bases and hit .392. I had 119 RBIs, but Jim Zapp got 137. I tease him all the time, "Hell, if it hadn't been for me, you wouldn't have that many because I was on base every time you got a RBI."

A member of the 1948 Black Barons, Zapp was a lifelong resident of Nashville, Tennessee.

"I talked to Larry Doby," Butch continued, "and he said that the first time he went into the clubhouse in Cleveland, not one ballplayer spoke to him. Can you imagine that? Your own teammates."

Doby was the second black to play Organized Baseball, the first in the American League.

Butch was on a roll:

> Nobody else can tell you what I'm going to tell you now. I hit Gaylord Perry when he was in the Giants organization. I hit against Sandy Koufax in an intrasquad game. I hit a home run against Don Drysdale when he was at Montreal, and when I got back to my position at first base, I heard someone holler to me, "You little hot dog! You little hot dog!" I looked over there and it was ol' Tommy Lasorda.

Lasorda was a pitcher for the Montreal Royals in the International League at the time. He went on to manage the Los Angeles Dodgers to four National League pennants and two World Series titles.

Butch reminded Lasorda of the incident at a Negro League event he attended in Nashville.

"I didn't say that," he said.

"Do you think I made that up?" Butch replied.

"When I get to talking with people and things come up, I say, 'Good God, I have more history than I think about.'"

Butch died in early 2011, almost two years after our telephone conversation.

One powerful quote he left behind was this one from the Nashville newspaper, the *Tennessean*: "No other athlete went through what Jackie Robinson had to go through in '47. Think about it: Martin Luther King hadn't even gotten married yet; Rosa (Parks) hadn't given up her seat yet. He was a brave man."[1]

So were Butch McCord, Artie Wilson, Bill Greason, Jim Zapp, Dave Hoskins, and other blacks who paved the way in baseball's minor leagues for others to follow.

After the 1952 season, when he became the first black to play in the Texas League, Hoskins revealed three death threats he received before a game in Shreveport, Louisiana. "First one said I'd be shot if I sat in the dugout. Second one said I'd be shot if I went on the field, and the third one said I'd be shot if I took the mound. I figured all three were from the same person. Probably someone just trying to scare me."[2]

Hoskins didn't tell anyone. He pitched the game and won easily—one of 24 victories for the year.

It was common for Negro League players to shave a few years off their age to enhance their chances of making it to the majors.

Sam Hairston, an outstanding Negro League catcher who appeared in four games for the Chicago White Sox in 1951, trimmed five years off his real age upon entering Organized Baseball at Colorado Springs, Colorado.

"Sportswriters in Colorado Springs always wanted to know how old I was," Hairston said. "I told them to go out on Highway 92 and stand by the side of the road, and I'd drive past 75 miles an hour and holler out my age."

Like many of the black pioneers, Hairston won the hearts of white fans.

"They loved him in Colorado Springs," said Don Gutteridge, Sam's manager there in 1950 and 1951. "He was so popular, they offered him jobs, anything he wanted."

One of the job offers was from the chief of police in Colorado Springs.

"Sam," he said, "would you like to stay here all winter and be a policeman?"

"Oh, my Lord, I couldn't arrest people," Hairston replied. "I couldn't do anything like that."

"I don't want you to arrest anybody," the police chief said. "I just want you to stand on the corner and smile."

These are stories worth remembering and telling again and again.

We are losing them as the Negro Leaguers fade into the past.

"Our time is limited," Greason said in 2007, at a reunion of five members of the 1948 Black Barons. "When you are 82, you don't have 82 more."[3]

It was just like old times for Willie Mays, far left, and four of his 1948 Birmingham Black Barons teammates at a baseball dinner in Beverly Hills, California, in 2007. Mays paid tribute to, left to right, Rev. Bill Greason, Artie Wilson, Jim Zapp, and Sammy Williams. "These guys," Mays said, "made it possible for me to come to the majors." *Courtesy Artie Wilson Jr.*

Willie Mays was there. So were Artie, Zapp, and pitcher Sammy Williams.

Williams was gone six months later. Artie died in 2010, Zapp in 2016.

Greason turned 93 in 2017, and Mays 86.

They are the last of the 1948 Birmingham Black Barons, a group of courageous, talented men on the front lines of tearing down pro baseball's color barrier.

That's a lot of history.

NOTES

PREFACE

1. *Long Beach Independent Press-Telegram*, March 23, 1958, 1.
2. *Oakland Tribune*, April 12, 1943, 18.
3. *Chicago Tribune*, July 17, 1943, 21.
4. *Oakland Tribune*, July 20, 1942, 12.
5. *Oakland Tribune*, April 12, 1943, 18.
6. *Pittsburgh Courier*, December 26, 1942, 16.
7. *San Francisco Chronicle*, March 1, 1993, D2.
8. *Pittsburgh Courier*, April 24, 1943, 18.
9. *Pittsburgh Courier*, April 24, 1943, 18.
10. *San Francisco Chronicle*, March 1, 1993, D2.
11. "Negro League Player Reflects on Life," CNN, August 31, 2014, http://www.cnn.com/videos/us/2014/08/31/nr-valencia-greason-former-baseball-player.cnn .
12. *Oklahoman* (Oklahoma City), August 22, 2012, 1C.
13. *Fresno Bee*, December 23, 1952, 17.
14. *Paris News* (Paris, TX), May 22, 1952, 11.
15. *Oklahoman*, August 3, 1952, 17.
16. *Sporting News*, August 13, 1952, 31.
17. *Fresno Bee*, December 23, 1952, 17.
18. *Fresno Bee*, December 23, 1952, 17.
19. *Sporting News*, January 28, 1953, 21.
20. *Pittsburgh Courier*, January 17, 1953, 14.
21. John Klima, *Willie's Boys* (Hoboken, NJ: John Wiley & Sons, 2009), 267.

22. Klima, *Willie's Boys*, 268.
23. *St. Louis Post-Dispatch*, June 1, 1954, 26.
24. Klima, *Willie's Boys*, 268.
25. *Los Angeles Times*, March 23, 1958, 60.

INTRODUCTION

1. *Fences*, directed by Denzel Washington, based on a play and screenplay by August Wilson (Hollywood, CA: Paramount Pictures, 2016).
2. *Sport*, February 1951, 66–67.
3. Roger Kahn, *A Season in the Sun* (New York: Berkley, 1978), 88.
4. Kahn, *A Season in the Sun*, 94–95.
5. *Lift Every Voice and Sing*, written by James Weldon Johnson, 1900.

I. JUST LIKE JACKIE

1. *Chicago Tribune*, August 19, 1946, 27.
2. Roger Kahn, *A Season in the Sun* (New York: Berkley, 1978), 87, 89.
3. Layton Revel and Luis Munoz, *Forgotten Heroes: Artie Wilson* (Carrollton, TX: Center for Negro League Baseball Research, 2013), 29.
4. *Sporting News*, August 18, 1954, 29.
5. *Pittsburgh Courier*, March 21, 1953, 19.
6. *Pittsburgh Courier*, September 24, 1949, 24.
7. Ed Mickelson, *Out of the Park* (Jefferson, NC: McFarland and Company, 2007), 169.
8. *Chicago Defender*, February 19, 1949, 14.
9. *Seattle Times*, March 20, 1956, 37.
10. *Seattle Times*, January 17, 1957, 17.
11. *Baseball America*, November 24–December 7, 1997, 3.

2. LET'S PLAY BALL!

1. *New York Times*, April 12, 1960, 28.
2. Christopher D. Fullerton, *Every Other Sunday* (Birmingham, AL: Boozer Press, 1999), 38.

3. Theodore Rosengarten, "Reading the Hops: Recollections of Lorenzo Piper Davis and the Negro Baseball League," *Southern Exposure* (Summer–Fall 1977), 69.

4. Rosengarten, "Reading the Hops," 69.

3. "LEAVE THE BUS HERE!"

1. Theodore Rosengarten, "Reading the Hops: Recollections of Lorenzo Piper Davis and the Negro Baseball League," *Southern Exposure* (Summer–Fall 1977), 71.

2. Rosengarten, "Reading the Hops," 73–74.

3. Christopher D. Fullerton, *Every Other Sunday* (Birmingham, AL: Boozer Press, 1999), 62.

4. *San Francisco Chronicle*, October 16, 1944, 3H.

5. *Oakland Tribune*, October 17, 1944, 20.

6. *Oakland Tribune*, October 20, 1944, 24.

7. *Rochester Democrat and Chronicle*, August 20, 1944, 26.

8. *Pittsburgh Courier*, April 8, 1944, 12.

9. *Cincinnati Enquirer* (Kentucky edition), June 1, 1944, 15.

10. *Pittsburgh Courier*, August 19, 1944, 12.

11. *Pittsburgh Courier*, September 30, 1944, 12.

12. Rosengarten, "Reading the Hops," 71.

13. *Pittsburgh Courier*, April 21, 1945, 12.

14. *Pittsburgh Courier*, April 28, 1945, 12.

15. *Pittsburgh Courier*, April 14, 1945, 12.

16. *Pittsburgh Courier*, May 5, 1945, 12.

17. *Pittsburgh Courier*, April 28, 1945, 12.

18. *Pittsburgh Courier*, April 21, 1945, 12.

19. *Pittsburgh Courier*, July 14, 1945, 12.

20. *Pittsburgh Courier*, July 14, 1945, 12.

21. *Pittsburgh Courier*, August 4, 1945, 12.

22. Branch Rickey, *Branch Rickey's Little Blue Book*, ed. John J. Monteleone (New York: Mountain Lion Book/Macmillan, 1995), 84.

23. Layton Revel and Luis Munoz, *Forgotten Heroes: Artie Wilson* (Carrollton, TX: Center for Negro League Baseball Research, 2013), 25.

24. *Chicago Tribune*, August 19, 1946, 27.

25. *Pittsburgh Courier*, August 24, 1946, 16.

26. *Sporting News*, October 2, 1946, 9.

27. *New York Age*, September 21, 1948, 27.

28. Larry Tye, *Satchel: The Life and Times of an American Legend* (New York: Random House, 2009), x (Preface).

29. *Council Bluffs Nonpareil*, October 13, 1946, 17.

30. Tye, *Satchel*, 172.

31. *San Francisco Call-Bulletin*, July 25, 1947, 13.

32. *Oakland Tribune*, August 21, 1952, 27.

33. *Oakland Tribune*, March 31, 1952, 22.

34. *St. Louis Star and Times*, August 25, 1947, 17.

35. Rosengarten, "Reading the Hops," 78.

36. *San Francisco Call-Bulletin*, July 25, 1947, 13.

37. *Pittsburgh Courier*, August 9, 1947, 15.

38. Rosengarten, "Reading the Hops," 78.

39. Bill Veeck, with Ed Linn, *Veeck—As in Wreck: The Autobiography of Bill Veeck* (Chicago: University of Chicago Press, 2001), 183.

40. Veeck, with Linn, *Veeck—As in Wreck*, 181.

4. THE BATTLE FOR ART WILSON

1. *Pittsburgh Courier*, February 19, 1949, 10.

2. Bill Veeck, with Ed Linn, *Veeck—As in Wreck: The Autobiography of Bill Veeck* (Chicago: University of Chicago Press, 2001), 257–63.

3. *Sporting News*, July 14, 1948, 8.

4. *Sporting News*, September 1, 1948, 4.

5. *Arizona Republic* (Phoenix), December 15, 1948, 6.

6. Veeck, with Linn, *Veeck—As in Wreck*, 171.

7. Neil Lanctot, *Negro League Baseball: The Rise and Ruin of a Black Institution* (Philadelphia: University of Pennsylvania Press, 2004), 466.

8. Document from National Baseball Hall of Fame files, Cooperstown, NY.

9. *Sporting News*, February 2, 1949, 24.

10. *Sporting News*, February 23, 1949, 2–8.

11. *Pittsburgh Courier*, February 19, 1949, 10.

12. *Arizona Republic* (Phoenix), February 12, 1949, 27.

13. *Philadelphia Inquirer*, February 12, 1949, 18.

14. *Sporting News*, February 23, 1949, 8.

15. *Pittsburgh Courier*, February 19, 1949, 10.

16. *Pittsburgh Courier*, February 19, 1949, 10.

17. *Pittsburgh Courier*, February 26, 1949, 10.

18. *Pittsburgh Courier*, February 19, 1949, 10.

19. *Sporting News*, February 23, 1949, 2, 18.

20. *Philadelphia Inquirer*, February 12, 1949, 18.
21. *Sporting News*, February 23, 1949, 14.
22. *Akron Beacon Journal*, February 25, 1949, 36.
23. *Arizona Republic*, March 8, 1949, 15.
24. *Arizona Daily Star* (Tucson), March 3, 1949, 20.
25. *Akron Beacon Journal*, March 28, 1949, 17.
26. *Akron Beacon Journal*, March 11, 1949, 43.
27. *Baltimore Afro-American*, March 5, 1949, 18.
28. *Sports Illustrated*, May 8, 1989, 117.
29. *Akron Beacon Journal*, March 11, 1949, 43.
30. *Sporting News*, April 13, 1949, 13.
31. *Akron Beacon Journal*, March 25, 1949, 42.
32. *Akron Beacon Journal*, March 28, 1949, 17.
33. *Sandusky Register*, March 4, 1949, 15.
34. *Chicago Tribune*, May 3, 1949, Part 3, 1.
35. *Sporting News*, May 11, 1949, 9.
36. *Sporting News*, February 23, 1949, 2.
37. *Sporting News*, May 25, 1949, 18.

5. TOILING ON TRIBE PLANTATION

1. *Sporting News*, April 13, 1949, 13.
2. *Oregonian* , April 23, 1952, Section 3, 1.
3. *Sporting News*, May 21, 1952, 23.
4. *Sporting News*, September 3, 1952, 30.
5. *Pittsburgh Courier*, April 2, 1949, 23.
6. *Oregonian*, April 7, 1949, Section 3, 1.
7. *Los Angeles Times*, March 20, 1949, 27.
8. Bill Swank, *Echoes from Lane Field* (Paducah, KY: Turner Publishing, 1997), 103.
9. *Sporting News*, June 1, 1949, 16, 18.
10. *Pittsburgh Courier*, April 16, 1949, 22.
11. *Sporting News*, June 1, 1949, 16.
12. *Sporting News*, March 16, 1949, 25.
13. *Smithsonian*, July 1991, 118.
14. *Oregonian*, April 13, 1949, Section 3, 1.
15. *Oregonian*, April 13, 1949, Section 3, 1.
16. *Oregonian*, April 17, 1949, Section 3, 1.
17. *Oregonian*, April 17, 1949, 34.
18. *Smithsonian*, July 1991, 123.

19. *Sporting News*, June 1, 1949, 22.

20. *Sporting News*, April 13, 1949, 13.

21. *San Diego Union*, April 21, 1949, B3.

22. *Arizona Republic* (Phoenix, AZ), July 23, 1949, 15.

23. Swank, *Echoes from Lane Field*, 100.

24. Swank, *Echoes from Lane Field*, 100.

25. *Smithsonian*, July 1991, 119.

26. *Smithsonian*, July 1991, 117–18.

6. A MIGHTY OAK GROWS IN OAKLAND

1. *Oakland Tribune*, June 14, 1949, 30.

2. *Oakland Tribune*, June 14, 1949, 30.

3. *Oakland Tribune*, June 15, 1949, 27, 30.

4. *Pittsburgh Courier*, June 25, 1949, 22.

5. *Oakland Tribune*, July 11, 1949, 20.

6. *Oakland Tribune*, May 7, 1949, 12.

7. *Feather River Bulletin* (Quincy, CA), August 20, 1986, 16.

8. *Oakland Tribune*, December 27, 1948, 16.

9. *Chicago Defender* (national edition), October 1, 1949, 18.

10. *Oakland Tribune*, June 26, 1949, 25.

11. *Oakland Tribune*, June 9, 1949, 22.

12. *Oakland Tribune*, May 27, 1949, 26.

13. *San Francisco Examiner*, May 27, 1949, 23.

14. *Oakland Tribune*, August 26, 1949, 27.

15. *Oakland Tribune*, August 28, 1949, 26.

16. *Oakland Tribune*, August 29, 1949, 22.

17. *Oakland Tribune*, February 23, 1950, 22.

18. *Oakland Tribune*, March 5, 1950, 30.

19. *Oakland Tribune*, August 15, 1949, 20.

20. *Oakland Tribune*, September 4, 1949, 11.

21. *Pittsburgh Courier*, August 6, 1949, 23.

22. *Los Angeles Times*, September 29, 1949, Part IV, 2.

23. *Sporting News*, October 12, 1949, 32.

24. *Reader's Digest*, May 1952, 96.

25. *Oakland Tribune*, June 21, 1951, 22.

26. *Oakland Tribune*, June 21, 1951, 22.

27. *Akron Beacon Journal*, March 14, 1949, 18.

28. *Oakland Tribune*, March 14, 1950, 38.

29. *Brooklyn Daily Eagle*, March 3, 1947, 11.

30. *Oakland Tribune*, October 12, 1950, 28.

31. *Oakland Tribune*, October 12, 1950, 30.

32. *Oakland Tribune*, October 17, 1950, 33.

7. CAUGHT IN THE MIDDLE

1. Branch Rickey, *Branch Rickey's Little Blue Book*, ed. John J. Monteleone (New York: Mountain Lion Book/Macmillan, 1995), 106.

2. *Philadelphia Inquirer*, April 10, 1947, 24.

3. *San Francisco Call Bulletin*, July 25, 1947, 13.

4. *New York Times*, May 17, 1982, C6.

5. Carl Erskine, *Tales from the Dodger Dugout* (Champaign, IL: Sports Publishing, 2001), 8.

6. *New York Herald-Tribune*, March 25, 1951, Section 3, 3.

7. *New York Times*, March 4, 1951, Section 5, 2.

8. *New York Times*, April 3, 1951, 33.

9. *New York Times*, April 11, 1951, 39.

10. *New York Post*, April 12, 1951, 50.

11. *Gastonia (NC) Gazette*, April 15, 1951, 23.

12. *Monongahela (PA) Daily Republican*, January 30, 1951, 2.

13. Monte Irvin, with James A. Riley, *Nice Guys Finish First: The Autobiography of Monte Irvin* (New York: Carroll & Graf, 1996), 142.

14. *Lebanon (PA) Daily News*, May 31, 1966, 11.

15. *New York Herald Tribune*, April 27, 1951, 24.

16. *San Francisco Examiner*, April 23, 1951, 36.

17. *San Francisco Chronicle*, April 23, 1951, 3H.

18. *Oakland Tribune*, April 22, 1951, A43.

19. *Sporting News*, May 2, 1951, 15.

20. *New York Post*, April 25, 1951, 79.

21. *New York Post*, April 25, 1951, 79.

22. *Sporting News*, May 2, 1951, 15.

23. *New York Daily News*, April 23, 1951, C20.

24. *New York Post*, April 25, 1951, 79.

25. Irvin with Riley, *Nice Guys Finish First*, 142.

26. *Sporting News*, May 2, 1951, 7.

27. *Brooklyn Daily Eagle*, April 27, 1951, 19.

28. *New York Post*, April 27, 1951.

29. *New York Times*, May 1, 1951, 37.

30. Thomas Kiernan, *The Miracle at Coogan's Bluff* (New York: Thomas Y. Crowell, 1975), 76.

31. *Oakland Tribune*, October 3, 1951, 36.

32. *New York Herald Tribune*, April 27, 1951, 24.

33. *Lebanon (PA) Daily News*, May 31, 1966, 11.

8. TRADING PLACES

1. Willie Mays, with Lou Sahadi, *Say Hey: The Autobiography of Willie Mays* (New York: Simon & Schuster, 1988), 56.

2. Mays, with Sahadi, *Say Hey*, 51.

3. *Brooklyn Daily Eagle*, May 25, 1951, 16.

4. Mays, with Sahadi, *Say Hey*, 56.

5. Birmingham Black Barons video documentary, Birmingham Civil Rights Institute, Richard Arrington Jr. Resource Gallery.

6. Mays, with Sahadi, *Say Hey*, 18.

7. *Brooklyn Daily Eagle*, May 25, 1951, 16.

8. *Minneapolis Star Tribune*, June 1, 1951, 19.

9. *Minneapolis Star Tribune*, May 30, 1951, 14.

10. *Minneapolis Star Tribune*, May 27, 1951, 34.

11. *Minneapolis Star Tribune*, May 30, 1951, 6.

12. *Minneapolis Star Tribune*, June 1, 1951, 17.

13. *Minneapolis Star Tribune*, June 5, 1951, 18.

14. *Minneapolis Star Tribune*, June 4, 1951, 22.

15. *Minneapolis Tribune*, June 22, 1951, 18.

16. *Oakland Tribune*, June 22, 1951, 26.

17. *Oakland Tribune*, June 24, 1951, 34.

18. *Sporting News*, June 4, 1951, 32.

19. *Oakland Tribune*, June 25, 1951, 19.

20. *Oakland Tribune*, June 24, 1951, 34.

21. *Oakland Tribune*, June 25, 1951, 19, 21.

22. *Oakland Tribune*, June 26, 1951, 23.

23. *Oakland Tribune*, September 11, 1951, 33.

9. LI'L ARTHUR REIGNS IN SEATTLE

1. *Seattle Times*, April 6, 1952, 41.

2. *Sporting News*, April 2, 1952, 13.

3. *San Diego Union*, April 18, 1957, A15.

4. *Sporting News*, May 21, 1952, 24.

5. *Oregonian*, January 14, 1953, Section 3, 1.

6. *Seattle Times*, January 25, 1956, 23.

7. *Seattle Times*, March 14, 1953, 6.

8. *Seattle Times*, January 25, 1956, 23.

9. *Seattle Times*, January 25, 1956, 23.

10. *Seattle Times*, March 31, 1953, 26.

11. Ed Mickelson, *Out of the Park: Memoir of a Minor League Baseball All-Star* (Jefferson, NC: McFarland, 2007), 179.

12. *Seattle Times*, May 2, 1953, 6.

13. *Sporting News*, April 29, 1953, 13.

14. *Los Angeles Times*, June 22, 1953, Part IV, 3.

15. *Sporting News*, September 23, 1953, 26.

16. *Sporting News*, August 18, 1954, 29.

17. *Seattle Times*, July 8, 1954, 23.

18. *Sporting News*, May 5, 1954, 23.

19. *Sporting News*, May 5, 1954, 23.

20. *Sporting News*, June 9, 1954, 27.

21. *Seattle Times*, December 6, 1954, 22.

10. PREJUDICE IN PORTLAND

1. *Sporting News*, August 31, 1955, 25.

2. Jules Tygiel, *Baseball's Great Experiment: Jackie Robinson and His Legacy* (New York: Vintage, 1984), 103–4.

3. *The Jackie Robinson Story*, directed by Alfred E. Green (Hollywood, CA: Jewel Pictures, 1950).

4. *Clarion-Ledger* (Jackson, MS), July 1, 1984, 53.

5. Ed Mickelson, *Out of the Park: Memoir of a Minor League Baseball All-Star* (Jefferson, NC: McFarland, 2007), 139.

6. Branch Rickey, *Branch Rickey's Little Blue Book*, ed. John J. Monteleone (New York: Mountain Lion Book/Macmillan, 1995), 110.

7. *Oregonian*, May 16, 1955, Section 2, 1.

8. *Oregonian*, July 28, 1955, Section 2, 1.

9. Mickelson, *Out of the Park*, 155.

10. *Seattle Times*, June 29, 1955, 31.

11. *Seattle Times*, January 17, 1955, 20.

12. Mickelson, *Out of the Park*, 146.

13. *Los Angeles Times*, March 6, 1956, Part IV, 3.

14. *Oregonian*, March 28, 1956, Section 2, 3.

15. *Seattle Times*, May 25, 1956, 27.

16. *Oregonian*, July 12, 1956, Section 2, 1.

17. *Fairbanks Daily News-Miner*, July 12, 1956, 10.

11. SAY HEY, IT'S MR. HEY HEY!

1. *Arizona Daily Star* (Tucson, AZ), April 25, 1956, D3.

2. *Sporting News*, May 23, 1956, 25.

3. *Sporting News*, May 23, 1956, 25.

4. *Seattle Times*, July 5, 1957, 15.

5. *Seattle Times*, January 17, 1957, 15.

6. *Seattle Times*, January 17, 1957, 15.

7. *Los Angeles Times*, June 23, 1957, C2.

8. *Sacramento Bee*, August 24, 1957, D2.

9. *Sacramento Bee*, August 27, 1957, C2.

10. *Sacramento Union*, August 27, 1957, 6.

11. John E. Spalding, *Sacramento Senators and Solons* (Manhattan, KS: Ag Press, 1995), 158.

12. *Los Angeles Times*, June 23, 1957, C2.

12. THE COMEBACK

1. *Honolulu Star-Advertiser*, July 22, 1962, 27.

2. *Oregonian*, July 19, 1962, Section 3, 1.

3. *Oregonian*, August 1, 1962, Section 3, 1.

4. *Tri-City Herald* (Pasco, Kennewick, Richland, WA), August 24, 1962, 22.

5. *Salem (OR) Statesman-Journal*, August 25, 1962, 10.

6. *Tri-City Herald*, September 7, 1962, 21.

13. TALKING BASEBALL (SELLING CARS)

1. *Oregonian*, June 19, 1955, Section 3, 4.

2. Roger Kahn, *A Season in the Sun* (New York: Berkley, 1978), 95.

14. THE BALLPLAYER, THE BOY, AND THE CIGAR

1. Ralph Mauriello, *Tales Beyond the Dugout* (Tecumseh, MI: DiggyPOD, 2017), 2.

2. Mauriello, *Tales Beyond the Dugout*, 3.

3. Dick Dobbins, *The Grand Minor League: An Oral History of the Old Pacific Coast League* (Emeryville, CA: Woodford Press, 1999), 227.

4. *Pittsburgh Courier*, April 7, 1951, 16.

5. Dobbins, *The Grand Minor League*, 227.

6. *Sports Illustrated*, May 8, 1989, 116.

7. *Sports Illustrated*, May 8, 1989, 117.

15. THE LAST .400 HITTER

1. Eric Enders, *The Last .400 Hitter*, 2000.

2. Enders, *The Last .400 Hitter*.

3. *Oregonian*, May 6, 1953, Section 3, 1.

4. Dick Dobbins, *The Grand Minor League: An Oral History of the Old Pacific Coast League* (Emeryville, CA: Woodford Press, 1999), 228.

5. Enders, *The Last .400 Hitter*.

6. Willie Mays, with Lou Sahadi, *Say Hey: The Autobiography of Willie Mays* (New York: Simon & Schuster, 1988), 28.

7. *Oregonian*, November 14, 1995, B2.

8. *Oregonian*, August 7, 1995, D1.

9. *Oregonian*, October 21, 1994, D1.

10. *Oregonian*, January 31, 1997, D1.

11. *Oregonian*, May 24, 2004, D6.

12. *Los Angeles Times*, February 13, 2007, D8.

13. *Oregonian*, November 1, 2010.

14. Section 597 of City of Birmingham ordinance passed September 19, 1950.

16. EXTRA INNINGS: A LOT OF HISTORY

1. *Tennessean* (Nashville), April 15, 2007, C1–C7.

2. *Sporting News*, March 4, 1953, 15.

3. *Los Angeles Times*, February 13, 2007, D8.

APPENDIX

Arthur Lee "Artie" Wilson Career Statistics

Threw right and batted left-handed
Height: 5-foot-10
Weight: 162 pounds
Born: October 28, 1920, Springville, Alabama
Died: October 31, 2010, Portland, Oregon (age 90)
U.S. professional leagues in which Artie Wilson played:
Negro American League (NAL)
Pacific Coast League (PCL)
National League (NL)
International League (IL)
American Association (ΛΛ)
Northwest League (NW)

Table 16.1.

YEAR	CLUB	LGE	G	AB	R	H	2B	3B	HR	RBI	SB	BB	SO	BA
1944	Birmingham	NAL	65	266	51	92	9	6	0		17			.346
1945	Birmingham	NAL	59	235	51	88	8	2	3	23	15			.374
1946	Birmingham	NAL	Records not available.											
1947	Birmingham	NAL	53	212	42	79								.373
1948	Birmingham	NAL	76	333	78	134	19	8	2	41	10			.402
1949	San Diego/Oakland	PCL	165	607	129	211	19	9	0	37	47	62	58	.348
1950	Oakland	PCL	196	848	168	264	27	17	1	48	31	68	79	.312
1951	New York	NL	19	22	2	4	0	0	0	1	2	2	1	.182
1951	Ottawa	IL	2	7	2	2	1	0	0	0	1	0	0	.286
1951	Minneapolis	AA	17	59	12	23	2	1	2	13	0	13	8	.390
1951	Oakland	PCL	81	349	39	89	8	1	0	22	6	14	36	.255
1952	Seattle	PCL	160	683	95	216	15	8	1	59	25	35	20	.316
1953	Seattle	PCL	177	638	80	212	23	14	2	76	9	47	25	.332
1954	Seattle	PCL	163	660	92	222	24	16	0	50	20	32	28	.336
1955	Portland	PCL	155	616	88	189	20	2	2	23	12	34	36	.307
1956	Portland	PCL	8	8	0	2	0	0	0	0	0	0	0	.250
1956	Seattle	PCL	93	265	33	78	9	4	0	25	6	24	19	.294
1956	Portland/Seattle Totals	PCL	101	273	33	80	9	4	0	25	6	24	19	.293
1957	Sacramento	PCL	75	315	34	83	10	6	0	17	3	11	12	.263
1958–1961	DID NOT PLAY													

1962	Portland	PCL	25	55	3	9	0	1	0	0	2	0	2	10	.164
1962	Tri-City†	NW	14	42	7	9	0	0	0	0	2	1	6	14	.214
NEGRO LEAGUES*			**253**	**1,046**	**222**	**393**	**36**	**16**	**5**	**42**	**64**				**.376**
MINORS			1,331	5,152	782	1,609	158	79	8	374	374	161	374	365	.312
MAJORS			**19**	**22**	**2**	**4**	**0**	**0**	**0**	**2**	**1**	**2**	**2**	**1**	**.182**

† Tri-City club represented Kennewick, Richland and Pasco, Washington
* Incomplete career marks

BIBLIOGRAPHY

Adelson, Bruce. *Brushing Back Jim Crow*. Charlottesville: University of Virginia Press, 1999.

Bush, Frederick C., Bill Nowlin, Carl Reichers, and Len Levin, eds. *Bittersweet Goodbye*. Phoenix, AZ: Society for American Baseball Research, 2017.

Clark, Dick, and Larry Lester. *The Negro Leagues Book*. Cleveland, OH: Society for American Baseball Research, 1994.

Dickson, Paul. *Leo Durocher, Baseball's Prodigal Son*. New York: Bloomsbury, 2017.

Dobbins, Dick. *The Grand Minor League: An Oral History of the Old Pacific Coast League*. Emeryville, CA: Woodford Press, 1999.

———, and John Twichell. *Nuggets on the Diamond*. San Francisco, CA: Woodford Press, 1994.

Erskine, Carl. *Tales from the Dodger Dugout*. Champaign, IL: Sports Publishing, 2001.

Fullerton, Christopher D. *Every Other Sunday*. Birmingham, AL: Boozer Press, 1999.

Golenbeck, Peter. *Bums: An Oral History of the Brooklyn Dodgers*. Mineola, NY: Dover Publications, 1984.

Holway, John B. *Blackball Stars*. New York: Carroll & Graf, 1992.

———. *The Complete Book of Baseball's Negro Leagues: The Other Half of Baseball History*. Fern Park, FL: Hastings House, 2001.

Irvin, Monte, with James A. Riley. *Nice Guys Finish First: The Autobiography of Monte Irvin*. New York: Carroll & Graf, 1996.

Kahn, Roger. *A Season in the Sun*. New York: Berkley, 1978.

Kelley, Brent, *Voices from the Negro Leagues*. Jefferson, NC: McFarland, 1998.

Kiernan, Thomas. *The Miracle at Coogan's Bluff*. New York: Thomas Y. Crowell, 1975.

Klima, John. *Willie's Boys*. Hoboken, NJ: John Wiley & Sons, 2009.

Lanctot, Neil. *Negro League Baseball: The Rise and Ruin of a Black Institution*. Philadelphia: University of Pennsylvania Press, 2004.

Mauriello, Ralph. *Tales Beyond the Dugout*. Tecumseh, MI: DiggyPOD, 2017.

Mays, Willie, with Lou Sahadi. *Say Hey: The Autobiography of Willie Mays*. New York: Simon & Schuster, 1988.

Medeiros, Mark D., and Paul J. Zingg. *Runs, Hits, and an Era*. Chicago: University of Illinois Press, 1994.

Mickelson, Ed. *Out of the Park: Memoir of a Minor League Baseball All-Star*. Jefferson, NC: McFarland, 2007.

Moffi, Larry, and Jonathan Kronstadt. *Crossing the Line: Black Major Leaguers, 1947–1959*. Jefferson, NC: McFarland, 1994.

O'Neal, Bill. *The Pacific Coast League: 1903–1988*. Austin, TX: Eakin Press, 1990.

Powell, Larry. *Black Barons of Birmingham*. Jefferson, NC: McFarland, 2009.

Raley, Dan. *Pitchers of Beer*. Lincoln: University of Nebraska Press, 2011.

Rickey, Branch. *Branch Rickey's Little Blue Book*. Ed. John J. Monteleone. New York: Mountain Lion Book/Macmillian, 1995.

Riley, James A. *The Biographical Encyclopedia of the Negro Baseball Leagues*. New York: Carroll & Graf, 1994.

Snelling, Dennis. *The Greatest Minor League*. Jefferson, NC: McFarland, 2012.

———. *Lefty O'Doul: Baseball's Forgotten Ambassador*. Lincoln: University of Nebraska Press, 2017.

Spalding, John E. *Sacramento Senators and Solons*. Manhattan, KS: Ag Press, 1995.

Swank, Bill. *Echoes from Lane Field*. Paducah, KY: Turner Publishing, 1997.

Thomson, Bobby, with Lee Heiman and Bill Gutman. *"The Giants Win the Pennant! The Giants Win the Pennant!"* New York: Kensington Publishing, 1991.

Tye, Larry. *Satchel: The Life and Times of an American Legend*. New York: Random House, 2009.

Tygiel, Jules. *Baseball's Great Experiment: Jackie Robinson and His Legacy*. New York: Vintage, 1984.

Veeck, Bill, with Ed Linn. *Veeck—As in Wreck: The Autobiography of Bill Veeck*. Chicago: University of Chicago Press, 2001.

White, Gaylon H. *The Bilko Athletic Club*. Lanham, MD: Rowman & Littlefield, 2014.

INDEX

ABOUT THE AUTHOR

Gaylon H. White is author of *The Bilko Athletic Club*, called "one of the best sports books of 2014" by Bruce Miles of the *Chicago Daily Herald*. He teamed with Ransom Jackson, two-time National League All-Star, to write *Handsome Ransom Jackson: Accidental Big Leaguer*. The book was a grand slam with Allen Barra of the *Chicago Tribune*, who wrote, "We can only hope that among today's players there's someone as sharp and funny as Handsome Ransom Jackson to remember them." Both books were published by Rowman & Littlefield.

The Los Angeles-born White graduated in 1967, from the University of Oklahoma, with a bachelor's degree in journalism-broadcasting. He was a sportswriter for the *Denver Post, Arizona Republic*, and *Oklahoma Journal*, before working almost 40 years for such varied companies as Hallmark Cards, Goodyear Tire & Rubber Company, Control Data Corporation, and Eastman Chemical Company.

At Eastman, White worked closely with industrial designers, and in 2015, the Industrial Designers Society of America selected him as one of its 50 most notable members from the past 50 years.

He and his wife Mary live in Kingsport, Tennessee. They have three children and seven grandchildren.